CRIME, ABORIGINALITY AND THE DECOLONISATION OF JUSTICE

CRIME, ABORIGINALITY AND THE DECOLONISATION OF JUSTICE

2nd edition

Harry Blagg

University of Western Australia

THE FEDERATION PRESS
2016

Published in Sydney by
      The Federation Press
      PO Box 45, Annandale, NSW, 2038.
      71 John St, Leichhardt, NSW, 2040.
      Ph (02) 9552 2200. Fax (02) 9552 1681.
      E-mail: info@federationpress.com.au
      Website: http://www.federationpress.com.au

First edition   2008
Second edition   2016

National Library of Australia
Cataloguing-in-Publication entry

      Blagg, Harry
      Crime, aboriginality and the decolonisation of justice / Harry Blagg

      2nd ed.
      Includes bibliographical references and index.
      ISBN 978 176002 057 6 (pbk)

      Restorative justice – Australia.
      Aboriginal Australians – Criminal justice system.
      Criminal justice, Administration of – Australia.
      Aboriginal Australians – Legal status, laws, etc.
      Customary law – Australia.

340.5294

Typeset by The Federation Press, Leichhardt, NSW.
      Printed by OPUS Group in Australia.

Contents

To Gillian, for everything

Preface

A lot, and virtually nothing, has changed since the publication of the first edition of this book in 2008. By this, I mean that there has been a frenzy of government policy and practice initiatives in relation to Aboriginal issues but these have yielded little in terms of improved conditions for Aboriginal people, particularly in relation to the litmus test for justice-related reforms – meaningful reductions in the over-representation of Indigenous Australians in the justice system. The 2008 edition of this book went to press as the full force of the *Northern Territory National Emergency Response Act 2007* (Cth) ('the intervention') was unleashed onto remote Aboriginal communities in the Northern Territory, spearheaded by camouflage-clad soldiers and armed police, storming the Australian desert.

Approaching a decade later, there are few signs of positive improvement as the result of intervention policies – while rates of incarceration in the Northern Territory have risen alarmingly. It is disheartening, therefore, to be observing in Western Australia in 2015 the same narratives in circulation: unsubstantiated claims of rampant sexual abuse in remote Indigenous communities taking on the status of self-evident truths; a one-sided 'debate' about the 'sustainability' of these communities and threats of mass closure. Demonstrating that, where issues of importance to Indigenous people are concerned, the gulf between Indigenous and non-Indigenous Australians is as wide as ever. The Aboriginal domain is subject to constant intrusion from governments for whom its continued existence remains a source of mystery and consternation, and who still view 'progress' in terms of the assimilation of Indigenous people into the mainstream polity as just another minority group.

In the wake of the intervention, I was fortunate enough to travel across the Northern Territory on a number of research projects. These included: a project funded by the Australian Criminological Research Council, with my colleague Dr Thalia Anthony, which inquired into the impact of the policing surge that spearheaded the intervention, particularly its impact on driving-related matters (see Anthony & Blagg 2012, 2013); research with Charles Darwin University's Northern Institute on Night Patrols and Men's Safe Houses on remote communities; and a number of practice evaluations on behalf of Red Dust Role Models,[1] an NGO working with young people on remote communities. These projects, in their different guises, unearthed similar feelings of alarm at the speed with which intervention strategies were undermining social cohesion on remote communities and stripping communities of the capacity to self-govern. These three research projects took place just as some of the mythologies, distortions, outright lies and misrepresentations that had justified intervention were being exposed. There were no 'petrol barons' exchanging petrol for sex with children; and women on communities such as Mutijulu – highlighted as a dysfunctional community plagued by sexual violence – were incensed by the negative portrayal

---

1   Red Dust Role Models is a not-for-profit organisation promoting health development for young people in remote Australia: <http://www.reddust.org.au/>.

of their community in the media. Furthermore, despite the massive investment in new police facilities on remote communities, statistical research in the Northern Territory in the wake of the intervention found no discernible increase in the rate of prosecution for family and domestic violence, or notifications of child sexual abuse, but a massive 250% increase in charges for vehicle-related offending (Anthony & Blagg 2012, 2013). The most notable and significant change in penal practice since 2006-2007 in the Northern Territory lies in the dramatic increase in the imprisonment of Indigenous women. While this is a national trend, the picture is bleakest in the Northern Territory where the rate of imprisonment of Indigenous women more than doubled, from just over 50 per hundred thousand to 110 per hundred thousand, between 2006 and 2011 (Australian Bureau of Statistics 2011). The cruel irony is that an intervention ostensibly aimed at protecting Indigenous women from abuse shepherded in an era of 'punitive excess' (Cunneen et al 2013) which was to sweep up Aboriginal women in large numbers.

Research in the Northern Territory also found that policing remains an ongoing source of concern in Indigenous communities. Empirical research found that the increased police presence was welcomed by some (Pilkington 2009), but there were also concerns that the police were not willing to work in partnership with communities, tended to ignore community elders, and were not focused on issues of concern to the communities (Allen Consulting Group 2010; Pilkington 2009).

Policing traditionally provided the sharp instrument of colonial dispossession. Notwithstanding the good relations that often spring up between Indigenous communities and police officers on a local level, policing as a system of regulatory practices imposes a set of expectations and standards that Indigenous communities find difficult to meet and, furthermore, give marginal relevance to their own priorities.

Even where there may be agreement on ends (safer communities, reduced levels of alcohol consumption, better services), there remain fundamental disagreements about methods – government often employing the punitive apparatuses of the state to achieve its aims, with little attention paid to the impact these methods have on the fabric of community life. We have yet to fully imagine a form of state policing in Indigenous communities that recognises and acknowledges Indigenous priorities and ways of resolving conflict as directly relevant to the maintenance of peace and security. While police priorities and goals remain fixed by the centre and imposed from above, without reference to the priorities of the communities they police, we are fated to repeat the mistakes of the past. The continued denial of Indigenous jurisdiction on the basis of entrenched beliefs about the absolute sovereignty of settler law lies at the heart of the problem. This second edition has been updated to take account of some developments post the 2007 intervention. However, these developments have not altered the fundamental nature of the relationship between Indigenous Australians and the white mainstream.

Patrick Dodson, who led the 1991 Royal Commission into Aboriginal Deaths in Custody, sombrely notes that some 25 years later, 'the criminal justice system continue[s] to suck us up like a vacuum cleaner and deposit us like waste in custodial institutions' (Gordon 2016). Dodson mentions the case of Ms Dhu (called this for cultural reasons) whose death in police custody in Western Australia in 2014 led to a sustained campaign by her family and the Western Australian Deaths in Custody Watch Committee for justice. In many respects her death is a case study on the malign indifference to Indigenous suffering, not just of our system of policing, but of a host of kindred institutions. Ms Dhu had been a victim of domestic and family violence but, as in the case of so many Indigenous women globally, instead of being treated as a victim, she was processed as an offender when reporting abuse, detained under a Warrant of Committal for unpaid fines and confined in the Hedland police lock-up for four days in lieu of the fines. The coronial inquiry into Ms Dhu's death in custody heard that though sick from septicaemia caused by a broken rib, she was denied access to medical care, despite crying out in pain and vomiting in the cell: she was assumed by the police and by nurses at the hospital, to be 'making it up', 'faking it', a 'druggy', and 'an alcoholic'. Taken three times to the hospital, she was denied admission each time. The nurse who refused to admit Ms Dhu 'rolled her eyes', according to a police witness, when Ms Dhu reported being in pain, interpreting it as 'attention seeking' behaviour (ABC News 2015). By the time police finally accepted she was sick, rather than experiencing 'cold turkey' drug withdrawal symptoms, it was too late, and she died on the way to hospital. Ms Dhu's case also reinforces the need to take into account systemic violence by the state when discussing violence against Indigenous women. The mainstream system seems incapable of keeping Indigenous women safe: calls for more police in Indigenous communities to tackle violence need to take into account the history of physical and sexual violence by mainstream law enforcement agencies against Indigenous women, who find it difficult to be taken seriously as victims: the space of the victim is a white space in settler societies. Any intersectoral collaboration between Indigenous and non-Indigenous organisations in the family violence space must take into account Indigenous women's vulnerabilities to state violence.

There are other areas of continued concern. Since the first edition was released, the issue of Foetal Alcohol Spectrum Disorder (FASD) has been forced onto the agenda by Indigenous women. FASD is a non-diagnostic umbrella term encompassing a spectrum of disorders caused by prenatal alcohol exposure (Douglas 2010). Prenatal alcohol exposure may cause damage to the frontal lobe of the foetal brain, resulting in cognitive deficiencies (Kulaga 2006). Deficiencies may include impairments in learning, attention, memory, sensory perception, and language. However, the question of FASD cannot be isolated from the history of colonial settlement and the multiple traumas resulting from dispossession which make Indigenous young people prone to suicide, addiction (for example, the drug 'ice' being the latest in a long line of substances worrying Indigenous communities) and alcohol misuse. It follows that resolving the problem cannot be decontextualised from the imperative to decolonise relationships between Indigenous people and the settler mainstream.

In 2015, three senior Bunuba women, June Oscar, Emily Carter and Maureen Carter, from Fitzroy Crossing, initiated a partnership between Nindilingarri Cultural Health Service, Marninwarntikura Women's Resource Centre, The George Institute for Global Health and the University of Sydney Medical School to conduct the first population-based Australian study of FASD prevalence. Known as the Lililwan Project, it also sought to develop individual treatment plans for children, educate the community on the risks of alcohol consumption during pregnancy and provide support for parents, carers and teachers. The population study reported rates of FAS/pFAS of 12 per 100 children. This is the highest reported prevalence of FAS/pFAS in Australia and similar to rates reported in 'high-risk' populations internationally (Fitzpatrick et al 2015). These findings reinforced demands for alcohol restrictions in the town. The findings are also raising questions about the role of Indigenous organisations in providing the 'external brain' for young people with FASD. There are dangers that young people found to be FASD impaired will wind up detained indefinitely if found unfit to stand trial. Indigenous organisations are seeking the resources to provide the care and support for these young people, particularly 'on country' and away from the pressures of community life. Indigenous people need to be involved when decisions are made about young people and resourced to run and manage diversionary alternatives (Blagg, Tulich and Bush 2015). Once again we are faced with two alternatives: go on as we are, repeating failed strategies of colonial era social engineering; or create a new partnership with the Indigenous domain that respects Indigenous culture.

Along with my colleague Dr Tamara Tulich, I am working with Indigenous community-owned and place-based agencies in the west Kimberly to develop diversionary pathways for youths found, or believed, to have FASD. Our approach reflects many of the themes set out in this book and includes a focus on therapeutic alternatives to the mainstream system that divert young people into community owned and 'on country' programs. The women of Fitzroy Crossing have also been innovative in terms of the struggle against family violence, as ongoing research funded by Australia's National Research Organisation for Women's Safety Limited (ANROWS) is discovering. Indeed, issues related to FASD are inseparable from the family violence issue: underpinned, as they are, by the experience of colonial dispossession. As I argue later: on the whole, Indigenous women see the solution to violence in holistic terms, where women are empowered to take charge of their lives. Unlike mainstream feminist approaches, however, there is a sharp focus on community healing. For Indigenous women, who have historically been the victims of forced sterilisation, cultural genocide and other strategies designed to kill off the Indigenous Other, the right to have and nurture a family, care for children, be in a family unit, are fundamental to their sense of justice.

Background work with Dr Thalia Anthony for a new research project on Night Patrols in central Australia and Western Australia which began in 2016, is finding that Indigenous communities still see their Night Patrols as an invaluable mechanism for keeping the peace in line with Indigenous culture. In post-intervention Northern Territory the number of patrols funded by government have increased considerably, however there are ongoing concerns about the strings attached to this funding. We are finding that the mainstream 'crime prevention' model being imposed onto patrols from above is blind to the cultural dynamics that make patrols successful. Some women's patrols – by far the most enduring, stable and successful patrols in the Northern Territory – are disbanding because the cultural knowledge senior women bring to the patrol is devalued in comparison with bureaucratic skills. At the risk of sounding alarmist, there is the possibility that many patrols will be eventually be run by white organisations and staffed by white people to meet essentially white expectations of community safety in Indigenous communities.

I remain extremely grateful to the many Indigenous people who have welcomed me onto their country and shared their experiences. Particular thanks are owing to Maureen Carter of Nindilingarri Cultural Health, June Oscar from Marninwarntikura Women's Resource Centre and the Elders from Kimberly Law and Culture, all in Fitzroy Crossing, Western Australia. Special thanks to Thalia Anthony for being such an amazing fellow traveller on spectacular journeys through Central Australia. Ditto Emma Williams. Thanks also to Tamara Tulich and Zoe Bush, intrepid partners on the FASD research. Many thanks to Heather Nancarrow and colleagues at ANROWS, Aunty Eileen Cummings, Nangala Woodley, Donella Raye and Nicole Bluett-Boyd for being great colleagues. Not forgetting colleagues and students at UWA, especially Tara McLaren.

Harry Blagg
Perth, Western Australia

References

ABC News, 'Police Thought Dying Aboriginal Woman Ms Dhu was Faking it, Coronial Inquiry Told' <http://www.abc.net.au/news/2015-11-23/inquest-into-death-of-dhu-in-police-custody/6963244>.

Blagg, H, Tulich, T and Bush, Z (2015) 'Diversionary Pathways for Indigenous Youth with FASD in Western Australia: Decolonising Alternatives' *Alternative Law Journal* 40(4) 257.

Douglas, H (2010) 'The Sentencing Response to Defendants with Foetal Alcohol Spectrum Disorder' *Criminal Law Journal* 34, 221, 226.

Fitzpatrick, J et al (2015) 'Prevalence of Fetal Alcohol Syndrome in a Population-based Sample of Children Living in Remote Australia: The Lililwan Project' *Journal of Paediatrics and Child Health* 51(4) 450, 451.

Gordon, M (2016) 'Patrick Dodson Makes Impassioned Plea for 'a Smarter Form of Justice' *Sydney Morning Herald*, 13 April 2016.

Kulaga, V (2006) 'Cognitive Processing Speeds Among Children Exposed to Fetal Alcohol' *Journal of FAS International* 4(3) 1.

1

Decolonising Criminology

This book explores the problematic relationship between the Australian criminal justice system and Aboriginal people. It sets out from the premise that, in many crucial respects, the fundamental nature of this relationship has remained unchanged since invasion when the system was employed as a tool of dispossession. Aboriginal people in Australia are among the most imprisoned people in the world. The reasons why this continues to be the case, despite a number of innovations introduced in the wake of the 1991 Royal Commission into Aboriginal Deaths in Custody (RCIADIC) (Johnson 1991), has been the source of debate among politicians, policy-makers and criminologists; some of whom point to the various 'pull factors' which draw Aboriginal people into the system in large numbers, while others focus on the 'push factors' which ensure that high rates of Aboriginal offending increase the likelihood of enmeshment in the system. In the years since the landmark inquiry into Aboriginal deaths in custody, there has been a sharpening of the dichotomy between official rhetoric on the one hand (which highlights the importance of diverting Aboriginal people from contact with the system) and the reality of increasing rates of Indigenous incarceration on the other.

However firm the commitment of government and policy-makers may be to the ideal of diversion and the construction of credible alternatives to involvement in the system, the fact remains that these policies co-exist with a suite of laws, practices and mentalities that tend to cancel them out. For the police (the system's key gatekeepers and primary decision-makers), the policy of arrest as a strategy of last resort takes second place in frontline policing still fixated on managing the *Aboriginal problem*, for which arrest and detention are most often viewed as *first resort* tools of order management.

Besides being massively over-represented as offenders in the criminal justice system, Aboriginal people are subject to extreme levels of victimisation in their own communities, making them the most victimised as well as the most imprisoned section of society. Levels of violence are so extreme that there are concerns that Aboriginal communities are wiping themselves out (Atkinson 2000); 'killing our future' Jackie Huggins calls it (cited in Cripps 2005); some Aboriginal people themselves talk of 'self-genocide' (Blagg, Morgan, Cunneen & Ferrante 2004), while Mick Dodson describes a seemingly endless cycle of inter-generational violence, where victims become offenders:[1]

> [V]iolence is undermining our very life's essence, it is destroying us, and there are very few Aboriginal families that are not struggling with the debilitating effects of trauma, despair and damage resulting from their experiences with violence. (Dodson 2003: 1)

Violence in Aboriginal communities has become the focus for official intervention over recent years. The most recent, and most publicised, example followed claims of widespread physical and sexual violence in remote communities of the Northern Territory in 2006. I discuss this example in some detail in later chapters, as it illustrates with alarming clarity the tendency of the mainstream to intervene in Indigenous society in ways that exacerbate rather than heal problematic situations. Aboriginal activists such as Judy Atkinson, Jackie Huggins and Mick Dodson were highlighting a problem which, they believed, required significant investment in a multiplicity of strategies underpinned by dialogue with Indigenous communities and informed by principles enshrined in the United Nations Declaration on the Rights of Indigenous Peoples, particularly what has become known as 'FPIC' (Art 10) demanding that policies likely to impact on Indigenous people receive their 'free, prior and informed consent'.[2] Instead, the response has been anything but consensual and informed and has relied on simply imposing white governance and control onto Indigenous communities in an unmediated fashion. The lessons of recent government-initiated and led interventions around violence and sexual abuse in Indigenous communities confirm a tendency towards coercive assimilation, underpinned by a belief that Indigenous communities are dysfunctional and incapable of even a modest level of self-government.

The questions raised in this book, then, are these: can government intervene in the issue of violence without further entrenching those systemic tendencies towards punitive capture of Aboriginal people? Can non-Aboriginal systems of law and justice deal with, or even understand, the needs of Aboriginal victims? Can government find new ways of working through dialogue with Aboriginal people, and with Aboriginal law and culture, which reduce levels of violence?

Disentangling the various threads connecting Aboriginal people with the criminal justice system is a painstaking task. This is due in large part to the constitutive role the system has played in mediating between Aboriginal people and a rapidly expanding settler society; a process which inevitably cast the justice and policing systems as the sharp instruments of dispossession. The justice system, and the mesh of carceral institutions which support it, represents part of a panoply of interconnected regimes and institutions evolved to resolve 'the Aboriginal problem'; but it has been, and remains, of central importance in framing and representing the Aboriginal problem as essentially *a problem of order*. Discourses of crime carry with them a particularly powerful resonance. Naming actions as criminal silences the kind of dissent possible when these actions are named another way – political, for example: the criminalisation of Aboriginal people's resistance to colonisation played a role in silencing criticism of the mass dispossession of Indigenous people and through this, the theft of land. Historically, the Australian criminal justice system, with its victim/offender dyad, its foundations in private property, its tendency to individualise events, has played a defining role in fashioning and reinforcing a white collective consciousness capable of inverting the realities of history to one where the white collective can believe itself to be the collective victims of Aboriginal criminality – a drama played out on a regular basis through representations of Aboriginal offenders in the media and shrill headlines condemning rampant child sexual abuse in Indigenous communities.

My argument is that to fully understand the extraordinary levels of Aboriginal over-representation in the criminal justice system as offenders, and the extraordinary rates of Aboriginal victimisation, requires a highly nuanced and variegated analysis situating this phenomena within an historical framework formed by processes of colonial dispossession, genocide and assimilation, and forms of resistance to these processes. Our focus on isolated criminal justice *institutions* (court, prisons, lock-ups, jails) should not blind us to the wider interest these institutions served, or that they formed part of a much broader system of controls designed to formalise white power and privilege. The focus on institutions must therefore take account of the fact that they were, and in some senses remain, nodal points in a broader fabric of colonial *relationships*. We must also recognise that what Patrick Wolfe (2008) refers to as the 'eliminatory' practices of the past have had real consequences in terms of social disorganisation, anomie and, particularly, inter-generational trauma, poor mental health, disability, alcoholism and violence. Simply removing the controls of the mainstream society is not enough: 'decolonisation' must be accompanied by massive investment in relevant social programs, healing processes and empowerment strategies.

As a discipline, criminology is essentially concerned with identifying the causes of crime and deviance and the ways the criminal justice system deals with these phenomena. Criminologists face having to sift through a disparate collection of variables before making judgements about what causes crime and why people are affected by it. Depending on the particular approach or stance the criminologist adopts, he or she might lend greater weight to one set of variables at the expense of another. But most criminologists, schooled in western positivist sciences or more radical 'conflict' philosophies, accept as given a number of ontological and epistemological positions regarding the social world and how it is to be interpreted.

The ontologies and epistemologies of Aboriginal people may be cheerfully ignored as constitutive factors when we 'read the data' on arrests, convictions, imprisonment and recidivism. One of the issues we need to interrogate is this knowledge/power relationship, where 'we' as experts, the bearers of scientific truths, are able to construct the field of inquiry in ways which allow us to determine what the facts are, what is knowable, what is available as knowledge, what is worth knowing and what isn't; judging some things as relevant, others irrelevant. This is a form of knowledge/power, which places us as criminological researchers in the dominant position. It is reinforced when we limit ourselves as researchers to simply compiling the data, having discussions with one another and with the centres of power in government and government agencies, rather than engaging in dialogue with Aboriginal people themselves as bearers of *Indigenous knowledge*. Indigenous knowledge is locally contextualised and usually passed down orally, it provides a counterweight to scientific rationalism.

Aboriginal people, while acknowledging the impact other forms of disadvantage have on their life paths and life chances, might narrate the story differently. From an Indigenous perspective *it is precisely their identity as Aboriginal people and attempts by the state to (variously) eliminate, restructure and re-constitute this identity that is the core issue*. Viewed 'other wise' Aboriginality ceases to be a variable to be weighted and measured against others, and instead becomes the over-determining factor. If we move out of the academy altogether and pitch our tent somewhere closer to the Aboriginal domain, and set out from within 'Aboriginal terms of reference', we might see the situation differently. We can't pretend that real Aboriginal people don't exist as we focus instead on the representations and artefacts visible to us as data on our computer screens, or assume to know what the solutions are to the multiple problems Aboriginal communities face, on the basis of research from overseas or from mainstream communities on the Eastern seaboard of Australia.

When we enter the Aboriginal domain, we pull with us a baggage train of theories and perspectives on crime and victimisation drawn from western research. Some hasty 'consultations' with Aboriginal workers, and/or elders, add local colour, but we often interpret what we hear and see with reference to pre-determined and pre-configured theories and solutions. Yet, it becomes quickly apparent to researchers able to suspend their preconceived notions that our 'domain assumptions' about social reality and the suite of solutions we habitually pull – like a rabbit from a hat – to solve what we perceive to be the 'problem', are misdirected.

Anne Worrall, for example, ably summarises a number of pertinent points in her critique of the 'What Works' doctrine and its relevance to the remote site of One Arm Point in the far north of Western Australia. The 'What Works' orthodoxy, Worrall argues, has underwritten an approach to community corrections fixated on a:

> model of focused, accountable, standardised intervention into the lives of offend-
> ers, based on the actuarial concept of risk assessment, the science of cognitive
> behavioural psychology, the morality of individual responsibility and the politics of
> restorative justice. (Worrall 2000: 243)

Worrall assesses how the 'What Works agenda' travels to remote Australia – specifically to the community of One Arm Point, a 'real place ... also a symbolic place' standing in for all the places where 'What Works might not work' (Worrall 2000: 244). She concludes that the orthodoxy is inevitably 'transformed beyond recognition' (Worrall 2000: 246) when practised in remote areas where all the realities of life and the values, beliefs and practices of Aboriginal people have to be taken in to account. Part of the task of the criminologist in relation to criminal justice and Aboriginal people is to enter into a dialogue with the Aboriginal domain and work in partnership with the network of representative structures through which the Aboriginal domain attempts dialogue with white society. The free-floating intellectual, armed with the orthodox techniques of mainstream social science, is not well positioned to arrive at solutions to the problem of Aboriginal over-representation or victimisation.

None of the foregoing discussion should be interpreted as a rejection either of sound research techniques or of good data collection – provided they are grounded in Aboriginal realities. The issue of statistics remains a critical one. Information about the criminal justice system became a key battleground in the post-RCIADIC era, as fledg-ling Aboriginal representative organisations – such as the various Aboriginal Justice Councils – took on the centres of power in the criminal justice agencies and the police, and attempted to implement those recommendations concerned with accountability and transparency. It remains of critical importance today. Criminal justice agencies have had a tendency to hoard data to meet their own internal reporting requirements rather than seeing data as a mechanism for making agencies accountable to outside bodies (Beyer 2003; Blagg, Morgan, Cunneen & Ferrante 2004).

The RCIADIC maintained that Aboriginal people needed to be involved in monitoring the criminal justice system and providing direct advice to government

– Aboriginal people being 'the best source of advice on issues impacting upon them' (Recommendation 62) – and recommended that Aboriginal Justice Advisory Councils be established in each State and Territory (Recommendations 2 & 3). During the 1990s, the operations of the criminal justice system in relation to Aboriginal people was stripped of its veil of secrecy, and criminologists played a vital role in demystifying the role of policing, in particular, as the crucial point of contact between Aboriginal people and the justice system as a whole (Harding, Broadhurst, Ferrante & Loh 1995; Cunneen & Robb 1987; Gayle, Bailey-Harris & Wundersitz 1990).

A statistical snapshot

Aboriginal people are significantly over-represented at every stage of the criminal justice process and particularly at the deep end. This is the case across Australia, although rates of over-representation vary between States.

A snapshot of arrest and imprisonment rates of Indigenous people in Australia reveals that rates of contact continue to soar across Australia. Between 2000 and 2013 the adult Indigenous imprisonment rate increased by 57%, widening the gap as the non-Indigenous rate did not show significant change (Australian Government Productivity Commission 2014). Recent data (Australian Bureau of Statistics (ABS) 2014) indicates that the difference between Indigenous and non-Indigenous imprisonment has steadily increased since the early 2000s. Indigenous people constitute around 28% of prisoners (sentenced and remand) in Australia generally, while they constitute roughly 2% of the population. In 'frontier' States such as Western Australia, the Northern Territory and Queensland they make up a significant proportion of the prisoner population. In Western Australia, for example, where they are 3.6% of the population they represent 40% of the adult prison population generally, over 50% of the women's prison population and a staggering 78% of the juvenile detention regime (ABS 2014; Australian Government 2014). For Indigenous people the age-standardised imprisonment rate was 18 times the non-Indigenous age-standardised imprisonment rate (3013.4 prisoners per 100,000 Aboriginal and Torres Strait Islander adult population compared to 166.6 prisoners per 100,000 adult non-indigenous population) (ABS 2014). In the Northern Territory, which has shown the highest increase in the rate of imprisonment of Indigenous people in the last decade, Indigenous people make up 86% of the prisoner population (ABS 2014) and approximately 30% of the total Northern Territory population.

The Indigenous age-standardised imprisonment rate was fifteen times the non-Indigenous age-standardised imprisonment rate (2390.2 prisoners per 100,000 Indigenous adult population compared to 155.2 prisoners per 100,000 adult non-Indigenous population) (ABS 2014). Queensland has experienced a surge in imprisonment rates in the past few years, even by Australian standards: Indigenous people comprise 32% (2243 prisoners) of the adult prisoner population.

The age-standardised imprisonment rate for Indigenous people was 11 times the non-Indigenous age-standardised imprisonment rate (1557.9 prisoners per 100,000 compared to 143.1 prisoners per 100,000 adult non-Indigenous population) (ABS 2014).

Systemic bias

These massive levels of Indigenous over-representation in the criminal justice system and the generally poorer standards of care in regional prisons (where Aboriginal people tend to be incarcerated) has led observers to conclude there is evidence of structural bias in play. Some see this bias less as a product of explicit racism than an unwillingness to acknowledge and accommodate the unique cultures and experiences of Aboriginal Australians. One report suggests:

> It is partly derived from the 'Eurocentric' construction of the criminal justice system which has its basis in property rights and individual responsibility and which does not easily accommodate Aboriginal cultural values and practices that do not conform to these norms. (Office of the Inspector of Custodial Services 2005: 56)

The Victorian Aboriginal Justice Agreement (1999) (VAJA), makes reference to racism and discrimination as factors contributing to the over-representation of Indigenous people in the criminal justice system. The agreement recognises that Aboriginal people continue to be over-represented at all levels of the criminal justice system at 'unacceptable and disproportionate rates' (VAJA 1999: 12). Consultations with Aboriginal communities undertaken for the VAJA identified a range of factors contributing to this over-representation, including:

- A cluster of underlying issues, such as extreme social and economic disadvantage, dispossession, and alienation from traditional land and culture;
- Vulnerability to crime, linked to high rates of victimisation, social disadvantage, family violence, drug and alcohol abuse;
- Lack of confidence in justice and related institutions due to cultural alienation and the role such institutions played historically, leading to unwillingness to access services; and
- Endemic and entrenched forms of racism, including racial vilification and stereotyping, that operate as a mechanism for excluding Aboriginal people from full participation in the life of the Victorian community.

VAJA maintains that the criminal justice system reinforces social values that are frequently at odds with those of the Indigenous community. The justice system has played a direct role in imposing an alien set of values on Aboriginal people, then criminalising when they will not, or cannot, conform to them. Notions of 'acceptable behaviour' are 'defined exclusively for the non-Indigenous community' (VAJA 1999: 14), while the values, beliefs and practices of Indigenous people are marginalised or treated as forms of anti-social behaviour.

VAJA goes on to stress the salience of institutional forms of racism in maintaining the dominance of non-Indigenous values and principles and in marginalising those of Indigenous people. Institutional racism is the most insidious form of racism because it is difficult to quantify, indeed those who practise it generally deny its existence:

> Institutional racism is typically initiated by persons of relative power and authority who see themselves as 'just doing these job' in accordance with supposedly fair and universal criteria. (VAJA 1999: 14)

Bowling (cited in Macpherson 2003: 21) argues that 'discrimination can occur irrespective of the intent of the individuals who carry out the activities of the institution'. We need, he suggests, to focus attention on the *outcomes* of activities and processes rather than *intentions* and *attitudes* of individual players.

The ongoing over-representation of Indigenous Australians in the criminal justice system cannot be accounted for solely in terms of the prejudices of individuals within the system, or greater levels of offending by Indigenous people – although that may play an accompanying role. They are, rather, a reflection of the multiple-layered patterns of disadvantage and extreme forms of marginalisation experienced by Aboriginal people and their status as a colonised people.

The use of the construct of systemic racism has not been without its critics. Weatherburn, Fitzgerald and Hua (2003) argued that, while Australia has historically been racist in its treatment of Aboriginal people, high rates of Aboriginal incarceration simply reflect higher rates of Aboriginal offending, especially serious crime. Weatherburn et al argue that since the 1991 RCIADIC, too much attention has been given to fixing the criminal justice system rather than impacting on the social and economic causes of crime. They are particularly critical of the rise in the use of diversionary sentencing, which simply delays the inevitable, while having no impact on serious offences such as domestic violence. Weatherburn et al consider that the focus should be on reducing Aboriginal crime – not on changing police and criminal justice processes to respond to that crime. The authors suggest that programs to reduce substance abuse, family violence and unemployment are the key to reducing Aboriginal crime and are critical of the focus on systemic bias which they believe has come to dominate criminological thinking, to the exclusion of criminal behaviour.

Weatherburn et al (2003) pick out the work of Cunneen for particular attention as representing a tendency to see Aboriginal involvement as a result of systemic bias. Cunneen (2006) responds to Weatherburn et al's critique on a number of levels. First, by pointing out that though they talk of over-representation in *prison*, the works they are critical of mainly focus on over-representation in police custody. Secondly, by criticising Weatherburn et al's tendency to construct a simple dichotomy between systemic and offending oriented explanations, Cunneen writes:

> [T]he Weatherburn approach ... constructs a simple binary explanation for Aboriginal over-representation in prison as either the result of systemic bias *or* offending levels by Aboriginal people. This binary approach is simplistic on a number of levels. (Cunneen 2006: 334)

Cunneen goes on to illustrate the depth of research that has been conducted on Aboriginal justice issues, including the Royal Commission itself, which includes work on the link between offending and economic factors, work on Aboriginal victimisation, Indigenous family violence programs, Indigenous self-policing initiatives and a host of issues that go well beyond simply reducing the whole question of over-involvement to discussions of systemic bias:

> The need for a multifaceted conceptualisation of Aboriginal over-representation which goes beyond single causal explanations (such as poverty, racism, etc) has been acknowledged for decades. An adequate explanation involves analysing interconnecting issues which include historical and structural conditions of colonisation,

of social and economic marginalisation, and institutional racism, while at the same time considering the impact of specific (and sometimes quite localised) practices of criminal justice and related agencies. (Cunneen 2006: 334)

Cunneen also makes the very pertinent point that Weatherburn et al completely ignore the role of Indigenous organisations in increasingly identifying and dealing with over-representation, including establishing the research agenda. The various Aboriginal Justice Councils have tended to adopt a very sophisticated approach to the question of over-representation, balancing the need for systemic reform to the system with early intervention initiatives, diversionary strategies and policies that lift rates of Aboriginal employment.

In more recent work, Weatherburn (2014) maintains the stance that, whereas racism and colonialism were influential in shaping relations between Indigenous and non-Indigenous peoples 'back in the day', they have given way to a set of contemporary crime problems amenable to mainstream solutions, as they reflect a range of crimino-genic conditions typical of marginal groups, such as unemployment, alcohol abuse, and so on.

If we envisage the problem as exclusively, or even mainly, a problem of crime, deterrence and punishment, we need look no further than the suite of strategies forming the core of the What Works doctrine. Aboriginal crime problems are different only in scale and should be amenable to orthodox forms of intervention. What is more, Aboriginal people might be arrested, incarcerated and imprisoned more often because they offend more often. If we adopt Cunneen's suggestion, however, we are faced with having to engage with a broad range of concerns that occasionally take us beyond the domain of criminology – often because mainstream criminology refuses to acknowledge them. The broader landscape involves understanding those colonial discourses through which Aboriginal people have been rendered knowable and amenable to domination by a powerful alien culture and how, in turn, these practices have been resisted by Aboriginal people. Doing justice to Aboriginal people requires, I want to suggest, that the criminologists come to terms with the specificity of Aboriginal people's situation as a colonised people, and the historically specific ways criminal justice has, and continues to be, employed as an instrument of colonial governance. Unless we make sense of this we cannot understand the depths of Aboriginal people's sense of alienation from, and frustration with, existing systems of justice. Moreover, we also fail to make sense of the complex strategies employed by Aboriginal people to resist these strategies of domination.

There are a number of possible lenses through which to view the question of systemic bias in the criminal justice system. Interest in systemic bias within the justice system emerged in the United States in the 1960s to describe discrimination against black people by the police and the justice system (Cunneen 2006). The key difference between the situation of black people in the United States and Indigenous people in Australia (and the United States) is that black Americans view progress in terms of acceptance as citizens, and demand equal treatment 'under the law'. Indigenous people position themselves differently and, while they may view fair and just treatment by the justice system as important, there is also a strong belief that this is still under someone else's law, an alien law that has been imposed on them without their consent and without recognition that they possess their own body of law. Viewed through this lens, the *bias* has less to do with 'discrimination' per se. I would suggest that the most damaging bias against Indigenous people is not the denial of *equality*, but the denial of Aboriginal *difference*.

Research finds little evidence of bias against Indigenous offenders at the sentencing stage of the criminal justice system (Bond & Jeffries 2011a&b) Indeed, there is a history of higher courts providing a 'discount' for Aboriginal offenders; in some instances, this was to even out the impact of discrimination at earlier stages of the criminal justice system, by the police, regional Magistrates and Justices of the Peace. Courts were particularly anxious to ensure that Aboriginal offenders who faced, or had experienced, Aboriginal penalties did not receive a double punishment (Northern Territory Law Reform Committee 2004).

The problem is that, with a few gestures towards cultural diversity, mainstream courts behave as though settler law was applicable to and appropriate for Indigenous people (Zdenkowski 1994). Thalia Anthony (2013) points to what she calls the 'recognition dilemma' in criminal sentencing (Anthony 2013: 4), where the courts, to some extent, acknowledge Indigenous alterity while upholding the system's essential 'whiteness'. The courts attempt to accommodate Indigenous difference through the conventional legal framework. Judicial discretion is employed to 'individualise' sentencing by taking into account relevant 'factors' in the accused background and life circumstances (Anthony 2013: 6). These may include factors particular to Aboriginal people: such as 'cultural' obligations, for example, where the accused's offending behaviour is a consequence of carrying out Aboriginal law – such as being involved in carrying out 'traditional' punishment involving the use of violence (Law Reform Commission of Western Australia 2006). Anthony concludes that attempts to 'reconcile' Indigenous and non-Indigenous notions of law through either lenient or harsher sentences are misdirected (Anthony 2013: 208). Instead she calls for a 'transformative' approach privileging 'domains of Indigenous sovereignty' and new forms of legal pluralism (Anthony 2013: 208). I return to these issues in a later chapter.

The problem of imposing Eurocentric structures onto Indigenous people is not restricted to law. The Euro-American criminological tradition, whether right or left realism, critical theory or administrative criminology, tends to operate without a theory of colonialism and its effects. Most comparative criminology is largely concerned with Europe and America. Many surveys of international trends in areas such as victimisation and rates of imprisonment tend to gloss over deeper cultural differences between societies in their search for uniform and measurable variables. They also construct a narrow definition of 'crime' as an object of inquiry, excluding crime committed by states. Morrison (2004) is critical of the 'exclusionary tactics' employed by mainstream criminologists intent on 'defining genocidal killings as outside the scope of the criminological enterprise' (Morrison 2004: 341). Others, notably Cohen (2001) and Bauman (2001), offer some compelling evidence that western social and political science generally neglected the Holocaust and other genocidal events as temporary interruptions to the flow of modernity rather than products of it. Yet, a comprehensive study of Aboriginal people and crime is incomplete without reference to the genocidal propensities of colonial powers and the settler state in the creation of present circumstances.

Settler colonial difference

Settler colonialism differs from other brands of colonialism in that it embraces not simply the exploitation but the wholesale appropriation of land, as though it were always/already the property of the European, awaiting 'discovery'. This ontology of settlement is, according to Patrick Wolfe (2008), inherently eliminatory (though, he insists, not inevitably genocidal). Settlement requires the extinguishment of Indigenous ownership of land, not always the extinguishment of the people themselves: genocide remains one among a range of strategies including forced assimilation, dispossession, enforced mobility and concentration in places of confinement. Settler colonists attempted to uproot Indigenous occupants and *replace* them in the soil: transplanting the Global North into the Global South.

> The magical trick that settler colonialism performs is to denaturalize the right to belong of the local population – to make them foreigners, while naturalizing the foreigner as the person who has the right to belong. Foreigners become natives and natives become foreigners. (Pilay 2015)

Settler colonial societies hold on to a particularly rich and thematically nuanced repertoire of self-exculpatory and self-aggrandising narratives, including biblical-scale imaginaries of redemption and renewal, promised lands flowing with milk and honey, and such like. Such narratives obscured the crimes of land theft and the necessary denial of Indigenous sovereign law. As Lisa Ford suggests, the eradication of Indigenous law became the 'litmus test of settler statehood' (Ford 2010: 9).

There was also a symbiotic relationship between frontier violence and the rule of law. Violence created the space (both metaphorically and figuratively) for law to be implanted, and the implanted law retrospectively legitimated the fruits of the founding violence and its methods. Agamben (1998) demonstrates how the imperative to create order from chaos permits sovereign power to authorise what he terms a 'state of exception' and suspend law. Colonial violence, therefore, was not the negation of law but the establishment of the preconditions under which western law could be implanted. Furthermore, the state of exception created zones where 'the monopoly of violence could still fall outside the hands of the state' (Evans 2005: 70). Settlers often took the initiative in localised massacres and genocides (Reynolds 2013). Critical scholarship on settler colonialism suggests that the administrative power of the formal state was not the decisive factor in genocidal actions by colonists. Genocide, according to Wolfe, was:

> not dependent on the presence or absence of formal state institutions or functionaries. Accordingly ... the occasions on or the extent to which settler colonialism conduces to genocide are not a matter of the presence or absence of the formal apparatus of the state. (Wolfe 2008: 11)

Indigenous peoples suffered violence from the formal apparatuses of the settler state *and* from settlers themselves. As I suggest in a later chapter regarding the relevance of references to the 'good community' as a basis for restorative alternatives to 'state justice', such binaries overlook the degree to which colonisation has been achieved, and maintained, through the dominance of both the settler state and the mainstream settler community as the key beneficiaries of the colonial project.

Criminologists have been criticised for ignoring the uses made by colonial powers of the criminal law as a mechanism of oppression and as a means of legitimating colonial power. Sumner (1982) suggests that colonial history remains too disturbing for criminologists because it lays bare the shoddy foundations of modern western societies, based not on principles of democracy and freedom, but on colonial pillage and the oppression of colonised peoples. John Pratt (2006) provides a lucid example of the particular ways colonial imagery produces particular crime discourse in his study of crime rates in New Zealand. He contrasts the geniality and friendliness of New Zealand with its high rates of incarceration, before dismissing the idea that incarceration rates reflect high rates of crime. Instead, Pratt points to the mythology of New Zealand as a 'paradise', one, which was both like, and superior to the country left behind:

> What better identity to affirm, then, what better way of defining oneself and what better way to find reassurance at the end of the long journey than to be able to claim not only that the new country was like the old, but it was also markedly superior to it – not just a younger more pristine Britain in its physical characteristics, but a morally and socially 'Better Britain' as well. (Pratt 2006: 547)

The paradise had to be safeguarded against all manner of danger and the state became 'the guarantor of these aspects of paradise that the initial settlers and subsequent generations were trying to create, or had come to New Zealand in anticipation of finding'. (Pratt 2006: 548). This meant, among other things, subjugating Indigenous Maori. The need to defend the powerful *conscience collective* that had formed on imagery of New Zealand as a colonial paradise has entailed high rates of incarceration and generally punitive ideas in relation to the uses of imprisonment. Maori people have borne the brunt of law and order strategies in New Zealand: they represent 50% of prisoners while only 15% of the population (Pratt 2006: 542).

Maona Jackson has made a consistent case for looking at Maori involvement in the criminal justice system in colonial terms, suggesting that the New Zealand state established a set of Pakeha values as the only legitimate ones, while deliberately marginalising Maori beliefs, this inevitably led to high rates of Maori incarceration. The system is essentially unreformable because it is based on Pakeha beliefs. The solution lies in establishing parallel Maoris structures founded on Maori beliefs and values (Jackson 1992: 1995).

This is not to say that European and American criminology, or the broader social science projects from which criminology has drawn upon, has no relevance. There will inevitably be a strong overlap between a post-colonial criminology and western criminology, particular the radical western tradition. As Webb (2003) and Bull (2004) point out, while Maona Jackson's work has eschewed western criminology and affirmed commitment to a strictly Maori philosophy, his work bears comparison with culture conflict theory and critical criminology. Bull (2004), for example, illustrates the usefulness of conflict and critical criminology in studying the impact of land appropriation by the Crown on Maori, while demonstrating the need to refine the theories in the light of colonial practices (Bull 2004: 498).

We cannot simply invent a new criminological language that excises criminology from its roots in western social science, and from the language and meanings embedded in it. Dipesh Chakrabarty (1992) draws our attention to Derrida's critique of 'western metaphysics' in *Writing and Difference*, where Derrida argues that while we may wish to dismantle what he calls 'western metaphysics' (which includes western philosophy and social science) we do not have the tools to do so because there is no alternative language (the language we have access to having been formed in and by western ontologies and epistemologies). So where do we go? Derrida maintains that we can only use the language against itself. Citing Levi Strauss's critique of anthropology, he suggests that the language of European philosophy and social science remains simultaneously 'both indispensable and inadequate' when examining colonial practices. The use of Levi Strauss in this context is fortuitous for us, because Levi Strauss was reflecting on his field encounters with Indigenous people in South America, where he found that the tool box of ideas he had brought with him from Europe were not up to the task – but remained, nonetheless, the only tools he had. They became a starting point for examining the field, but needed to be constantly updated, reviewed, revised and reconfigured in dialogue with the realities, myths, beliefs and practices of the new world he encountered.

Of course, one of the definitive shifts in thinking within anthropology since Levi Strauss has been an increased stress on research reflexivity, which has problematised the very notion of the 'field' as an independent reality 'out there' having an autonomous existence outside of the categories 'we' (white anthropologists, criminologists, administrators etc) employ to create it. The painful process of 'decolonising anthropology' (Gullestad 2006), for example, has involved an awareness of these processes and an increased willingness to examine critically those aspects of white European culture, which enabled us to appropriate much of the world, not simply territorially, but also at a profoundly cultural level. Following Chakrabarty we may consider having to 'provincialise' criminology. By which I mean seeing criminology, with all its strengths and weaknesses, as a product of a particular set of narratives created by what Van Swaaningen (1997) pithily described as a series of dead Europeans and living Americans.

Chakrabarty and his colleagues, in what became known as the 'subaltern studies' group, explored the relationship between colonial structures and the creation of dominant and subordinate cultures. The continuing relevance of colonialism in the context of Indigenous Australia, however, has been questioned by some theorists. Some recent critical anthropological writing, for example, has attempted to shift discussion of Aboriginal issues beyond the colonisation/ decolonisation binary, tied – it is claimed – to outdated notions of left and right politics and some generally wearied clichés about identity and self-determination. In their introduction to a series of essays on new anthropological writings – and threaded through the various (though not all) contributions to the edition – Cowlishaw, Kowal and Lea (2006) maintain that a number of profound shifts have taken place in the whole discourse of Indigenous affairs when:

> [A]n Indigenous elder calls for welfare payments of remote community members living in Darwin's 'long grass' to be cut, it is not analytically adequate to dismiss this as some kind of false consciousness, even if we might cringe at the alacrity with which such opinions are gleefully reported. (Cowlishaw, Kowal & Lea 2006: ix)

The incident referred to here involved a widely publicised event in which a Larrakia elder (the traditional owners of the Darwin area) berated a number of 'long grassers' (generally people from remote communities living rough in and around Darwin) about their disrespectful, anti-social behaviour and suggesting they return to their communities.

Cowlishaw, Kowal and Lea abstract the comments of these Indigenous elders from their political and cultural contexts. To begin with, the actions of the Larrakia Nation, which has included developing a number of 'cultural protocols' – codes of behaviour for visitors to follow when in Darwin focused on respectful behaviour – have been made in the context of intense pressure from government, the media and sections of the white community for 'long grassers' to be removed from the town, some of the pressure has been directed at the Larrakia themselves. The issue of 'anti-social behaviour' and public incivilities became a hot political issue in the lead up to the recent election in the Northern Territory, and saw the introduction of new police 'move on' and anti-social behaviour orders. Enormous pressure was placed on the Larrakia to distance themselves from the behaviour of outsiders. Is this indicative of people abandoning Aboriginal culture, or does it simply illustrate the kinds of pressures currently being brought to bear on urban Aboriginal people, who may see their *survival* as Aboriginal people being tied to keeping other Aboriginal groups out of their country? What we might be witnessing here is the shredding of some lingering illusions about pan-Aboriginality, where local difference gives way to a broader Aboriginal identity, and the reassertion of traditional notions of ownership of country by a single group.

The authors receive a mild rebuke from Dipesh Chakrabarty who, in a foreword to the text, suggests that the authors are too eager to abandon 'old apparatuses of understanding' which have, admittedly, shown some 'wear and tear' (Chakrabarty 2006: iii). He writes:

> [T]he colonial model is not so easily disposed of. For the Aboriginal populations of this country have suffered *systemic* and *systematic* discrimination. Explaining such a systemic and/or systemic discrimination calls for a larger historical category (like colonialism, racism and so on). The figure of mobility – or any other figure of indeterminacy – cannot explain why certain disadvantages tend to become systemic. In the absence of a better explanation, the colonial paradigm retains a residual attraction, at least for the time being. (Chakrabarty 2006: iv)

Despite their 'wear and tear', constructs such as racism, colonialism, colonial discourse and systematic racism continue to have a place in the analysis of relationships between Indigenous people and criminal justice. There is still a need for critiques of criminal justice taking colonialism as a point of departure and challenging the legacy of what Spivak (1996) calls the 'colonial imagination' continues to have on our thinking. Working in the difficult and challenging space between Indigenous and non-Indigenous domains requires that we constantly face up to, and challenge, the often subtle and insidious ways in which our own privileged position as – usually – white researchers informs our relationship with Aboriginal people.

Part of the process of decolonising criminology involves being aware of the racism inherent within the workings of the criminal justice system and sensitivity to the narratives and discourses of marginalised voices. There has always been a link between positivist research methods and the colonial project. Seeing the Indigenous world from that privileged standpoint of what Stuart Hall has called that ubiquitous 'white eye' (Hall 1995) gives us the power to gaze at the other while blanking out ourselves. 'We' and our own cultural baggage, are rendered unseeable though the deployment of scientific methods focusing attention on the subject (Aboriginal crime, Aboriginal violence) while excluding from scrutiny the cultures, desires and practices of the subjects doing the looking: permitting us to sermonise on Aboriginal crime and violence without having to take account of the fact that, in Aboriginal cultural memory, we arrived uninvited, proceeded to trash the place, desecrated its most sacred places, destroyed its native flora and fauna, appropriated the bodies of the women, humiliated the men, ran off with the children, disrespected the religion, introduced poisonous and illicit substances, and flogged and killed with relative impunity.

What weight can and should we attach to such factors when seeking causes for over-representation in the criminal justice system and for endemic violence in some Indigenous communities? Do they simply represent a tragic backdrop against which to establish debates about present circumstances? A set of 'distal' rather than 'proximate' causes, to be gestured at but essentially excluded from, our analysis of contemporary issues, as in Don Weatherburn's (2013) work? It is convenient for us to view the past as another country, yet for Indigenous people our past is their present, and their future, as long as they remain prisoners of our incapacity to acknowledge the extent to which the traumas of (denied) colonial violence continue to reverberate within Indigenous families and communities.

As we shall see in later chapters, many Aboriginal people maintain that dispossession, loss of land and culture, the desecration of Aboriginal sites, the breakdown of skin and moyete systems (traditional rules for identifying appropriate marriage partners), the unwillingness of white authorities to acknowledge the jurisdiction of Aboriginal laws, have *direct and immediate* relevance both to criminal behaviour and to processes of criminalisation.

A group of highly respected Indigenous women elders I met with in the town of Fitzroy Crossing in 2015, who work around issues such as alcohol abuse, Foetal Alcohol Spectrum Disorder (FASD) and family violence, suggested that many Indigenous young people grow up with a profound sense of loss and grief which, these women suggested, is shaped both by personal experience (deaths, violence, family dislocation) and an inherited sense of loss and grief stemming from dispossession. This combination, they maintained, led to a sense of fatalism and lack of worth, leading often to suicide, violence, alcohol and drug abuse and anti-social behaviour. For many Aboriginal communities the damage of colonisation survives in the present, it is not a thing of the past, it continues to shape people's inner and outer realities.

The RCIADIC recognised the importance of social and historical forces when developing the notion of 'underlying issues', to describe the complex interplay of structural, personal and historical factors underpinning Aboriginal involvement in the system. Commissioner Patrick Dodson provided the following explanation of underlying issues in his report on Western Australia:

> In determining what constitutes an 'underlying issue', I have examined all social, cultural, legal and economic matters as they directly and indirectly affect the constantly high rate of imprisonment of Aboriginal people in this State. In sum, an 'underlying issue' can be defined as understanding the 'why' and 'how' of high rates of Aboriginal incarceration. (Dodson 1991: 5)

The issues identified by Dodson include a number typical of conditions of 'powerlessness' and 'ongoing marginalisation':

[T]he ongoing effect of mission and other-forms of institutionalisation on the socio-cultural and economic lives of Aboriginal People; and some of the adverse effects of contemporary Aboriginal social life brought about by Aborigines themselves, as well as those from outside of Aboriginal society. Underlying issues are therefore those phenomena that arise in considering the legal, cultural, social and economic factors as they occur independent of the other society or through their interrelatedness to it. (Dodson 1991: 6)

Dodson, therefore, resists simply locating underlying causes in the actions of government, institutions, and other external structures. He identifies the 'adverse effects brought about by Aborigines themselves', through their interaction with justice and other systems, the internalisation of oppression and the tendency towards self-destruction.

Any attempt to fully explore the linkages between Aboriginal people and criminal justice must take into account a number of factors. First, Aboriginal justice issues have a *radical specificity*, a degree of difference, which sets them apart from those surrounding other groups: we cannot simply collapse Aboriginal justice issues into established conceptual categories such as disadvantage, multiculturalism, class, gender or race. Secondly, it is necessary to recognise that, while there are numerous intricate crossing points, hybrid zones and liminal spaces between Aboriginal and non-Aboriginal worlds (of an increasingly dense and complex nature – as I will discuss later), there remain aspects of Aboriginal social reality which are profoundly incommensurable to our own, and which have to be accepted, and respected, in difference.

The anthropologist Von Sturmer suggested that, 'Aborigines read life backwards and forwards. We read it forwards; the past is only a means to an end; a teleology not characteristic of Aboriginal thought' (Von Sturmer, cited in Williams 1986: 7). Many Indigenous peoples weave in and out of modernity on a daily basis (Calanicos, 1995), combining time in the western present with time in the ancestral past. The notion of 'progress' as employed by Indigenous people differs from enlightenment notions of linear progress that assume a process of shedding archaic traditions and embracing individual autonomy. Instead, it may involve the capacity to achieve a constructive balance between modern and pre-modern modalities of living. This is a journey through time that is circular rather than linear, collective rather than individual.

Attempts to 'liberate' Aboriginal people from beneath the dead weight of tradition have generally had catastrophic consequences. Aboriginal people have resisted attempts to remake them in the mould of white society and have fought a long and bitter rear guard action to hang on to their law and culture (Davenport, Johnson & Yuwali 2005). They do not seek 'inclusion' into the mainstream culture and take a degree of pride in living Otherwise (Povinelli 2001, 2006). As Frances Morphy notes in relation to the Yolngu people of Arnhemland:

It is not simply that Yolngu value their difference and assert their 'right' to be different. From their point of view it is not a matter of choice. They feel themselves to be fundamentally and intrinsically different from 'white' people because of their relationship to their country and its ancestral forces. (Morphy 2007: 31)

In 1968, Stanner spoke of the 'great Australian silence' in relation to Indigenous people (Stanner 1968). In 2014, it is still possible for an Australian Prime Minister to speak of Australia as an 'unsettled' or 'scarcely settled, Great South Land', rather than a country with an uninterrupted occupation for 40,000 years. Indigenous peoples cannot gain purchase on the narrative structures of late-modernity. They belong to Europe's discursive past (our 'primitive' selves), so we find it difficult to see their *ongoing* struggles for recognition of Indigenous claims (which, because they inevitably involve land, appear quaintly anachronistic, the stuff of historical and anthropological research, rather than criminology).

The tendency to erase Indigenous suffering is apparent in the way Australia memorialises its past as a convict settlement. While sites such as the Port Arthur convict prison enjoy World Heritage status, the carceral history of Indigenous Australia has been deliberately obliterated. For example, Rottnest Island off the coast of Perth in Western Australia, a holiday destination 'blessed with a casual atmosphere, picturesque scenery, dazzling marine life and some of the world's finest beaches and pristine bays …',[3] was the site of a brutal regime. It was the only penal establishment in Australia specifically for Aboriginal people, many of whom were from the distant Kimberley region in the State's far north, transported several thousand kilometres from home for defending their lands against white invasion: between 1838 and 1931 some 369 Aboriginal prisoners died on Rottnest Island (five by hanging) (Green 1998). There are no monuments celebrating Rottnest as part of Australia's penal past; instead, the cells that warehoused Indigenous suffering have been knocked together to form *bijou* studios for guests at what is now the Rottnest Lodge. For most white people, the concentration camp on Rottnest, like other sites of colonial brutality, has been consigned to the deep past: for Aboriginal people, it remains part of a collective injustice, that still awaits recognition and restitution.

In the following chapters I aim to explore some of the limits of criminological knowledge in 'explaining' Indigenous people's interaction with mainstream justice through an examination of intrinsic Indigenous *difference*.

Notes

1   'Violence, Dysfunction, Aboriginality' speech to the National Press Club by Professor Mick Dodson: 'I am talking about violence that is now so entrenched in our relationships that the victims become the perpetrators of violent acts which continue to the next generation of children, so that even before those children reach adulthood, they in turn become perpetrators of violence against members of their own families' (Dodson 2003).

2   United Nations Declaration on the Rights of Indigenous Peoples, 107th plenary meeting, 13 September 2007. At Art 10: 'Indigenous peoples shall not be forcibly removed from their lands or territories. No relocation shall take place without the free, prior and informed consent of the indigenous peoples concerned and after agreement on just and fair compensation and, where possible, with the option of return'.

3   See <http://www.experienceperth.com/destinations/rottnest-island>.

2

Criminal Justice as Waste Management: Modernity and its Shadow

In recent years there has been a resurgence of interest in cross-national and comparative criminology. Much of this interest has focused on the ways criminal justice policy, philosophy and practices 'travels' (or not) between nation sovereign states (Sparks & Newburn 2002). Cultural globalisation provides a backdrop to these debates; in particular those perceived tendencies towards convergence with American-style crime control policies as representative in some crucial respects of late-modern culture (Garland 2001); as well as a recognition of the pressures towards the creation of supranational structures providing common points of reference on issues of international significance such as human rights, and drug/people trafficking.

Contemporary societies cannot exist in isolation from one another or from the multiple and far-reaching transformations engendered by globalisation. While economic changes, particularly those linked to international financial systems, are the most rapid, even instantaneous, the restructuring of other social institutions goes on apace. Globalisation is occurring on numerous levels, encompassing economic, social and cultural forms of integration. Yet there is an awareness among sociologists that globalisation is a complex and uneven process which includes within itself the paradox that cultures become more, rather than less, aware of their particularities and idiosyncrasies – through processes of *glocalisation*. The more progressive aspects of globalisation have seen an increased interest in institutions of global governance as well as a vibrant international human rights discourse capable of critiquing national legal systems. The success of human rights discourses in providing a transnational meta-narrative in this way reveals that reports proclaiming the death of the grand narrative may have been somewhat exaggerated.

Globalisation does not mean the dissolution of the nation state, far from it. What globalisation appears to be doing is to supplement and extend, as opposed to simply displace, the nation state. It has blurred the boundaries of state sovereignty in some areas, sharpened it in others. One outcome of this has been the replacement of the process of government with structures of 'governance', which Giddens (1998) suggests: are 'either … not part of any government … or are transnational in character' (Giddens 1998: 33). Sociologists tend to agree that what distinguishes this era is the increasing *density, intensity, scale and durability of global networks* (Beck 2000; Giddens 1998). There is also significant agreement that the process is probably irreversible and beyond the capacity of any one national government or bloc to control.

There is now a burgeoning literature on global 'policy convergence' and 'policy transfer', generally interpreted to mean the process whereby the institutions and structures of policy formation developed in one society are transferred to another (Dolowitz & Marsh: cited in Lendvai & Stubbs 2007): generally from global north to global south. 'What is common to all this literature', Clarke et al suggest, 'is the rather linear notion of movement being described. Policy ideas or models are rendered as 'objects' to be loaded up on a truck at point A and unloaded at point B' (Clarke et al 2015: 15). Policy transfer often, in fact, involves processes of dialogue, interpretation and negotiation. Lendvai and Stubbs (2007) describe a globalised, transnational environment where policies are constantly being translated, rather than simply transferred. As Edward Said observes in *The World and the Text*:

> Like people and schools of criticism ideas and theories travel – from person to person, from situation to situation, from one period to another. Cultural and intellectual life are usually nourished and often sustained by the circulation of ideas. (Said 1984: 3)

Said offers the caveat, however, that such movements 'are never unimpeded', they undergo processes of 'representation and institutionalisation different from those at the point of origin'. Said observes that travelling ideas tend to dissipate as they traverse time and space, they become domesticated and assimilated, their meanings transformed, even lost, in translation. In settler colonial societies the issue of policy transfer becomes yet more complex. Settler societies borrow, translate and adapt ideas from other sovereign nation states, or via the network of transnational bodies developed by western nation states to manage globalisation. There is then a secondary process as these policies are imposed on the Indigenous population.

Societies such as Australia have become net importers of American crime-speak (zero tolerance, three strikes, judicial activism, revolving doors, adult crime/adult time etc) as well as a host of measures, policies and procedures designed to fix the problem (increased prison building, gated communities, mandatory sentencing, naming/shaming juveniles). However, set against the integrationist argument that criminal justice policies have become uniform and homogenised, are a set of arguments pointing to the continuing salience of local factors in shaping policy. O'Malley (2002), and Jones and Newburn (2002) point to the persistence of beliefs and values that set limits on the importation of correctional and judicial strategies. Australia, despite the tendency to adopt American crime-speak, has, according to O'Malley (2002), resisted mass imprisonment as a solution to crime problems (a view which, problematically, ignores the ubiquity of mass-imprisonment for the Indigenous population – as we have seen).

Mainstream criminological theory remains wedded to a number of conceptual orthodoxies, which prevent exploration of the complex internal ordering of post-colonial social formations. Cavadino and Dignan (2006), for example, in their critique of the global homogenisation thesis, maintain that there are a number of distinctive political economies – categorised in their work as neo-liberal, conservative corporatist, social democratic, and Orientalist corporatist – each manifesting its own specific set of values that influence its degree of punitiveness: hingeing on socially embedded beliefs about whether deviants should be included or excluded from society.

Cavadino and Dignan (2006) place Australia in the 'neo-liberal' category; meaning that Australia has been strongly influenced by contemporary American philosophies privileging individualism, minimal state intervention and residual rather than active welfare. They suggest, however, that Australia also has traces of 'social democracy'. This picture, while impressionistically plausible, has a number of inherent flaws. First, the tendency to reduce complex social formations to simple types, (neo-liberal, corporate etc) elide significant differences in historical experience and social structure – the generalisations come at the cost of neglecting cultural and social nuance, and local structures of sentiment and feeling. Secondly, there is an absence of analysis of colonialism, and how colonial structures bifurcate, fragment and refract processes, ideologies and practices into racially distinct forms. Settler colonial societies such as Australia, Canada and New Zealand, like apartheid South Africa, are not one society, but remain socially and culturally bifurcated between a, largely, white settler mainstream and an Indigenous minority. It is possible to argue, in relation to Australia, that there remain strong, rather than weak, currents of social democratic practice influencing criminal justice practices, but these currents flow in the direction of non-Aboriginal Australians. Aboriginal Australia has been the object not just of 'neo-liberal' principles of punishment but traditional mechanism of colonial order maintenance. These objects have meshed together to form a kind of *neo-liberal/colonial assemblage* that retains elements of traditional frontier policy sutured onto modern discourses enshrining individualist solutions and social responsibilisation.

Running in parallel with neo-colonial/neo-liberal practices are a suite of innovations – around alternative sentencing, alternatives to custody, drug diversion, youth conferencing, post-prison re-entry and reintegration, supported parole, supervised release initiatives, therapeutic jurisprudence – which smack of social democratic and inclusionary thinking. These, however, have yet to benefit Indigenous offenders, who continue to be incarcerated in increasing numbers: indeed all such practices have done in some States is to further bifurcate the system along racial lines, increasing the *rate* of over-representation, further marking off the Aborigine as the natural and incorrigible offender.

The fundamental factor limiting the relevance of comparative, cross-national and cross-cultural criminology to the study of Aboriginal Australians – or any other Aboriginal people – lies in the notion of the *nation state* itself as the point of departure for comparative inquiry. In many crucial respects Indigenous people constitute a separate society, but they do not have a separate state structure. Indigenous people, as Marshall-Beier points out, lack the basic requirement for being taken seriously within 'mainstream scholarship', a 'Westphalian state' (Marshall-Beier 2004: 83): statehood being viewed as the only acceptable and legitimate form of political organisation possible; there can be no political process without the authority of the state. Marshall-Beier argues that this notion of state-centred power, coupled with a view of Indigenous society as existing in a Hobbesian state of nature, without structure and order, has rendered Indigenous people invisible to western scholarship – other than as a disadvantaged group. Moreover, this 'invisibility' (which he sees in the works of cross-national 'international relations' scholarship, but the implications are much broader) has legitimated a tendency to 'characterise the settler states resident on their [Indigenous people's] territories as *former* colonists, thereby mystifying the contemporary workings of advanced colonialism' (Marshall-Beier 2004: 4).

Indigenous people become absorbed into the larger national entity and collapsed into established 'cross-cultural' and multicultural categories. They become just another cultural or ethnic group adjusting to the demands of the mainstream culture. Yet, Aboriginal people articulate a set of demands that set them apart from immigrants and other minorities, as I will return to later.

Mass imprisonment

Levels of Aboriginal incarceration bear comparison with the 'mass imprisonment' (Garland 2001) or 'hyper-incarceration' (Wacquant 2001) phenomenon identified in the United States – described by Garland as the 'systematic imprisonment of whole groups of the population' (Garland 2001: 2) – the groups in question in the United States being young urban black and Hispanic males. Garland forwards a number of reasons for the emergence of mass imprisonment: including truth in sentencing, mandatory sentencing, zero-tolerance policing and, particularly, the war on drugs. The mass imprisonment thesis has been criticised for extrapolating from American experiences. Other societies – Australia, the United Kingdom and Western Europe, for example – while undoubtedly subject to authoritarian populist strategies – have not experienced the explosion of imprisonment found in the United States.

If, as suggested earlier, we look less at aggregated statistics and focus on race, the picture looks different. In Australia, Indigenous people represent a fraction of the population in comparison with blacks in the United States. As noted in Chapter 1, there has been an explosion in the incarceration of Indigenous people as a percentage of the prison population, the system is moving in the direction of being an Aboriginal prison system. This has been masked by a process, which has resulted in the decarceration of many white offenders, through diversion, greater use of community-based services, the greater use of fines (which work in favour of the affluent and waged). Aboriginal people have not benefited from these reforms because they represent too great a risk for diversion, often fail necessary eligibility requirements for community-based alternatives, are a bad risk for parole, and are usually unemployed and homeless.

It is also necessary to separate Aboriginal justice issues from those effecting ethnic minority groups. Indigenous people were the subject of a specific set of colonial practices premised on the well-embedded belief that their evolutionary time was up and they were destined for extinction. Aboriginal people were modernity's 'waste': the criminal justice system became one of a number of sites of *waste management*[1] for those stigmatised as belonging to a doomed race, and a warehouse for those who resisted the process. The use of the carceral system in this way was a feature of Australian colonial expansion. The danger of simply importing the cultures of control and 'mass incarceration' theses, as developed by Garland, to the Australian context, lie in the fact that Garland's elegant and persuasive analysis is premised on the belief that there was a rupture, or break, with liberal welfare policies of the post-war era replaced by a new focus on retribution and incapacitation. This assumes a periodisation that does not necessarily transfer itself to the colonial setting. This is largely because Aboriginal people had never been included in the benefits of the welfare era; they had always remained outside the public realm and were subject since colonisation to strategies designed to further their elimination.

I would like to introduce what Edward Said (1993) referred to as a 'contrapuntal' dynamic – or counterpoint to this kind of periodisation. A post-colonial analysis may stress the pervasive *continuities* between technologies of control over time for colonised peoples and the possibilities that the post-colonial social formations of settler societies are capable of maintaining a number of radically divergent practices bifurcated according to Indigenous and non-Indigenous status. Socioeconomic and penal policies in the colonies do not fit the established periodisations mapped out in many western texts, from punitive to liberal welfare, to neo-liberal etc. These had an effect but were not in dominance, they tended to be over-determined by strategies intended to eradicate the Aboriginal race.

Western penological strategies were intended to manage dangerous populations. We may develop a case for arguing that colonial discourse framed the template for control of populations deemed *unnecessary*, as opposed to simply *dangerous*. Looked at in this way, can American correctional policies be said to simply be catching up with colonial practices in settler societies and other colonial regimes? Employing correctional strategies as a means of warehousing a 'doomed race'? The recognition that the colony frequently acted as a laboratory for technologies of repression eventually to be repatriated to the colonial centre was apparent to Hannah Arendt, who pointed out that it was in colonial Africa that the ideologies and beliefs that would form the basis for European totalitarianism were nurtured and prefigured (Arendt 1973); and to Franz Fanon, who maintained that German fascism largely refined technologies of repression widespread in Europe's colonies (Fanon 1990).

It seems that advanced western societies at certain times create, or identify, a surplus population that cannot be accommodated economically or socially and for whom special measures are contemplated. Robert Staples and Sydney Willhelm have made a bleak assessment of the future for black men in the United States, who have become, Staples argues – like Maori, Native American and Aboriginal men before them – the 'excess baggage' of white dominated societies, and are increasingly being placed in conditions which 'threaten to institutionally decimate' them (Staples 1994: 67).[2] While Willhelm maintains that the wholesale removal of blacks from the labour market – a process he terms the 'economics of uselessness'– is creating not a black underclass but a strata of déclassé individuals 'no longer needed for their labour' (Willhelm 1994: 48). He draws on Sartre's idea of 'conditional genocide' to describe a future in which blacks will be forced to accept a reduced and destitute existence in isolated ghettos or risk extermination if they rebel. This tacit 'understanding' between black Americans and the centres of power, he argues, mirrors past 'understandings' with Native Americans: stay on the reservation or be annihilated (Willhelm 1994: 51).

Feeley and Simon (1992) suggest that the emergence of the 'new penology' reflected 'the influence of a more despairing view of poverty and the prospects for achieving equality' (Feeley and Simon 1992: 468). At its core the new penology involved 'lowered expectations' (Feeley and Simon 1992: 469), abandoning any pretence that we can rehabilitate and reform, limiting ourselves instead to quotidian practices of surveillance and control. This new realism was the natural accompaniment to a broader set of pessimistic ideologies portraying the dispossessed as an urban underclass, to be feared and despised and, above all, strategically and ritually exorcised from the moral nexus of civil society as essentially beyond redemption. Garland makes similar claims in his 'cultures of control' thesis, in which he maintains that the rise of 'punitive sanctions and expressive justice' (Garland 2001) signify a radical departure from liberal strategies of social engineering in favour of punitive segregation and control of offenders. Lois Wacquant's work is closer in orientation to critical race theorists like Staples and Willhelm in the sense that he directly links late-modern penologies to broader shifts in the management of problem racial groups: whereas for writers such as Feeley and Simon and Garland, race – while acknowledged as important – is not granted such definitive status.

In an important article in the journal *Punishment and Society*, Wacquant (2001) speaks of a 'deadly symbiosis' between prison and ghetto in America; where race has ceased being a social welfare issue and becomes an issue of penal management, and he situates these developments within an 'historical sequence of 'peculiar institutions' that have shouldered the task of defining and confining African Americans' (Wacquant 2001: 95). These two situating factors: the historical management of the dispossessed within a diversity of institutions, regimes and enclosures; the contemporary symbiosis between prison and ghetto, lifts the debate from within the narrow confines of the penological regime alone and firmly positions it within contemporary crises around the management of race. Wacquant suggests that, because of sweeping economic changes, a *carceral continuum* exists between prison and ghetto, with the ghetto becoming more like the prison, and the prison more like the ghetto (Wacquant 2001: 97).

The new language of created by these transformations condenses blackness and criminality within a tightly unified discourse. It is a frightening picture of mass imprisonment and a form of sociocide that retains the body (which becomes a commodity within new corporate/incarceral assemblages without which these new privatised systems could not yield profits) while eliminating social identity. Black Americans are corralled along a 'school to prison' pipeline, fixed in place (ghetto/prison), through a form of spatial and carceral apartheid.

Zygmunt Bauman discusses 'globalisation' as a process which increasingly emancipates the 'first world' from the constraints of time and place, while simultaneously chaining the 'second world' (the 'locally tied') to the painful deprivations of an increasingly more impoverished and socially restricted locality. So, while the inhabitants of the first world live in a 'perpetual present', enjoying a life over-flowing with incident:

> People marooned in the opposite world are crushed under the burden of abundant, redundant and useless time they have nothing to fill with. In their time 'nothing ever happens' ... They can only kill time as they are slowly killed by it (Bauman cited in Beck 2000: 56)

Bauman's focus on the 'locally tied' versus those unconstrained by time and place, while providing a vivid metaphor for the uneven impact of globalisation, has some limitations when applied to Indigenous people, however. Bauman's work has been influential in shaping our understanding of late-modernity, or what he prefers to call 'liquid' modernity, due to its increasing tendency towards individualism, transnationalism, privatisation and fluidity – a domain of shifting allegiances and identities, rootless nomadism and fractured identities (see, for example, Bauman 2004). This emphasis on liquidity and mobility is dangerous because it elides the continuing importance of struggles and contestations around belonging to place in the Global South (Escobar 2001). Even Manuel Castells, whose work on 'networked societies' (2010) charted the emergence and domination of the 'space of flows', which had enormous influence on the mobilities and globalisation literature, expresses concern that the focus on movement should not eclipse the importance of place, particularly in the context of nurturing social solidarity (Castells 1999: 297).

Globalisation does homogenise and standardise on some levels while, paradoxically providing mechanisms for the definitively local to flourish. To the extent that is does restructure and realign relationships between global agency and the sovereign nation state it can open up new pathways for Indigenous people to operate outside its debilitating structures of control. Aboriginal artists in remote communities advertise their work on the Internet, travel to Berlin, London and New York to exhibit their work and thereby by-pass the suffocating paternalism and the patronising racism that too often informs Australian views of them and their work.[3]

Globalism may also allow Aboriginal people to recover elements of traditional culture previously repressed by religious and governmental institutions. The products of the global culture, which rapidly destroy barriers of time and place have had an enervating impact and have made a renaissance in traditional culture possible. The introduction of the motor car into remote regions in the 1960s made it possible to revive initiation ceremonies – participants were now travelling thousands of kilometres to attend ceremony, rituals were revived – moreover the journey itself provided an opportunity for creating solidarity and cultural cohesion, involving sharing traditional songs and stories (Peterson 2000).

Aspects of modernity – good roads, modern communication, four-wheel drive vehicles – opened up possibilities for visiting and reconnecting with country. The current cycle of 'law business' in the desert and central regions of Australia would not be possible without modern means of transport and communication. Modern forms of communication have allowed some Aboriginal people to break free of the 'outback ghettos' into which many were herded by governments and missions, and live on traditional homelands while still being connected to the modern world, creating 'hybrid economies' and communities free of alcohol and family violence. Moreover, Indigenous people have employed the technologies of the global world to develop links with each other, and develop joint strategies on issues such as Indigenous human rights, via the UN Convention on the Rights of Indigenous People, social and culture intellectual property, as well as share information on land rights and justice reform.

For Aboriginal people, participating in globalism does not necessarily imply the renunciation of tradition. As we shall see, the well-established strategies of absorbing and taking hold of white materialism (accepting government rations, for example) has not involved relinquishing Aboriginality, it represents, rather, a mechanism for ensuring the survival of the essential nucleus of Aboriginal culture.

It is dangerous to overstate the degree of homogenisation instituted by processes of globalisation and overlook the extent to which social change is driven by a host of countervailing forces. Elizabeth Povinelli argues that, far from late-modernity standardising and homogenising the world, it is shadowed by a diversity of radically incommensurate worlds (or what Frazer (1992) calls 'subordinate counter-publics') evolving 'new ethical and epistemological horizons' within 'the complicated space and time of global capital and liberal democratic regionalism and nationalism' (Povinelli 2001: 319). Povinelli sees a diversity of 'competing social visions' (2001: 319) in play, set against powerful pressures towards rationalisation, closure and commensuration. Critical writing from within anthropology has adapted these insights to explore the shadow cultures and counter-publics forming on the margins of the modern world.

The risk society

Risk society theories maintain that the management of risk has become a key organising principle of daily life in the affluent west. Developed from the works of Beck (2000) and Giddens (2001) and taken forward in the criminological writing of O'Malley and others (see O'Malley 1998), risk society theory has become pivotal to the way many contemporary criminologists theorise the role of the state, global institutions and allied networks in the development and implementation of crime-related policies. According to the thesis, reducing risk has become an over-riding preoccupation of governments who have become steadily more risk averse: and it is shaping the way existing institutions do business, as well as bringing into being a suite of new institutions tasked to define, assess and manage risk. Risk society theories complement the gloomy prognoses that the future is unlikely to produce the prosperity and, above all, security assumed by architects of post-war society. Rather there is a deepening pessimism and widespread cynicism regarding the role of government, industry, scientists and experts generally to speak the truth – or even speak plainly – let alone build a more secure world. The contract with government has shifted from one where government would provide for the future, to one where government would play a minimalist role in the provision of security. Given also that these governments increasingly operate according to neo-liberal principles, where government 'steers' rather than 'rows', the contract would be executed in partnership with an array of other institutions including the private sector. This is the second key motif in risk society thinking: the transformations taking place in the willingness and capacity of the state to provide security to citizens outside of an alliance with other players. There is an increased patchwork of security provision suturing together a growing private sector – which is increasingly dwarfing government – with traditional providers.

In many respects criminal justice policy has always involved the identification and management of risk. Hudson (2003: 46) isolates, however, a shift away from the management of individual risk to the control of aggregate risk. In the contemporary context, she suggests, aggregated risk-focused policies are targeted at 'potential rather than actual offenders and victims' (Hudson 2003: 46) while new legislation increasingly moves towards 'risk assessment for (assumed) actual offenders which are based upon aggregates, on group characteristics rather than on knowledge of the individual about whom the assessment is made' (Hudson 2003: 46).

Hence, assignment to a particular category of offender judged to be of high risk in terms of recidivism – a statistical rather than a clinical assessment – may be sufficient to place an ex-offender on a register or ensure longer periods of supervision and parole (Hudson 2003). The aspect of the risk society thesis that has generated the greatest interest among criminologists has been the nexus between risk assessment, risk control and the general retreat from, or death of, the 'social'. Risk is not born socially, rather it is increasingly being privatised and the domain of 'private prudentialism' (O'Malley 1992).

Aboriginal people, as I have already suggested, have never been defined as a 'part of the public'. They have traditionally represented the other from which the public needs to be protected. Government has never taken responsibility for their security, paid the wages, nurtured their children – there never was a golden age of welfare or social democratic institutions concerned with their wellbeing. The story in relation to risk, therefore, needs to be read differently. While there are strategies in train designed to 'responsibilise' Aboriginal communities and introduce 'prudentialism', this should not be interpreted as the ending of a 'welfare state' era, with all the associated network of welfare institutions found under European social democracy. Indigenous people were never the recipiemts of this kind of largess, instead there was a form of 'passive welfare' in which dole cheques were dropped into under-resourced, makeshift camps – built to temporarily house groups assumed to be on the road to extinction. Aboriginal people have always been, in Hudson's terms, the subject of risk assessment on the basis of 'group characteristics' and fears about what they might do if left unchecked and uncontrolled. Is the 'risk society', then, less a new phenomenon, than another instance of modern western society adopting and refining group-based control strategies developed in the colony?

I have suggested thus far that western theory fails to take into account the experiences of *racism, colonialism and difference*, particularly the ways the settler state employed the law as a means of managing conflicts between races, and quite explicitly legitimated land theft through the imposition of white legal constructs (Anthony 2013).

Broadhurst (2002) suggests that attempts to explain over-representation by convention means have been 'largely unsuccessful' (2002: 256) and calls for an 'integrated approach' to the subject involving 'comparative, cross-disciplinary, and critical methods' to conceptualise the problem (2002: 256). Broadhurst finds that Australian theorists have tended to rely on traditional criminological theories to explain over-representation, from socio-biological through to social deprivation, strain, social disorganisation and conflict theories and there have been few attempts to develop 'multi-factorial and synthesis theories of Indigenous crime causation' (2002: 261) and defends theories focusing on colonial constructions of Aboriginalism and Orientalism as devices for understanding the situation of Aboriginal people. However, he argues that these perspectives assume a placid and docile population, whereas Aboriginal people have demonstrated a considerable capacity of resistance. He also finds merit in the works of anthropologists such as Trigger (1992) and Rowse (1998) who demonstrate the mechanisms through which Aboriginal people have been able to oppose and disrupt the process of colonisation through the maintenance of a separate Aboriginal identity (Broadhurst 2002: 24), and he sees parallels with 'sub-cultural theory' in terms of that theories emphasis on hedonism, autonomy and opposition. Broadhurst argues that high rates of imprisonment of Aboriginal people in States such as Western Australia and also in the Northern Territory are best viewed within a framework created by 'frontier culture', 'that is, a settler society that see itself as vulnerable and threatened by 'outsiders' of whom Aborigines – 'the exotic other' sustained by Aboriginalism – represent a traditional and recurring example' (Broadhurst 2002: 273).

He sees the frontier metaphor as justifying punitive responses to crime: social order and cultural boundaries need to be constantly defined and imposed in the face of the threat posed by the Aborigine. 'Frontier' is the site for 'moral ambiguity' and considerable uncertainty; it requires considerable attention in terms of policing and, occasionally, repression. Broadhurst's use of frontier is best applied in metaphorical rather than descriptive/territorial terms. Western Australia and the Northern Territory are both frontier States, however, the conflict between the justice system and Aboriginal people in those States is not confined to the 'outback'. It takes place in urban areas such as Darwin and Perth – the Northbridge area of the latter represents a kind of frontier where the unsettling presence of Aboriginal youth disturbs the ordered flow of post-modern time (middle-class entertainment, conspicuous consumption, al fresco dinning). Urban, as well as rural and remote, Aboriginal people are significantly over-represented in the criminal justice system in the Northern Territory (Cunneen 2001b). In Western Australia, while arrest rates are high in areas such as the remote Kimberley region, the difference between rates is highest in the more urbanised south-west, where Aboriginal people have been found to be between 11 and 13 times more likely to be arrested than non-Aboriginal people, as opposed to eight times in the Kimberley (Ferrante, Loh, Maller, Valuri & Fernandez 2004).

The degree to which colonial conditions spawned an approach to punishment for the Aboriginal population different from the system reserved for whites, illustrates the need to treat cautiously those periodisations in the development of penal regimes derived from European and American criminology. Punishment had a different trajectory for Aboriginal people. As Finnane and McGuire (2001) note, in excess of 100 Aboriginal people were judicially executed in the 19th century: the ultimate penalty was viewed by colonists as the educative instrument for 'savages', and it was retained for Indigenous people after it was abolished for whites in Queensland, Western Australia and South Australia. Execution in public, involving Indigenous spectators, at the scene of the crime, would offer a 'moral' lesson to blacks and reassure whites that the Aboriginal menace was met with vigilance. Even when such brutal strategies fell into misuse, imprisonment was employed as a means of managing the dispossessed:

> Incarceration within unique institutions, segregation from the settler population and surveillance and regulation through an expanding bureaucracy were strategies of social control increasingly deployed in an attempt to address the distinctive challenges posed by a dispossessed indigenous population. (Finnane & McGuire 2001: 279)

We have tended to use abnormal total institutions – those normally employed in the west to exclude, stigmatise and denigrate – as routine mechanisms for managing contact with Aboriginal people. As John Pratt (1998) has pointed out, these institutions were implanted along with an ideology which viewed involvement in them as a sign of moral failure and a lesser eligibility principle that ensured the standards of care provided would remain inferior to those found in the outside worlds. Frontier institutions played a role, not in assimilating Aboriginal people into the mainstream, but in inscribing the stigma of difference. Stigma, according to Goffman (1990), refers to 'an attribute that is deeply discrediting' (1990: 13). 'By definition ... we believe the person with a stigma is not quite human. On this assumption we exercise varieties of discrimination, through which we effectively, if often unthinkingly, reduce his life chances' (1990: 15).

This is not to say that all Aboriginal people accepted the stigma of difference. For non-Aboriginal people, the stigma of involvement in the justice system represented a means of confirming the difference of race.

Enigmas of arrival: migration, disorganisation and diaspora

Immigrant experiences are deeply embedded in the psyche of western criminology. The immigrant and the immigrant community were the natural subject for criminological inquiry. Various forms of social disorganisation theory – the classical lens through which the experience of diaspora was framed – have had considerable impact on the ways modern criminology observes deviant behaviour. The birth of the great modern cities of the United States and, to a lesser extent, Western Europe, provided a social laboratory where the consequences of cultural conflict and social dislocation could be studied alongside various strategies and techniques of adaptation, co-existence and integration. Park's (1915) and Shaw and McKay's (1942) seminal work in Chicago were formulated through observations of a city in constant flux, as new immigrants, fleeing the conflicts, revolutions, counter-revolutions and pogroms of Middle and Eastern Europe, arrived in Chicago seeking a better life. Shaw and McKay (1942) were concerned with the impact these changes had on crime rates. Their fieldwork found the city to be in dynamic movement, developing outwards from a central hub (these days a CBD) in a series of concentric circles. Crime rates were not distributed evenly across the city but were concentrated in the zones adjacent to the city centre and diminished further away from the centre. When ethnic groups moved outwards and acquired the trappings of citizenship, they did not take the propensity for crime with them; this remained embedded in the locality they left behind, to be inherited by the next ethnic immigrant out-group. High crime rates were a manifestation of the social disorganisation inevitable when groups uproot themselves, or are forcibly uprooted, from one place and relocate themselves, or are relocated, somewhere else. Cunneen and White place this gloss on the work of Shaw and McKay:

> They argued that delinquency can be viewed as part of the natural social process of settling in experienced by new immigrants. Specifically, these communities were seen to exhibit a high degree of social disorganisation. (Cunneen & White 1995: 50)

The overall message contained in the works of the Chicago school is one of adaptation. The dominant language, culture, religion, values and political processes have to be learned, or at least negotiated: some aspects of the old culture are left behind, others modified, others kept private, others displayed as emblems of cultural difference. Immigrants learn, and modify, the rules of the new society. Young people, because much of their lives take place in the public realm, are the ones who most routinely come into contact with what Althusser referred to as the 'repressive' and 'ideological' apparatuses of the state (Althusser 1971): as represented by the police on the street and the teacher in the classroom: the latter have the task of creating decent citizens from the polymorphous mass of new arrivals. Youths form gangs to protect themselves and the neighbourhood; and to provide a form of status defence. But, when they formed neighbourhood sub-cultures they also performed an extraordinarily conformist act (no matter how deviantly oppositional in content the subculture is) because it replicates the dominant mode of stable integration; the settled neighbourhood group, a local community free of dreaded itinerancy and rootlessness. Gangs may be oppositional but they also conform with a number of the core beliefs, rituals and practices of the mainstream, they structure their lives around a territorial core (the neighbourhood) and develop internally highly stratified hierarchies celebrating many of the conservative attributes of mainstream beliefs (particularly those around masculinity and power) but living them out radically. Shaw and McKay's (1942) work illustrates the effects of rapid social change, where customary rules are made redundant. It fits well with the experience of Australian migrants, who are often labelled as outsiders and subject to racist treatment: the majority of whom, however, eventually 'fit in', leaving the latest group of arrivals – in recent years, people from the Horn of Africa who are rapidly replacing Vietnamese and Cambodian people – as a source of mainstream anxiety. What, however, do these theories say about Aboriginal people?

Aboriginal experiences of dispossession were not diasporic. They were never new arrivals to a new country. Their country was taken from them. A complete set of foreign laws, institutions, peoples, economies, beliefs, rituals, diseases, flora and fauna simply dropped on them uninvited. Despite attempts by the state to dismantle Aboriginal culture, Aboriginal people have retained strong links with country, law and language: culture for Aboriginal people is not a nostalgic memory of a foreign place kept alive through cultural rituals, but a compelling and immediate force in their lives; animate in the landscape around them and renewed on a daily basis though connection with kin. A sense of ownership, at least for Aboriginal people, is real not symbolic.

It is important that non-Aboriginal criminological researchers at least listen to and then weigh up the implications of what Aboriginal people tell us about their connections with the Australian continent, before imposing Eurocentric theories of order, symbolic attachment to place and vocabularies of meaning onto Aboriginal people. What Aboriginal people tell us is that they are in many crucial respects a separate society. We have then to imagine the implications, for theory and practice, of there being two separate social formations coexisting behind the carefully embroidered façade of one state, one language, one system of law. Nurturing these two social formations are two conflicting founding mythologies; one – the dominant one – is concerned with Australia as a 'new' society, the other is concerned with perhaps the oldest continuing culture anywhere in the world.

Some of the most cogent and forceful contemporary criminological writing is concerned with problems of inclusion and exclusion and the ways structured inequalities based on ethnicity and race in the United States and western Europe, create polarised and unequal societies. In the case of Indigenous peoples, however, the issues are not simply about racism, inequality and disadvantage – important though these issues are. Davenport, Johnson and Yuwali (2005) in their work on the Martu people of Western Australia go to the core of the issue when they write:

> The Martu cannot be viewed as an unfortunate projection of wider society. They have a distinct society. That society, grounded in the law, provides meaning, richness and aspiration. It sets priorities; people's decisions and actions are founded upon it. It influences the forms of social groupings and transactions and requires that people fulfil obligations. It allows creative accommodation of new resources and

situations, but it is essentially constant, unchangeable. To Martu, its prescriptions are paramount. (Davenport, Johnson & Yuwali 2005: 175)

Here lies the rub. Mainstream Australia might have less difficulty with Aboriginal people if they played the game according to the rules of 'multiculturalism', where a degree of difference is permitted provided that it is not perceived to be a threat to 'the Austinian paradigm of the indivisible sovereign' (Haverman 1999: 4), that has been taken on by the modern nation state. Being a 'distinct society', as the Martu believe themselves to be, represents a threat to national sovereignty. Even radical criminology has difficulty in embracing the specificity, the uniqueness, of Indigenous aspirations.

Critiquing critical criminology

Critical criminology has played a crucial role in broadening the framework of criminological debate by introducing two important layers of inquiry; first, that the genesis of crime has to be located within the social, economic and political structures of society; and, secondly, that the criminal justice system itself is complicit in manufacturing the very deviance it seeks to eliminate, and actively reproduces rather than reduces social inequalities (Taylor, Walton & Young 1971; Van Swaaningen 1997) On the other hand, critical criminology has been criticised on a number of levels:

- it has a preoccupation with the processes of *criminalisation* which obscures the reality and real effects of *crime*; it tends to minimise the genuine and deep problems of the inner city;
- it focuses too much on *inter*-group victimisation at the expense of *intra*-group victimisation, and;
- has a tendency to romanticise atavistic street cultures.

Nevertheless, what was (and remains) exciting about the project of critical criminology was the overt commitment to human emancipation and social justice as a necessary component of criminology: its progressive and transformative dynamic. It is eloquently and persuasively expressed in Jock Young's masterful study of social inclusion and exclusion (Young 1999) where he sees the transition from the exclusive society in terms of the dilution of old, suffocating traditions:

> For, it is in the breakdown of tradition, the opening up of individualism, the melting of all that is solid and fixed, 'the uninterrupted disturbance of all social conditions' which holds the key to the future and the possibility of transformative change. (Young 1999: 559)

Young's work illuminates all that is positive and progressive in critical criminology while exposing its weakness in relation to the Indigenous people: for whom 'inclusion' can equal 'assimilation', and for whom the elimination of difference can equal cultural genocide. Indigenous peoples have been engaged in a protracted struggle since colonisation to prevent the meltdown of tradition. In the context of the post-industrial western society, Young's radical critique places emancipation from tradition at the centre of political struggle. Abstracted from its western context and imported into the post-colonial world, however, these ideals can become immensely disabling rather than enabling. Indigenous people want to have their differences, indeed their *radical alterity* acknowledged. Modernity's emancipatory project includes cultural secularisation, individualism and rationalisation: enlightenment ideals, which continue to carry considerable weight. Was not the 'breakdown of tradition', the melting of all that was solid in Indigenous life not the greatest tragedy in Australian history?

The discipline of anthropology has less difficulty in this regard because its sets out a position which authenticates tradition. It celebrates difference, diversity and plurality: while sociology tends – as a science born of modernity – to focus on social change, the transformative effects of markets and tendencies to global homogeneity. Sociology has been concerned with those institutions brought into being by the industrial transformations of the past several hundred years (Giddens 1998) while anthropology has been concerned with small-scale societies with their roots still in the pre-modern world (Canclini 2005). The weakness of anthropology traditionally has been its excessive focus on cultural autonomy and lack of a macro-social dynamic – an issue I return to in relation to anthropological interventions around Aboriginal violence – as well as some historically embedded assumptions about what constitutes 'authentic' Indigenous culture and tradition, which have tended to deny agency and cultural variation.

Anthropology's close engagement with Indigenous culture has had negative as well as positive dimensions. Anthropological knowledge of 'real' cultures has placed anthropology in a highly privileged position, as the custodian of real Indigenous knowledge, passing judgement on what is 'Aboriginal' and what is not. Barry Hill's illuminating study of Carl Strehlow (Hill 2003) finds Strehlow literally in possession of Arranda language, ceremony and artefacts, able to contemptuously dismiss all attempts by the Arranda to renew tradition on the basis of his superior knowledge, and ownership of 'real' Arranda culture. White essentialism of this kind cripples strategies by Aboriginal peoples to redefine their cultures. My main concern with anthropological approaches has less to do with what they *place in* but what they *leave out* of inquiries in the Aboriginal domain. While academic anthropology has developed a reflexive position in relation to tensions between the 'field' and the 'academy', it has still to come to terms with broader social formation. Studies of life in Indigenous communities are frequently bereft of a larger, macro social context: of how the social relationships and problems such as alcohol abuse and violence are mediated through contact with powerful colonial apparatuses of control and coercion.

Colonialism post-colonialism

The meaning of the prefix *post* in post-colonial has been the subject of debate. I employ the term, not as implying a condition *after* colonialism, rather as representing an ensemble of cultural, social, political conflicts and debates occurring within societies sharing an experience of colonisation. In the mainstream social sciences, such as sociology, colonialism is no longer a fashionable topic. It had its heyday in the 1970s and 1980s when third world liberation movements caught the imagination of new left sociologists. Colonialism tended to be studied through the lens of 'development' and underdevelopment, progressive Marxist movements, revolution and modernisation (Frank 1971). Indigenous people were rarely mentioned, largely because their struggles did not fit the pattern of modernist *national* liberation movements in a simple and convenient way. What was rarely questioned in the sociology of development and underdevelopment was the desirability of progress itself, understood in its rational enlightenment form. The Trotskyist thesis of permanent revolution provided a timetable for the inevitability of socialism: industrial development was an inevitable precondition for eventual liberation, with 'backward' societies racing forward to catch up to modernised societies by collapsing together developmental stages. The state become, in Lois Althusser's formulation, 'the site and the stake' of progressive struggles (Althusser 1974), to be captured and transformed. These transformations imply the inevitable destruction of traditional cultures: all that is traditional and solid melts into air. Colonialism was an inevitable, if regrettable, step along the road to modernity (Said 1993).

The major writers associated with post-colonial discourse – as diverse as Franz Fanon, Edward Said, Homi K Bhabha, Gayatri Chakravorty Spivak and Robert Young – offer an alternative view of the relationship between the colonist and colonised, which focuses on the extent to which colonisation operated at a cultural as well as an economic level. In Spivak's terminology, the process of colonisation involved a blend of not only physical marginalisation and the theft of land, but also a profoundly *epistemic* form of violence. This becomes important later when we assess the significance of debates about recognition of customary law. I argue that the criminal justice system played, and still plays, a role in this process of cultural deracination.

Edward Said's classic study 'Orientalism' can be criticised for being too bleak and pessimistic in relation to the capacity of the colonised to break free from the structures of knowledge/power imposed by the coloniser. I maintain that such intellectual pessimism is actually essential when dealing with the dire predicament of Australian Aboriginal people. In response to his critics, Said (1993), although still working within a Foucauldian framework, modified his thinking to include processes of resistance to colonisation, and attempted to demonstrate the limitations of colonial discourse through his notion of 'contrapuntality', representing the ways alternative counterpoints and meanings emerge, creating fresh social movements, philosophies and ideas that challenge dominant narratives.

Space precludes a full exploration of the post-colonial theory and its implications for the study of Indigenous peoples, however, it is important to note the extent to which the post-colonial theories have been concerned with deposing the western enlightenment tradition from its place at the centre of all knowledge. In this respect these theories have mirrored the deconstructionist philosophy of Jacques Derrida. As Robert Young suggests, if *deconstruction* is about anything, it is about the deconstruction of the assumed primacy of the west (Young 1990).

Post-colonial theories have been read in parallel with post-modern theory: and the former would agree that the modern world is characterised by uncertainty and fluidity. Old certainties about human progress, rationality, the role of experts, the infallibility of science, have been ditched as we struggle to come to terms with the realities of global climate change, endemic human conflict and the failings of modernist projects to satisfy the basic human needs of the majority on our planet, let alone create a better one. One outcome of this disenchantment with enlightenment principles has been an increased willingness to countenance other forms of knowledge and forms of social organisation based on other traditions (Gray 1995). Where post-colonial theory has differed from post-modern theory is around engagement with culture. For post-modern theory, all culture is provisional and constantly in flux, it rejects all forms of 'essentialism', there can be no 'identity' as such, all subjectivities are inscribed in and through discourse. Post-colonial theory embraces a more pragmatic view of identity and even supports what Spivak calls 'strategic essentialism' (Spivak 1996: 159).

Colonised peoples depend on the development of an oppositional identity as the basis for struggle with the colonising power: this identity offers self-worth, dignity and the renewal of pre-contact cultures. A 'strategic essentialism' forms part of Indigenous people's challenge to the dominant, hegemonic culture. The strength of post-colonial critique is that it seeks to 'deprivilege hegemonic narratives and to hear voices marginalised in the colonial encounter, taking heed of the subjugated knowledges they bear' (Marshall-Beier 2004: 87). A key problem for western thinking lies in the fact that Indigenous peoples may view liberation politics in an entirely different way from the enlightenment tradition. Going back to my earlier point, the colonial state, for many third-world liberation movements, became the focus of struggle. What is difficult to imagine are forms of resistance that do not seek to take over the state, or reproduce it, but actively seeks to create distance from state structures and recreate traditional forms of order.

Colonialism created a set of images and narratives the overall effect of which was to unify the colonists on the basis of shared whiteness, to a large extent, minimising pre-existing class and regional differences, provided these were Anglo-Celtic classes and regional differences. Benedict Anderson remarked that 'communities are to be distinguished ... by the style in which they are imagined' (Anderson 1991: 6). The colonial project created a particular form of national imagination, in which the European masses could achieve redemption by racially stocking new lands with their blood and toil (Said 1993). New Zealand, as Pratt (2006) describes it, was imagined as a 'paradise' that needed to be defended against the denigrating influence of the criminal 'Other'. Read in retrospect, it is impossible to ignore the fascist elements in colonialism: the racial triumphalism; the belief in the essential superiority of white Europeans; the contempt for the evolutionary inferior blacks; the mystical belief in their rights to populate the world. These principles unified groups who might otherwise have come into class conflict. It provided a basis for common ground between labour and capital: colonial intentions over-determined other relationships. As Sigmund Freud writes: 'There is an advantage, not to be undervalued, in the existence of smaller communities, through which the aggressive instinct can find an outlet in enmity towards those outside the group' (Freud 1989: 5).

In the colonial era, a shared sense of colonial privilege tended to unify groups who might on other levels appear to have radically different, even competing interests. In Australian history, differences and conflicts between government agencies, economic interests and church groups existed over ways and means, but there was considerable underlying unity of purpose over ends, over the fundamental superiority of white men, white civilisation, white law and white religion. Until the 1960s, a whole swathe of social, cultural, economic and administrative policies were premised on the 'doomed race' thesis (McGregor 1997). Extinction 'was regarded as the Aboriginals inescapable destiny, decreed by god or by nature' (1997: ix). Police officers and missionaries, anthropologists and stockmen, diggers and pastoralists, might have had conflicting ideas about the ways to treat the black, but each generally maintained the belief that the Aborigine was a lesser species, destined to disappear in the face of the superior white civilisation – whether the 'dying pillow' was to be smooth or not is of less historical significance than the fact that oblivion itself was inevitable. It has been these over-arching beliefs premised upon notions of race, which tie together what might seem on the face of it to be radically divergent – even conflicting – class structures.

Reflecting on his own work on the practices of church missionaries, anthropologist Robert Tonkinson admits that he underestimated their role as bearers of a 'powerful alien culture', (cited in Davenport, Johnson & Yuwali 2005) and it was the fact that this culture was 'powerful' and 'alien', rather than any *specific religious content*, that was the crucial factor. The fact that it was a Christian belief system was of less importance than the fact that it reflected a wholly foreign cosmology; a different and imposed system of knowledge and beliefs, customs and manners, ways of thinking and being: and the new demands for conformity it created within a set of asymmetrical power relationships. Moreover, the new belief systems were backed up by the power of the law and the police, who enjoyed a monopoly over the legitimate use of violence.

Colonial relationships were not simply imposed from the barrel of a gun. They were mediated by rations and material goods (from flour through to basic healthcare) which locked Aboriginal people into a set of subordinate relationships with the white people who were the owners and controllers of these powerful and desired goods, acquiring them often meant accepting enclosure in institutions (particularly missions). At the same time Aboriginal people were being systematically dispossessed of the only commodity that may have given them more than simple slave status: their land. The implications of this process – where Aboriginal people appear to 'give up' their Aboriginality and their claims to the land in exchange for the bounties of civilisation – lies, in many respects, at the heart of this study. Before we examine these implications in detail, let us explore further some other important conceptual devices of colonial discourse, beginning with one that is perhaps its most characteristic, the notion of frontier: the 'frontier' and 'frontier conditions' resonant with images of harsh terrain, harsh conditions and, of course, harsh justice.

The continuing relevance of 'frontier'

The Oxford English Dictionary defines the frontier as '[t]he part of a country which fronts or faces another country; the marches; the border or extremity conterminous with that of another; the borders of civilisation'. We have tended to assume that the frontier was a phenomenon of the 19th century and no longer exists. This view is entirely wrong. In Australia the frontier still exists, although the forms it takes shift and move over time. Zygmunt Bauman is surely correct when he maintains that far from frontier being a thing of the past, modernity relentlessly generates new frontiers as it marches forward, transforming the world as it goes. He writes that as a 'frontier civilisation', modernity 'recreates itself and rejuvenates itself through a constant supply of lands to conquer' (Bauman 1995: 141), and he has this to say about its civilising mission that has direct and immediate relevance to the current debate about Aboriginal cultures and violence:

> Modernity legitimizes itself as a 'civilizing process' – as an ongoing process of making the coarse gentle, the cruel benign, the uncouth refined. Like most legitimations, however, this one is more an advertising copy than an account of reality … what it hides is that only through the coercion they perpetrate can the agencies of modernity keep out of bounds the coercion they swore to annihilate; that one person's civilizing process is another person's forceful incapacitation. The civilizing process is not about the uprooting, but the *redistribution* of violence. (Bauman 1995: 141)

As part of the process of nation building, the Australian state claimed the monopoly on the use of force, and outlawed the existing body of law (by denying its existence *as law*) and its forms of censure and punishment (by labelling them as violence). Yet, settler law was implanted through violence. Violence created the space (both metaphorically and figuratively) for law to be implanted, and the implanted law retrospectively legitimated the fruits of the founding violence and its methods. Agamben (1998) demonstrates how the imperative to create order from chaos permits sovereign power to authorise what he terms a 'state of exception' and suspend law. Colonial violence, therefore, was not the negation of law but the establishment of the preconditions under which law could be implanted. Furthermore, the state of exception created zones where 'the monopoly of violence could still fall outside the hands of the state' (Evans 2005: 70). Settlers often took the initiative in localised massacres and genocides (Reynolds 2013).

The monopoly of state power has allowed the settler colony to gloss over this eliminatory violence and legitimise its own mechanisms of oppression. As we shall see when we discuss customary law issues, we have been culturally programmed to view some forms of outright coercion in ways which minimise the brutal violence contained in them – imprisonment, containment in insane asylums: our capacity to routinise coercion through institutionalisation (see Foucault 1991) has simply sanitised the practice: '[O]ne category of coercion is called "enforcement of law and order", while the nasty word "violence" is reserved only for the second' (Bauman 1995: 141).

Gillian Cowlishaw expresses this eloquently in her analysis of Aboriginal violence versus officially sanctioned violence in New South Wales: it is essentially a contrast between instrumental and expressive forms of violence:

> The cool, cruel violence of correction, containment, or punishment is deemed rational, while violent actions performed in rage are deemed irrational, uncontrolled, and frightening. The former is characterized by intentionality to affect another person; the latter may cause hurt, but it is defined by its expressive nature. (Cowlishaw 2003: 105)

The success of the civilising process in the colonial context has been to further legitimate colonial violence while underscoring the mindless, indiscriminate savagery of Aboriginal violence. Frontier, therefore, no longer involves a simple line in the sand, a stockade, and the perimeter of a vulnerable homestead: it is not simply about territory in the sense of mapping some consistent boundary between the savage and the civilised, in the 'outback' (Broadhurst 2002). The frontier traverses the inner spaces of society, not just its outer limits. It has also ceased to be a narrow line in the sand: the thin red line has become a blue line that is both denser and more networked than in the years of the colony.

If we imagine frontier in *relational*, rather than *territorial* and *institutional*, terms then we can see elements of frontiers existing wherever Aboriginal and non-Aboriginal Australia confront one another. It takes shape in urban, rural and remote locations, along city streets, in parks, public houses, schools, offices, hospitals, prisons and youth detention centres, courts, at public events, in swimming pools, within shopping malls. Just because we on one side of the frontier insist it does not exist – the construct having outlived its usefulness to us – does not alter the fact that those on the other side of it confront its continued existence in their daily lives. 'Indigenous peoples', Paul Haverman suggests, 'continue to experience the "frontier" everywhere, long after the "settlers", "civilizing mission" and appropriation of their lands has ostensibly ended' (Haverman 1999: 7).

Franz Fanon named the frontier as it is created by colonisation a *Manichean* divide. This suggests a frontier built on more than simple difference, but one founded upon a set of religious, cultural and moral dichotomies. Manicheanism was a form of religious dualism, which supposed a primeval conflict between light and darkness, good and evil. For Fanon, the colonist saw him/herself as representing light while the native represented darkness – a fact only confirmed by the evidence of the eye.

For Fanon, the relationships between the colonisers and colonised is based upon 'pure force' (Fanon 1990: 28). Fanon describes the relationship and the role of the police in sustaining them, thus:

> The colonial world is a world cut in two. The dividing line, the frontiers are shown by barracks and police stations. In the colonies it is the policeman and the soldier who are the official, instituted go-betweens, the spokesmen of the settler and his rule of oppression. (Fanon 1990: 29)

Fanon recognised that relationships within western societies were cemented through social relationships engendering 'respect for the established order' (1990: 28): close to the Gramscian notion of 'hegemony', where the government rules by shaping and winning consent, rather than through coercion and oppression. While in the colonies, 'the agents of government speak the language of pure force', they bring only 'violence into the home and mind of the native' (1990: 29). Fanon's account of colonial relationships was forged in the heat of anti-colonial struggle in Africa and, as in the works of John Paul Sartre and Albert Memmi, 'constructs two antithetical groups, the colonizer and the colonized' (Young 1995: 5) with each group retaining a distinct and separate identity. This kind of analysis, according to Young, carries the danger that it will 'reproduce the static, essentialist categories it seeks to undo'. It confirms the very colonial categories of difference it is committed to dismantling. Young goes on to identify newer currents in post-colonial writing stressing a more complex inter-relationship between what were the rigidly demarcated worlds of coloniser and colonised.

Relationships between Aboriginal and non-Aboriginal Australians have become more complex and textured, more focused on shaping consent. Historically, policies towards Aboriginal people were constructed on the premise that Aboriginal people were not 'part of the public' (Raferty 2006) and that their needs – such as health needs – could be simply satisfied. The legacy left by this kind of race thinking has included worse health for Aboriginal people. Over recent years, however, there have been changes in the delivery of health services to Aboriginal people to improve the situation. Most remote Aboriginal communities are serviced, maintained and supported – however poorly – by government organisations.

In the area of social order, however, this Manicheanist legacy remains stubbornly entrenched. Policing in relation to Aboriginal people has not ceased to be frontier policing, to the extent that it remains essentially concerned with policing the public boundaries between Aboriginal and non-Aboriginal domains and obsessively concerned with the threat of Aboriginal disorder. Events following the death in custody on Palm Island of an Aboriginal man, Doomadgee, (who sustained broken ribs and had his liver cut in two), are illustrative of this obsession. Noel Pearson's summary of events following the death – are worth recounting at length:

> An extraordinary police and judicial full-court press is inflicted on the Palm Island community following the subsequent riot: Tactical Response Group police storm homes with guns, people are banned from their island, bail is refused, police investigations are relentless, charges are laid. The police investigation of the death was utterly compromised, with all indications pointing to a flawed inquiry and no indication whatsoever of the police hierarchy acting to ensure confidence in the performance of the service's public duties. Three Palm Islanders are charged with riot offences, plead guilty and are convicted and sentenced by a highly experienced judge, but the Attorney-General instructs the DPP to appeal to the Court of Appeal which, in a breathtaking judgment by the chief justice, Paul de Jersey, increases the sentences and sends a mother of four children to prison. Her children are made wards of the state. The dead man's only child takes his own life in the period following his father's death. Remaining Palm Islanders charged with riot offences are awaiting trial. Hurley and his mates from the police service who exonerated him return to their jobs. (Pearson 2006)

Following widespread outrage at a decision of the Queensland DPP not to lay charges against the officer involved in the death of Doomadgee, the matter was subject to an independent review by Sir Lawrence Street, who recommended charges be brought against Senior Sergeant Hurley. However, further examination of the facts of the case concluded that there was insufficient evidence on which to base a prosecution of the police officers involved.

There are many facets of this case that deserve close scrutiny. For purposes of this inquiry, what remains of interest in the initial course of events is the Janus-faced nature of the system's response. The police involved in the original incident are given the benefit of the doubt; perhaps there is also a belief that a prosecution would not be in the public interest (Aboriginal people are not interpolated into this notion of the public). Aboriginal people are not given the benefit of the doubt. The disorder on Palm becomes – for a while at least – the issue of concern. 'Riots' cannot be tolerated and must be brutally put down, the death of an Aboriginal man on the floor of a police lock up presumably can be tolerated – or at least, the death does not signify *a crisis of order*.

Aboriginal people are policed – indeed, over-policed – at those points of intersection with the white domain, where they come to represent a source of potential danger to the non-Aboriginal world. They are under-policed – or, more precisely, under-serviced by the police – in their own communities, where there are no white interests to safeguard, no white public spaces to protect, and no white sensibilities to be shielded against the unsettling proximity of the Aboriginal Other. Many towns with a high Aboriginal population have high rates of police to citizen ratio. While some remote communities have no police presence at all.

Aboriginal people do not simply stand on the margins of white society as atomised, disadvantaged individuals looking in. They occupy a set of cultural and social spaces and places, and enjoy a deep connection with 'country', which endows their lives with meaning. I want to suggest that when we discuss culture in the Aboriginal context we do so in a way which acknowledges that culture is tied to Aboriginal law and, homologously, Aboriginal occupation of space and place. I will discuss Aboriginal law in detail later, first let us explore the substance of Aboriginal occupied space through a brief examination of the concept of Aboriginal domain.

Aboriginal domains

The notion of Aboriginal domain is a useful one for embedding discussion of culture in those spaces where Aboriginal forms of solidarity predominate. The construct was first employed by John Von Sturmer to describe instances where:

> the dominant social life and culture are Aboriginal, where the major language or languages are Aboriginal, where the system of knowledge is Aboriginal; in short where the resident Aboriginal population constitutes the public. (Von Sturmer 1984: 219)

Nicolas Petersen saw evidence that, far from closer relationships with western society eroding domain, it continued to exist in the Western Desert:

> Despite fifty years of government policy that has seen Aboriginal people in the greater Western Desert become inextricably enmeshed in the welfare state, with a dependence on the market for food and the Department of Social Security for income, *the social relations from their pre-settlement times remain relatively lightly transformed.* (Petersen 2000, emphasis added; see also Petersen 1991)

Trigger (1986, see also 1992) defines domain in terms of distinctive spheres of thought, attitudes, social relations and styles of behaviour (1986: 99). Like Trigger, Rowse (1992) gives the definition conceptual flexibility by suggesting that domain could be said to exist in smaller networks and spaces than implied in Von Sturmer's construct, with its implicitly geo-territorial turn. Rowse also contributes the notion of 'Aboriginal enclaves' to describe situations where non-Aboriginal structures 'could still be placed under pressure to adjust to Indigenous ways' (Rowse 1998: 21). Here non-Aboriginal agency has to take account of Aboriginal forms of meaning, patterns of living, reciprocity, law and culture.

I would like to refine further those characteristics of Aboriginal domain which allow us to make sense of continued and adaptive Aboriginal cultural investment in sites, places and spaces which may appear at first sight to have been appropriated (or extinguished) by mainstream society. First, Rowse suggests that Aboriginal people create and maintain domain within geographically quite small spaces. Let us flesh this out a little more:

Sites of domain may be diffuse and intermittent rather than dense and concentrated. Let us imagine 'domain' other than in those strictly territorial terms that restrict it only to that figurative and metaphorical 'outback'; some distinct chunk of Australia 'out there'. Shedding this reductionist view of domain allows us to think outside the binary oppositions, where 'real', 'full blood' Aboriginal people inhabit the outback while we inhabit (and unproblematically own) everywhere else. We can, therefore, transfer the concept of domain to urban as well as remote or rural locations. Aboriginal domains are dotted around urban Sydney, Brisbane, Melbourne, Perth, Adelaide and Darwin, as well as numerous country towns. These cities are cross-hatched by distinct and well-established trails ('runs' Nyoongar people call them), enclaves of Aboriginal space, ceremonial spaces, meeting places, neutral ground, drinking sites, significant parks, town camps, 'long-grass', and they are increasingly home to Aboriginal structures and organisations (medical, housing, legal, social etc).

The Aboriginal 'languages' spoken can include Aboriginal English, camp talk, Creole, as well as traditional languages. It is generally accepted that Aboriginal languages encapsulate more than traditional language but include those post-colonial forms of language born from contact between Aboriginal languages and English. These include Aboriginal English, pidgin and Kriol (Creole) (see Eades 1995). These operate to connect Aboriginal people and cement social relationships.

There can be a degree of liminality and flexibility, in terms of the boundaries of domain. The limits of domain may be contested, negotiated and fluid rather firmly fixed. The domain might be temporal as well as spatial. It might be Aboriginal domain at night, non-Aboriginal domain by day – some urban spaces and public transport become the domain of Aboriginal youth at particular times of the day or night. In urban areas and country towns the boundaries between white and black domain are essentially contested, and there is ongoing conflict over the occupation and, significantly, the use of space. Colonisation transformed many traditional spaces into public space. As we shall discuss later, attachment to this space may have deep historical meaning. In relation to Aboriginal youth culture, for example, the connection to place is not the same as the *symbolic* appropriation of local 'territory' (said to be a feature of western working-class youth culture, see Cohen & Robbins 1978) but to traditionally Aboriginal-owned sites appropriated by white society.

I have been critical, thus far, of a tendency to impose constructs detached from European ideologies onto Indigenous people. One particularly cherished set of images concerns the distinction between the state (bad) and community (good) – the latter being a repository of 'real', emotionally embedded relationships rather than those impersonal, increasingly bureaucratised relationships of the world 'out there'. This is a view underpinning communitarian justice. Aboriginal people, however, have had as much, sometimes more, to fear from white community and civil society, as it has from the state. The desire to build community by non-Aboriginal colonists led to the deracination of Aboriginal people. They were displaced to make way for community and represented its dark other. From an Aboriginal perspective, the arrival of white community inevitably presaged the destruction of their own.

The colonist and native hold counterpoising views about the nature of things, they interpret things differently, one's freedom is the other's slavery, one's liberty is the other's confinement (Fanon 1990). I was struck by the relevance of this when interviewing Aboriginal people as part of the Law Reform Commission of Western Australia's Aboriginal Customary Law Project (discussed in more detail later). It became clear that dissimilar, even opposite, meanings become attached to occupation of the same place, space and time from an Indigenous and non-Indigenous perspectives: with some Aboriginal people finding refuge and respite from the crises in their community and family life and from the constant racism of the white community in prison; the same Aboriginal people may feel imprisoned when on the streets, on trains and buses.

For many Aboriginal people daily life is lived within a panopticon of white eyes. These are the views of Aboriginal women in Bandyup Women's Prison during the consultations for the inquiry into Aboriginal Customary Law:

> Not all women find the experience wholly negative. They develop strong friendships and are safe from what they perceive to be a racist society and from family violence. 'Its 80% black here, so I like it – outside we are a minority, here we are the majority'. It's sad but true, we are safer here.

and

> Many women end up in jail because they are homeless, some because of alcohol and drugs, a number get themselves imprisoned to escape male violence. 'Jail is a kind of refuge for Aboriginal women'. (Prisoner consultations)[4]

Can prison therefore contain Aboriginal domain under certain conditions? The consultations found evidence of this (discussed later in the context of Aboriginal law). For many Aboriginal people, prison is a source of *pain,* but not necessarily of *shame.* It does not carry the same stigma within the Aboriginal domain to be incarcerated in a white jail. This opens up possibilities for living the prison experience within terms of reference different from those prescribed by white society and its judicial officers. Prison becomes a place for acquiring some of the bounties of white society, food, medical services, education, and for meeting with classificatory kin, conducting family business, taking a break, drying out. All of which comes at a cost, not just for inmates but for families and communities as well.

Difference, compromise and accommodation

Many Aboriginal people hold radically incommensurate views to mainstream Australians about the significance of becoming – voluntarily or involuntarily – involved with white society and the implications of accepting its goods and services. In *White Flower, White Power* (1998) Tim Rowse explores the ways white power was solidified through the distribution of rations in Central Australia. Rowse draws on Michel Foucault on two levels of his analysis. First, Foucault's insight into the transferability of techniques of management across disciplinary sites (in Foucault's work, techniques of normalisation traversed the prison, the asylum, the classroom). Secondly, the Foucaultian notion, widely accepted within post-colonial theory, that processes of colonisation required the construction of a corpus of knowledge about the colonised.

Rowse sees rationing as:

> a colonial technique which could be transferred across a diversity of institutions: the scientific party, the pastoral lease, the mission enclave, the police station, the welfare settlement. At each of these sites in central Australia from the 1880s to the 1960s, people were rationed. (Rowse 1998: 5)

Moreover, the relationships between coloniser and colonised created through rationing formed, 'a fruitful site for the production and testing of rationers' understandings of Indigenous people' (Rowse 2002: 5). Central to Rowse's thesis – and it is a crucial observation that has implications beyond the issue of rationing in the late 19th century – is his hypothesis that, while rationing may have ensured a degree of predictability and order at the frontier, it did so without necessarily establishing 'shared understandings' (Rowse 2002: 204). Both sides were able to exist holding radically incommensurable interpretations as to the meanings attached to the giving and receiving of rations. In Foucault's sense the institutions constructed disciplinary regimes concerned with changing the moral identities of the Aborigine. However, while they may have captured Aboriginal bodies and claimed dominance of many dimensions of their lives, they failed to dismantle the internal structures of Aboriginal society: Aboriginal domain survived.

This insight – how practices intended to (at least eventually) assimilate actively perpetuated difference between coloniser and colonised – has informed other important work on frontier contact. Davenport, Johnson and Yuwali's (2005) extraordinary study 'Cleared Out' traces the migration of Aboriginal people from traditional territories to settlements on the fringes of the western desert: a process beginning in the 1940s and completed in 1965 when a small group of Martu women and children were collected and brought in to the Jigalong Mission. The essential factors driving this process were the availability of food and other goods 'flour, sugar and tobacco', and access to kin who had already made the transition (Davenport, Johnson & Yuwali 2005). In doing so they were making decisions which were highly consistent with the demands of Aboriginal culture, staying close to kin and finding a reliable source of food. In Jigalong, Aboriginal people took the rations but resisted attempts to eradicate Aboriginal law and culture, maintaining 'their society and law, with a strong ritual life' (2005: 161), and, while the mission promoted an ideology in which the natives were civilised and Christianised the reality was different:

> In reality, the missions constituted a new frontier, in which contact between Aboriginal and European Australia was negotiated in an ideologically charged symbiosis: the Aboriginal people wanted food and supplies and the missionaries sought their souls. (Davenport, Johnson & Yuwali 2005: 164)

This frontier became another site of conflict and resistance. Each side had a different view of their obligations and entitlements. The missionaries saw the process as one in which Aboriginal people would eventually embrace Christianity and the ways of the European – albeit a diminished form of citizenship, appropriate for those stigmatised by their race. The Martu had a completely different interpretation of the contract. The Martu perspective on the agreement was that in return for goods and services they would accede to a degree of 'coercive authority' in areas of their lives (Davenport, Johnson & Yuwali 2005: 165). They had not, however:

> [s]igned up to missionaries' other evangelical agenda, to remake them and their society, and they were hostile to interference that contravened their Law. They

maintained their identity, their languages, their Law and their society (Davenport, Johnson & Yuwali 2005: 165).

These insights are important in allowing us to visualise a core reality. A history of protracted and intensive involvement in total institutions has not meant that Aboriginal people have come to share the values and goals of these institutions as their own. They have not shared in the vocabularies of meaning that capture by these institutions normally implies.

Colonial history has left its mark on the way Aboriginal and non-Aboriginal domains co-exist. Over the past few decades there have been some movement in the ways some government agencies and the judiciary have approached the issues raised by the persistence of the Aboriginal domain. There is a greater awareness of the intricate points of contact and the crossing points between domains. If colonial societies feared one thing more than any other it was 'hybridity', the dangers of racial and cultural pollution and miscegenation. Yet future improvements in relations between Aboriginal and non-Aboriginal people may rest on generating forms of hybrid structure in the liminal space between domains that, while opening up room for dialogue, do not attempt to dismantle or co-opt Indigenous domain.

Liminal, hybrid and incommensurate worlds

I have suggested that there exist regions of Aboriginal experience and ways of seeing the world that remain incommensurable to white society. By this I mean that there is no stable, reliable meeting point between these worlds; no necessary equivalent; no reliable commonalities; no common language or universal grammar that would render one side understandable to the other. We need to engage with Aboriginal people on the basis that we really do not know or understand aspects of their social reality and, more importantly, we cannot make sense of things from an Indigenous world view by simply extending our own brand of reason to cover the Indigenous world. Moreover, rather than these issues becoming simpler and easier to read over time, they are becoming increasingly more complex as they become over-layered with questions about land rights and land usage and Native Title. There are manifold layers of complexity, strea-ming from the incommensurability of Indigenous and non-Indigenous worlds, and from the fact that Indigenous social life itself is multiply ordered (and disordered) rather than uniform and standardised: a representation of Indigenous society that only exist in the minds of non-Indigenous people. As Povinelli points out 'when we begin with the thick sociological descriptions of contemporary Indigenous life, we often seem to encounter landscapes of indeterminacy, incommensurability, and incoherency' (Povinelli 2006: 15).

She correctly maintains that, rather than eliminate models of complexity in Indigenous life, we should 'embrace these conditions and begin developing models that reflect them' (Povinelli 2006: 151). We have to be aware that social life in Indigenous society is complex and variegated, not simple, static and unchanging. Part of the Orientalist thinking that framed and legitimated colonial possession of the Australian continent was the belief in Indigenous culture was unchanging and 'timeless', as opposed to the dynamic and progressive culture of the west (Jensen 2005). Aboriginal ritual and

CRIME, ABORIGINALITY AND THE DECOLONISATION OF JUSTICE

ceremonial life is complex and so are the relationships, rules and practices which have emerged to deal with the presence of whites.

The Law Reform Commission of Western Australia's (2006) consultations with Indigenous communities found that they did not want more interference with their law and, particularly, did not want their law to become legal text. What they were concerned about – and I discuss the issue in detail in a later chapter – was the increasingly *denser zone of contact between Aboriginal and non-Aboriginal law*, finding ways, as Povinelli expresses to 'navigate the multidimensional and multifunctional intersection of law, public culture, and practical knowledge, that they continually confront even when doing nothing more than drive to an outstation on a rutted road' (Povinelli 2006: 162).

There are numerous crossing points and in-between places, what the Native American philosopher Anne Waters calls 'interstitial space' (Waters 2001) between Indigenous and non-Indigenous worlds. These spaces are not necessary fixed and permanent, they remain tentative and unstable, constantly labile and necessarily uncertain. The status of meanings in these spaces require constant re-negotiation, constant nurturing; little can be – or become – taken for granted. These zones can provide fruitful environments for negotiation, compromise and partnership.

We need to explore, rather than ignore, liminal spaces between Aboriginal notions of ceremony and our own. In his seminal text *The Rites of Passage* (1960), anthropologist Van Gennep develops a perspective on ceremonial performances which sees them not as simply ritual but as marking forms of transitions: in his case in social status. I would like to adopt the idea – transgressively perhaps – to include syncretic changes in status relationships *between* social domains, rather than within them. Van Gennep names this transition space a *liminal state*: an unpredictable space where the authority of existing customary practice is reduced, creating a deliberate zones of ambiguity and uncertainty. Turner (1967), developing Van Gennep's insights, describes the liminal state as a kind of 'anti-structure', a space where the taken-for-granted rules and strictures of everyday life dissolve and need to be renegotiated.

The liminal space can nurture new forms of mutual understanding and become a place for 'Intercultural' dialogue based on respect for a 'pluriverse' of epistemologies and worldviews. It aims to create greater mutual understanding between the margins and the mainstream, north and south (Merlan, 1998; Escobar, 2001). Unlike multi-culturalism, intercultural dialogue is not premised on the belief that minority cultures will eventually be absorbed into the mainstream and that cultural difference is a problem to be managed. Instead, inter-cultural dialogue institutes a mix of engagement spaces where fresh understandings can be generated and inter-subjective experiences facilitated.

The danger with the intercultural approach for Indigenous people is that intercultural spaces may themselves becomes sites of assimilation, as Morphy and Morphy (2013) argue, '[t]he intercultural, once articulated as a conceptual space, has the potential to become the space where Aboriginal people gradually merge with the mainstream' (2013: 177). Helpfully, Cathy Walsh distinguishes between what she calls 'functional' and 'critical' interculturality; whereas 'functional' interculturality does not address underlying inequalities the seeks to maintain the system, the latter, 'seeks its major transformation in social, political, epistemic, and existential terms. That is, a new ordering of structures, institutions, and relations' (Walsh, 2007: 12).

Walsh identifies characteristics necessary for a critical praxis: transformative ideas and practices that seek to build new social structures and institutions respectful of difference. Similarly Walter Mignolo draws the distinction between 'multi-culturalism', which 'concede[s] "culture" while maintaining "epistemology"', and 'interculturality' which was devised by 'Indigenous intellectuals to claim epistemic rights' (Mignolo 2007, see also 2011).

Creating spaces for the emergence of transformative practice requires that we explore opportunities for intercultural dialogue. Mignolo correctly asserts that simply celebrating the performative elements of Indigenous culture is not the same things as acknowledging the salience of Indigenous knowledge. *Indigenous people demand a seat at the table, not just the chance to dance at the preliminaries.* These spaces will, of necessity, be fluid and liminal, rather than fixed and permanent, and provide a birthing space for new hybrid practices that recognise the extent to which Indigenous people have feet in two worlds. Canclini (2005) offers a useful definition of hybridity as representing a stream of 'socio-cultural processes in which discrete structures or practices, previously existing in separate form, are combined to generate new structures, objects and practices' (Canclini 2005: xxv). The concept of hybridity has a murky past. Robert Young (1995) expresses some ambivalence about the construct given its historical linkages with notions of racial miscegenation: although he acknowledges that 'there is no single, or correct concept of hybridity' (1995: 27). Homi K Bhabha focuses on the liminal moment and the 'third space' produced from the interaction between cultures. He celebrates the role hybridity plays in allowing otherwise subjugated, 'denied knowledge' to become part of the dominant discourse and 'estrange the basis of its authority – its rules of recognition (Bhabha 1994: 115). Hybrid movements create a 'third space' (Young 1995: 23; Bhabha 1994) where traditional values are re-articulated and translated in new ways. One needs to be cautious when adopting the notion of hybridity as employed by Bhabha to the Indigenous context, as he is writing about the experience of post-colonial, diaspora populations in Europe and America. In contrast, Spivak (1996) maintains that there is greater degree of incommensurabilty between 'subaltern' populations in the 'third world' and the west. In relation to Indigenous people – who are not diasporic but embedded in place – there may be even greater layers of incommensurability separating mainstream and Indigenous knowledge.

I want to promote the creation of hybrid spaces, or liminal zones, as a potentially rich, but necessarily uncertain, forms of decolonising practice. Hybrid and liminal space is, as I suggested earlier, always unstable and uncertain, fluid and protean, and always in a state of transition. Hybridity does not mean the wholesale merging of two laws and cultures – that would be assimilationist, given the cultural power of the non-Aboriginal world to determine the terms of this merger – but rather as an attempt to create syncretic processes in the points of intersection – those liminal zones. Our progressive contacts with Aboriginal interests are increasing taking place in this new liminal space. The processes around granting Native Title, for example, are creating their own particular 'recognition space'. The Native Title resulting from each determination can be considered to lie in a 'recognition space', between the particular Indigenous system of traditional law and custom, and the general Australian legal system' (Martin 2004: 68).

We should set out from the assumption that some key differences will not be made the same. We should explore the symbolic power of new rituals that exploit hybridity. They involve, in Canclini's terms, the combination of previously separate cultural processes to 'generate new structures, objects and practices' while, in Bhabha's terms, allowing hitherto 'denied knowledge' to be articulated within the dominant discourse. The new structures, objects and practices include:

- Circle Sentencing Courts;
- Aboriginal or Koori Courts;
- healing centres;
- Aboriginal self-policing initiatives (Night Patrols);
- community justice groups;
- elders groups;
- 'on-country' camps; and
- Homelands and Outstations.

I have attempted to illustrate this process in Figure 2.1 (see *opposite*). The non-Aboriginal domain is to the left of the diagram and the Aboriginal domain is to the right. In this approach, the core mysteries of Aboriginal law are left alone and instead there are hybrid initiatives intended to work within the liminal space between domains: creating new partnerships. Taking, for example, policing, we see the police as a mainstream body working within non-Aboriginal law; then moving to the right, Aboriginal liaison schemes which may work in Aboriginal communities but are structurally non-Indigenous; then there are Warden schemes, which, while situated in Aboriginal communities are structurally subordinate to the police; then there are sobering up facilities which are often (but not always) Aboriginal owned and managed; then there are Community Patrols which have no police powers, are independent of the system, work within Aboriginal terms of reference, and use Aboriginal notions of cultural authority. They are not traditional structures but they represent a mechanism by which Aboriginal people can manage problems in an Aboriginal way. We will discuss these initiatives in more detail later.

New initiatives of liminality and hybridity are important in the sense that they do not colonise Aboriginal domain but construct an ensemble of new spaces. Aboriginal people have been highly imaginative in the ways they have adopted non-Aboriginal belief systems to meet needs: and there have been all kinds of hybrid and syncretic processes around ritual and belief. Some highly traditional remote communities in Western Australia have embraced fundamentalist, Pentecostalist forms of Christianity; but without relinquishing customary law and culture. This may not be the contradiction it first appears: Pentecostalism, 'the song of the dispossessed' (Davis 2004) provides mystery and charisma, but it also pragmatically challenges problems such as alcohol and addiction within communities while giving powerful affirmation to the view of many Aboriginal people – that the world brought by the white man is corrupt, unjust and irredeemable. Such forms of syncretism are not uncommon among Indigenous peoples in South America, Canada and New Guinea, nor do they always displace traditional belief systems and Indigenous claims of authenticity and autonomy.

Figure 2.1: **LIMINAL SPACE. HYBRID INITIATIVES**

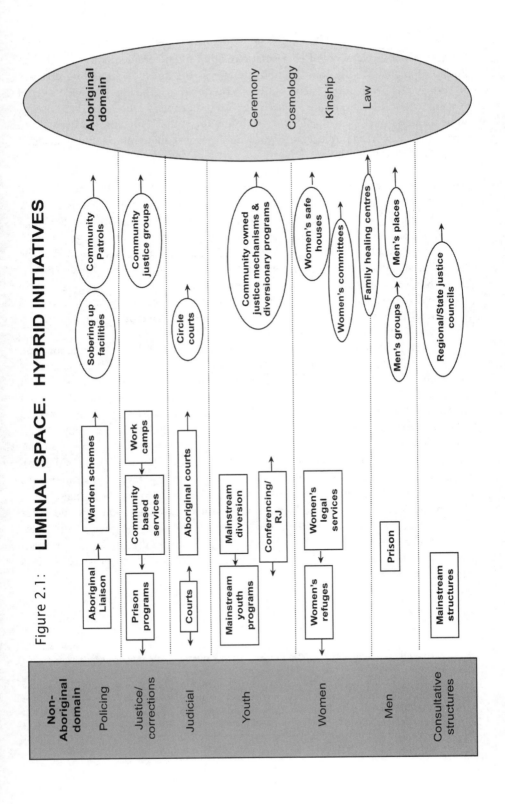

Syncretic accommodation

The performative elements of charismatic religion often complement – rather than simply supplant – Indigenous religious practices. The question should be not why do Indigenous peoples join them, but why wouldn't they? They may provide a set of explanations and solutions more in keeping with Indigenous world-views than enlightenment and rational secular belief systems. Therefore, rather than representing paths to modernity, away from tradition, they provide a means of maintaining tradition, albeit in a mediated and reworked fashion.

There are other considerations, Pentecostal churches provide a way of dealing not just with spiritual issues but also material ones, they have a foot in the white domain, are institutionally powerful and influential, they can capture resources. Moreover, they seem able to find ways to work which are non-racist and, importantly in Aboriginal communities, seem to speak directly to the needs of impoverished women, grandmothers and single mothers (Davis 2004). These have been the most dispossessed of the dispossessed and also those who have kept Aboriginal family life alive. These religions offer solutions to some of the problems brought by white society that Aboriginal culture wasn't evolved to handle (alcohol, addiction) and may – instead of threatening to erase Aboriginality – might provide some of the conditions for survival through a series of what Mosko (2001) calls 'syncretic accommodations'.

Accommodations of various kinds have provided the basis for Aboriginal survival. Tonkinson (2006) observed how the Martu people of the Western desert were able to accommodate themselves to mission systems of control on numerous levels, but never allowed the mission to remake them as white people and they constantly resisted attempts to dismantle Aboriginal law. The fundamental mistake non-Aboriginal society consistently makes is to mistake accommodation for assimilation. Generally, Aboriginal people take hold of the resources offered to them as means of holding together fundamental elements of Aboriginal law and culture, not to become white. In the case of the Martu, they were not approaching missions and feeding stations in an attempt to become white, but as a means of boosting their capacity to remain Aboriginal.

The issue of Aboriginal youth crime has dominated debates about law and order in some states since the early 1980s. On the face of things, Aboriginal youth issues are particular amenable to scrutiny from within mainstream criminological perspectives and surface appearances, however, obscure a number of deeper realities. This is explored further in Chapter 3.

Notes

1   Feeley and Simon employ the concept in their 1992 study of the new penologies, but it has also been employed by Bauman (2001) in a noteworthy survey of late-modern genocide (see also Haverman 1999).

2   According to Staples (1994) the only thing that could prevent them from joining Indigenous men is that America needs black men to fight its wars against Asians and South Americans – he could add Arabs and the Islamic world to the list today.

3   I am grateful to Howard Petersen for raising this issue.

4   Law Reform Commission of Western Australia, Thematic Summaries of Consultations, at <www.lrc.justice.wa.gov.au>.

3

Aboriginal Youth: Culture, Resistance and the Dynamics of Self-destruction

> I'm goin' out in a blaze of glory. They (the justice worker and the magistrate) talk about me not wasting my life. They don't know. It's wasted already. (Aboriginal youth, aged 15)

This chapter addresses the issue of young Aboriginal people and criminal justice. Statistics on Aboriginal youth involvement in the criminal justice system seem scarcely believable. In Western Australia, by age 18 around 80% of Aboriginal youth will have had contact with the system and on any day upwards of 80% of youths in detention in Western Australia are Aboriginal. The persistence of the problem has been referred to as a source of 'national shame' (House of Representatives Standing Committee on Aboriginal and Torres Strait Islander Affairs 2011) while a WA government inquiry talked of a 'broken' justice system (Community Development and Justice Standing Committee 2010).

It is no longer adequate or meaningful to talk about a juvenile justice system in Western Australia; what we have is a system concerned almost totally with the habitual confinement of Aboriginal children and young people. Contact with the system is repeated and protracted. It begins early – police often comment on the age Aboriginal youth come to their attention and frequently lament the fact that they cannot arrest them until they are 10 years of age (the norm in Australia) – and it occurs frequently. It is important to view the arrest and detention statistics in context. Other social indicators of inequality have remained relatively stable, abysmally so, for decades (Hunter 1993). Aboriginal infants have significantly higher chances of dying in their first years than non-Aboriginal children, they will go on to experience higher risks of chronic ill health, mental illness, poor educational achievement, greater risk of unemployment, suicide and self-harm in the community; they will die much younger than other Australians (for a full treatment, see Department of Indigenous Affairs 2010). A succession of coronial inquiries in the Kimberley, including a 2008 inquiry into 22 non-custodial, alcohol-related youth suicides (Hope 2008; see also Hope 2004) pointed to the bleakness of communal life and lack of investment in infrastructure, as well as the failure of government agencies to address the causes of unemployment.[1]

Aboriginal youths are over-represented at all stages of contact with the law: arrest, prosecution and detention. They are over-represented in the more punitive parts of the system and under-represented in less intrusive options (Cunneen & White 1995: 14). For many Aboriginal youth, becoming involved with the criminal justice system is an inevitable fact of life. How can we account for such dramatically high levels of contact with the system? In this chapter, I discuss possible reasons. As we have seen, criminologists are increasingly rejecting mono-causal explanations and are looking to a mix of theories and perspectives, a number of which mesh together the insights of critical western criminology with an analysis of the particular role colonial relationships play in constructing the criminal justice system and framing Aboriginal people's responses (Broadhurst 2002; Cunneen 2006). No single explanation can account for the phenomenon, and there is a strong case for an analysis which recognises both the 'push' and 'pull' factors at work. In this chapter, I suggest that responding to Indigenous youth who become enmeshed in the system remains a site of contestation between Indigenous communities and the mainstream.

Thus far I have argued that the western paradigm of criminological theory can only take us so far when attempting to make sense of Aboriginal relationships with crime and criminal justice. In many respects, developing a body of theory to explain youth crime and disorder provided the engine room for criminological theory in the United States and western Europe for a good deal of the 20th century, generating a rich treasure trove of ideas, critical debates, theories and perspectives. These theories do have some explanatory relevance in relation to Aboriginal youth and crime.

Labelling; processes of deviance amplification; folk devils and moral panics

These perspectives have obvious explanatory value in relation to the stereotyping and labelling of Aboriginal youths as offenders. Aboriginal youth are highly visible in public space and vulnerable to over-policing. Their extreme visibility and membership of a problem group marks them off as targets for heavy street policing in urban and rural settings, where policing is, 'focussed on high levels of public disorder and property crime involving young Indigenous people' (Hogg 2005: 342). Moreover, their deviance is highly newsworthy, coverage of Aboriginal youth issues focuses on criminality: 'The face of crime is Aboriginal' (Sercombe 1995). There are 'symbolic locations' (Northbridge in Perth, Fortitude Valley in Brisbane) where the presence of Aboriginal youth becomes a signifier of potential disorder and raises public anxiety – the police are called in to sort out the problem. The kinds of over-policing Aboriginal youth are subject to in public settings has a tendency to amplify deviant behaviour, in turn Aboriginal youth will tend to live out the stereotypes as they become increasingly more alienated from society (Blagg & Wilkie 1995; Broadhurst 2002; Cunneen 2001b).

Structural and cultural anomie

'Anomie' describes a process of normlessness and has been employed by criminologists to describe a diversity of situations where social norms and values break down under the pressures of social change and groups struggle to adapt. The absence of mechanisms of social regulation and the erosion of stable norms of behaviour can have devastating consequences: crime, deviance, drugs, alcohol and suicide can be viewed as indicators of anomie. Youth suicide in Aboriginal Australia has been described as the highest in the world (Tatz 2001a). Moreover, Aboriginal youths can be said to make realistic assessments of their life chances in a structural racist society and turn to deviance as a mechanism for achieving what society holds up as important (respect, money, power) but which is actually closed off to them.

Race, hegemony, conflict and resistance

A hegemonically powerful group class uses the criminal justice system to impose controls on a powerless out-group. Social and economic crisis stimulate policing solutions targeting a racial minority as representing a threat to society. The restoration of law and order becomes a national obsession. Particular moral panics (see above) crystallise public, media and state concerns about the problem group. The group, stigmatised on the basis of race and/or ethnicity, become subject to on-the-street racial profiling, kerbside justice, over-policing and systemic violence. Oppositional cultures of resistance emerge through which the outsider group, under increasing pressure from the state, expresses internal solidarity and creates a counter-hegemonic lifestyle and oppositional culture of resistance. Oppositional cultures are often hedonistic, blurring with criminal gangs and cannot offer long-term solutions.

Control, disorganisation, belonging and attachment

Aboriginal youth are often homeless, they have a low participation rate in terms of school and neighbourhood organisations, family life is haphazard and unpredictable and there is little scope to construct a stake in conformity: bonds of attachment to mainstream institutions are weak, while attachments to deviant peer groups are strong. Families often fail to produce a stable and consistent home environment. The legacy of removal policies and other child stealing strategies designed to render Aboriginal society dysfunctional worked. Many Aboriginal children grow up in highly disturbed environments – parents are often drunk, drugged or in prison – or are shipped off to family: grandmothers act as parents. Many children become wards of the state and/or drift on to the streets.

There is nothing 'wrong' with any of these perspectives. On the face of things, Aboriginal youth issues converge closely with those of marginalised youth from other racial backgrounds, and they have been subject to similar state strategies of marginalisation, criminalisation and control. At first it may seem that studying the structure and culture of Aboriginal youth and their struggles with the system is wholly achievable within the framework provided by mainstream criminological theory: and it is around Aboriginal youth culture that we would expect to see most evidence of syncretism and hybridity, as Aboriginal youth become drawn in to global youth culture and Aboriginal people generally become subject to the homogenising pressures of late-modern globalisation. As I have already stressed, however, these pressures towards conformity have to be set against other pressures towards difference. There are aspects of Aboriginal youth experience that are not neatly encapsulated in any of the major theoretical models that have informed mainstream criminology. Before dealing with these issues in any depth let us briefly review the international situation in relation to youth justice issues.

Concern about the behaviour of young people across the modernised world has stimulated the emergence of a veritable smorgasbord of programs and initiatives promising to resolve the juvenile crime problem (Muncie 1999). Reviewing the international comparative youth justice literature, Muncie and Goldson (2006: 197) identify 'multiple, overlapping and contradictory themes in contemporary international juvenile justice reform'. They identify a general process of retreat from the welfare state solution to the juvenile crime problem, and they support the thesis that youth crime and disorder has been 'repenalised' and treated more like adult crime. Muncie and Goldson (2006) suggest that the fashion for 'restoration' internationally has been employed as a 'responsibilisation' strategy, meaning that it has become a punitive sanction designed to make the offender wholly responsible, not just for the offence itself, but for any subsequent processes of reparation and reintegration: a form of 'punitive responsibilisation' (2006: 213). Muncie and Goldson also offer a bleak assessment of the impact of UN instrumentalities on domestic policy and practice in the sphere of juvenile justice, where rhetorical support and superficial adherence to instruments such as the UN Convention on the Rights of the Child masks the pursuit of policies, 'which exacerbate structural inequalities and punitive institutional regimes' (2006: 212). While giving broad support for this thesis as a general trend, the authors also signal a note of caution. They identify what they call 'marked and significant global variations' in rates of custody and adherence to UN instrumentalities and see the key to difference lying in the degree to which the issue of youth crime is 'depoliticised' in particular societies (Muncie & Goldson 2006: 212-13).

When we import theories from Europe or the United States we need to be constantly aware of the contexts in which these theories evolved. The Birmingham Centre for Cultural Studies was responsible for formulating a radical cultural studies linking cultural practice with the politics of class, race and gender (Hall & Jefferson 1978). They influenced a generation of progressive criminologists through their focus on crime and various forms of hegemonic crises. Superimposing this form of 'cultural studies' on Australian society can lead to portraying mainstream Australia as 'subaltern' to a hegemonically dominant 'Britain': Australian 'history from below' often takes as its point of departure, attempts to construct an Australian identity separate from that of the colonial centre (Stratton & Ang 1996). While important, this focus on the hegemonic power of Britain can obscure the realities of colonial dispossession by Australian settlers and the underlying unity between the settler and the colonial authority. The notion of diaspora has also been employed to explore the experience of ethnically 'Other' immigrants (those not from the 'mother country' or Europe) navigating their way through multicultural Australia (Stratton & Ang 1996; Jensen 2005). Neither method of situating alternative cultures – cultural marginalisation or diaspora – provides a reliable lens through which to observe Aboriginal youth culture.

Aboriginal youth culture

Aboriginal youth, like their counterparts across the world, are consumers of western global youth culture. It is possible to look at Aboriginal youth culture as forming a bridge between traditional Aboriginal identity and modernity – as Aboriginal people gradually lose connection with traditional culture and embrace dominant global western culture. On the one hand, we have a parent culture which remains committed to aspects of traditional culture and, on the other, a younger generation rapidly breaking free of these constraints, with ensuing generational conflict. Many Aboriginal adults themselves take precisely this view and have, for example, expressed concerns about the corrupting power of black American rap and hip-hop culture, which Aboriginal youth consume through the media and through the youth detention system, creating what they called a 'niggerized Aboriginal culture' where a street and prison 'blackness' replaces Aboriginality as the basis for culture (Blagg, Morgan, Cunneen & Ferrante 2005). It is possible to see evidence of this process at work when talking to Aboriginal youth, many of whom have abandoned their parent's passion for country and western music in favour of the sharp urban rhythms of black hip hop. Yet, there are dimensions of Aboriginal youth culture which resist accommodation into the global youth culture model, and there are strong continuities between Aboriginal generations beneath the superficial overlay of globalism. In Canclini's (2005) formulation, Aboriginal youth may spend more time 'in modernity' than their parents, but they also 'leave' it as well, because their lives are also structured by the demands of the Aboriginal domain which sets down obligation and expectations as well as providing cultural maps of meaning.

Aboriginal youths tend to see themselves as Aboriginal first and black second (Crime Research Centre and Donovan Research 1999) and have a strong sense of their Aboriginality even when this is accompanied by cynicism about community elders (Law Reform Commission of Western Australia 2006). Aboriginal youth are entangled in the same set of structural and cultural dynamics as their parent cultures: which are a product of the fact they are Aboriginal in a society where Aboriginality is still viewed as a problem to be managed. While they may be developing solutions to the problematic based on new syncretised styles there are numerous continuities between Aboriginal parent and youth cultures. A distinctive feature of Indigenous youth experience involves being a product of a culture that has been the target – not of policies of diaspora, exclusion and marginalisation – but of genocide. Many Aboriginal children today have parents who were part of the stolen generation.

Youth, family and genocide

Cunneen and White (1995) isolate a number of cultural and historical factors relevant to an inquiry into Aboriginal youth and the justice system. They point to the significant cultural differences between notions of childhood and adulthood in Indigenous societies and the ways colonisation interfered with Indigenous practices in relation to childrearing, particularly through the theft of land and deliberate policy of child removal which targeted Indigenous children as a means of transforming and pacifying Indigenous society (Cunneen & White 1995: 137). Aboriginal children bore the brunt of policies founded on the back of anxieties about miscegenation and the menacing threat of a 'half-caste' population diluting the white race.

Cunneen and White (1995) make the point that early colonial warfare aimed to eliminate Aboriginal people as a group and made no distinction between ages – children were as vulnerable to murder as their parents. Later, children became the focus of various forms of protection policy. Relating the practices of the NSW Aboriginal Protection Board, established in the early 1900s, Cunneen and White show that the aims of the board were: to reduce the Aboriginal birth rate by removing adolescents – girls especially – and to prevent Aboriginal children from identifying with their communities and families by isolating them and preventing return to their families (1995: 138).

This suggests that it is the *Aboriginality* of Aboriginal youth that marks them off for special treatment by the system, and there is an historical link with historical strategies of genocide and assimilation. It is not simply culture, or group conflict, race difference, or marginality and exclusion, it is a specific set of differences unique to the history of Indigenous contact with colonial power: the strategies, techniques and technologies deployed by colonial powers to 'manage' the problem; the specific philosophies of evolution linked to these strategies, techniques and technologies (particularly the embedded belief in the 'doomed race' theory); and the consequent – and deliberate – attempts to refashion the Aboriginal world through the targeting of children.

A number of scholars have noted the deep bifurcation in official policy towards children and families of Aboriginal and white descent (Human Rights and Equal Opportunity Commission 1997; Haebich 2000) in the protection and assimilation eras. While white families were being shaped and supported by a range of state measures designed to strengthen the family unit as the basis for national progress, Aboriginal families were excluded from the system of rights and entitlements, 'their [Aboriginal] families were not to be sites for forging strong productive citizens. They were officially discouraged from producing offspring' (Haebich 2000: 160).

The 'Stolen Children' Inquiry discovered that the traumatic consequences of separating children from their mothers were well-known in social work and children's services from the ground-breaking work of Winicott, Bowlby, Melanie Klein and others. Strong, healthy bonds of attachment were recognised to be of crucial importance in creating healthy children and this view permeated thinking in post-war children's departments. However, attitudes towards Aboriginal children and families were premised on the need not to nurture but to dismantle Aboriginal family and communal life; and this led to a suite of policies and practices which denied Aboriginal people access to the public realm and its benefits and entitlements, because Aboriginal people were not viewed as 'part of the public', they could not therefore be the beneficiaries of public policy.

Children and young people were the particular target of policies designed to eradicate Aboriginality. Some commentators have suggested that, whereas many Aboriginal adults have constructed enclaves within daily life that insulate them against the worst excesses of racism against Aboriginal people, and have benefited from some government policies (self-determination, Native Title), Aboriginal children continue to experience systemic racism in their daily contact with white institutions. Evidence suggests that Aboriginal youth are more likely to be involved in the criminal justice system than are Aboriginal adults (Cunneen & White 1995: 141). Butler (1994) suggests that, while there have been shifts towards policies of self-determination policies in fields affecting adult Aboriginal people, Indigenous children and young people are still in 'terra nullius', governed by policies which fail to acknowledge the 'Indigenous status of children' (Butler 1994: 4). Government policies in education, child protection etc, acknowledge issues related to marginality, deprivation and disadvantage, and they acknowledge 'multiculturalism', but they ignore the 'special needs' emerging from the history of colonial dispossession (Butler 1994: 4). They focus on 'welfare' rather than the rights and entitlements. In this sense, strategies of inclusion or de-marginalisation can be dangerous because they may perpetuate assimilation where they are premised upon the eradication of difference.

Mandatory sentencing

Aboriginal youth are at serious risk of enmeshment in the criminal justice system, and they are over-represented in those offences liable to attract imprisonment. For example, Aboriginal youth have been the target of Western Australia's mandatory sentencing laws. Until 2001 both the Northern Territory and Western Australia had 'three strikes'-style mandatory sentencing legislation focused on property crime. The Northern Territory repealed its mandatory sentencing laws when a Labor government was elected to power. Repealing the legislation represented a recognition of Aboriginal people's profound hostility to legislation which, according to the Aboriginal Social Justice Commissioner, had 'targeted Indigenous people and had been costly and ineffective in deterring crime' (Aboriginal and Torres Strait Islander Social Justice Commissioner 2001). This left Western Australia as the only Australian jurisdiction still imposing mandatory sentences for property-related crimes: three home burglaries – or 'strikes' – would trigger automatic detention of six months. Having listened to the widespread concerns of Aboriginal people, The Law Reform Commission of Western Australia called for the repeal of the laws (Recommendation Eight, Law Reform Commission of Western Australia 2006b). The Commission noted that in 2001, 80% of the children picked up under the laws were Aboriginal and that 90% of these were from regional areas (the overall Aboriginal percentage rose to 87% in 2005, it is unknown how many were from regional areas). Because there are no regional youth detention facilities, Aboriginal children are taken thousands of kilometres to Perth, away from family, in contravention of human rights standards (Morgan, Blagg & Williams 2001).

For government, the laws are too politically sensitive to tamper with, having become a symbol of political potency, symbolising the government's willingness to take a 'tough stance' on law and order – in a state where law and order issues have framed the agenda for elections. The WA government's stance remained unchanged despite overwhelming evidence that the laws had not had their desired effect (in relation to deterring property crime) and have unfairly targeted Indigenous youth (Morgan, Blagg & Williams 2001). The WA DPP and the Department of Justice also want the laws to stay, the latter stating that they are an 'appropriate way to deal with serious and repeat offenders' (Law Reform Commission of Western Australia 2006b: 86). This cynical comment only reveals the deeply political nature of the laws because, as the Law Reform Commission of Western Australia shows (2006a, 2006b), 'serious and repeat offenders' would certainly be subject to imprisonment without these particular laws and the laws are simply dragging in less serious offenders into the system.

The three strikes mandatory sentencing laws are especially problematic given that they 'redistribute' discretion to the pre-trial decision-making stage (Morgan 2000), thereby increasing already powerful gate-keeping powers of the police and, essentially eliminating judicial checks on discriminatory and capricious police powers. The laws also prevent courts taking into account relevant aspects of customary law in mitigation and will inhibit the capacities of community-based Aboriginal initiatives – such as Community Justice Groups – from developing diversionary mechanisms (Law Reform Commission of Western Australia 2006b: 87). Morgan, Blagg and Williams (2001) also demonstrated that many of these young people might be victims of 'justice by geography' and may have been the beneficiaries of diversionary alternatives had they committed their 'strike' offences in the metropolitan areas. This is due to the greater sophistication of diversionary systems in the metropolitan area, including a greater awareness of the processes by Children's Court Magistrates, who regularly refer cases back to Juvenile Justice Teams for diversionary conferencing. Since mandatory regimes work on an accumulation of offences, early diversion from the system by way of a formal caution, and/or referral to a juvenile justice team, may prevent a young person from developing the necessary 'repeat offender' profile.

The Stolen Children Inquiry pointed to the continuities between traditional practices of child removal and contemporary law and order strategies. Cunneen and White (1995) (see also Cunneen 2001b) maintain that criminalisation represents the modern strategy for the control and separation of Aboriginal children. While old methods of welfare removal may have fallen into disrepute, criminalisation provides a ready mechanism for the capture and incarceration of Aboriginal youth, the Human Rights and Equal Opportunity Commission's (1997) Inquiry into the 'Stolen Generation' makes this point:

> [T]he police play a pivotal role in the separation of Indigenous children and young people from their families and communities. The Inquiry has already documented this role in the history of removal policies. However, police still have a major function in bringing about separations. Most obviously, Indigenous children and young people are separated from their families and communities by being placed in police custody and held in watch-houses, lock-ups or cells. (Human Rights and Equal Opportunity Commission 1997: 13)

Early involvement

Early involvement in the system remains a key cause of long-term enmeshment. The Royal Commission into Aboriginal Deaths in Custody (RCIADIC) noted in relation to Aboriginal youth, 'as well as having early contact with the criminal justice system they had repeated contact with it'. This latter point is one of great significance (Johnson 1991, vol 5: 18). This holds true for girls as well as boys. Rowena Lawrie, in her consultations with women prisoners in New South Wales found:

> Most of the women surveyed had long histories of involvement with the criminal justice system. 60% of the women surveyed had been convicted of a criminal offence while still juveniles and at least 36% of them received their first conviction between 11 and 12 years of age. Ninety-eight per cent of the women surveyed had prior convictions as adults and at least 26% had between 15 and 30. (Lawrie 2002: 17)

Clearly, early involvement with the police, courts and corrections, far from deterring criminality more often has the effect of increasing the likelihood of long-term contact.

David Garland points out that one of the consequences of mass imprisonment in the United States has been that many young people receive their most significant form of socialisation not within civil society but within the confines of the prison:

> This means that imprisonment has become one of the social institutions that structure this group's experience. It becomes part of the socialisation process. Every family, every household, every individual in these neighbourhoods has direct personal knowledge of the prison – through a spouse, a parent, a neighbour, a friend. Imprisonment ceases to be the fate of a few criminal individuals and become a shaping institution for whole sectors of the population. (Garland 2001: 6)

In the United States, the prison experience has spawned cultures where prison values provide a template for action outside as well as within the confines of the prison. Oppositional cultures emerge which deliberately create style from prison values, dress, macho posturing, misogyny, an obsession with 'respect' – as one commentator suggests, the convict culture has become the template for street culture in the United States (Miller 2001: 157).

There has been little equivalent research in Australia on this phenomenon. Aboriginal people, however, have particular concerns about the consequences of mass imprisonment on their young people. The issues here are complex: prison, as we have noted, is a source of *pain* but not of *shame*. It has been called a rite of passage, a badge of honour (Beresford & Omaji 1996). On the other hand, we know that Aboriginal communities – particularly women – hold prison responsible for generating a 'bullshit' version of Aboriginal law and sustaining a distorted notion of male entitlements under Aboriginal law. They see the constant, repetitive involvement in prison as part of the cycle of Aboriginal communal violence (Blagg 2000a, 2001).

Prison has lost whatever deterrent impact it might have had for many Aboriginal males through gratuitous over-use, and is blamed for perpetuating male cultures of violence. It is in these institutions – rather than simply within traditional Aboriginal law and culture – that men nurture and refine narratives of entitlement to violence based upon a distorted interpretation of Aboriginal law; what I have called Aboriginal male myths of cultural entitlement to violence (Blagg 2001). These myths are rarely challenged in prison programs – run largely (when they run at all) by white psychologists and social workers employing cognitive skills programs that bear no relevance to Aboriginal ways of seeing the world (Morgan & Mottram 2006)

Western Australia spends a considerable amount of money incarcerating Aboriginal youths, on the basis of quite trivial offending. On 23 May 2005, a 15-year-old Aboriginal boy attempted to steal a two-dollar ice cream from a supermarket in Onslow.. Western Australian authorities then spent roughly $10,000 to escort the youth nearly 1000 miles to Perth, where he faced the Children's Court. By his release on 4 June, he had been jailed for 12 days. The child was subject to a conditional release order at the time of the offence, which might have accounted for the prosecution; nevertheless, this matter could have been dealt with locally by a caution.

Cultures of resistance

Oppositional cultures develop a set of attitudes values, and behaviours deliberately in opposition to those of the mainstream, and they provide an alternative source of status and respect. In the last instance, however, oppositional cultures – while allowing short-term scope for spontaneity, autonomy and hedonism – have the tendency to simply cement subordination in the longer term; they prepare lower working-class young people for the place society had ordained for them anyway, at the bottom of the hierarchy (Willis 1981). Bourgois' study of the 'inner city street culture' of El Barrio (East Harlem, New York), provides a vivid illustration of this process: he describes these cultures as 'a complex and conflictual web of beliefs, symbols, modes of interaction, values, and ideologies that have emerged in opposition to exclusion from mainstream society', they offer a platform for a 'spontaneous set of rebellious practices' (Bourgois 1999: 8). Living on the margins propels them into 'lifestyles of violence, substance abuse and internalised rage' (1999: 9). The awesome contradiction at the centre of street culture is that it is:

> predicated on the destruction of its participants and the community harbouring them ... although street culture emerges out of a personal search for dignity and a rejection of racism and subjugation, it ultimately becomes an active agent in personal degradation and community ruin. (Bourgois 1999: 9)

Aboriginal youth culture shares some of the features referred to by Bourgois, in the sense that it is pre-occupied by the search for dignity and respect, Aboriginal youth have a sharp awareness of racism and subjugation and their life styles (drugs, alcohol, petrol sniffing, fighting, continuous contact with prison) are self- (and other) destructive: but there are also salient differences. To begin with, the Puerto Rican parent culture of El Barrio is diasporic, and the youth sub-culture is concerned with controlling 'the street', forming defensive perimeters to protect themselves from the wider society. The ownership of the street, or the neighbourhood, remains symbolic; they only 'own' it to the extent that they are able to occupy it and police access to it. They will never have the deeds to it; these remain the property of someone else. This relationship with a diasporic landscape differs from the ways Aboriginal youth work on their relationships with place and space, these remain embedded in the entanglements of colonial occupation, and the consequent co-existence of two domains. Aboriginal youth, like their parent culture, claim the land (as the land claims them) and believe themselves bound to it: the sense of ownership is not symbolic but historical and cultural.

There are other sites of difference. The cultures of resistance formed by margina-lised and socially excluded youths in western societies have an ambivalent relationship with the dominant culture. While they may be rebellious, they also sign up to many of the cultures goals and broader aspirations. In Bourgois' study of El Barrio he finds that many of the young people who wind up selling crack were at one stage 'pursuing the immigrant's dream' of mainstream success, wanting real work and status (Bourgois 1999: 137). The inner structures of the classic sub-culture are in many respects a mirror of the mainstream, but it takes the mainstreams most conservative values and lives them out radically. Aboriginal people have rarely desired such close entanglement with mainstream culture. The 'resistance' is not simply resistance to brutal strategies of 'exclusion' – in Bourgois' terms, but resistance to a host of strategies of assimilation, cultural genocide and dispossession. This is not to say that Aboriginal youth don't desire many of the things the mainstream has, but they want them in combination with a range of traditional Aboriginal demands. It is interesting that Aboriginal youth are rarely involved in the drug market – though they are consumers. Selling drugs provides a means of social mobility, and offers status and respect in the ghetto: the war on drugs has provided the means for the mass imprisonment of black and Hispanic youth in the United States. While Indigenous youth are massively over-represented in Australia's detention systems they are rarely imprisoned for drug-related offences.

Aboriginal youth culture: peer groups and gangs

Studies of deviance focus heavily on the role of the peer group in creating conditions for criminal and anti-social behaviour. Classically, young people form into groups or gangs for leisure, power, social defence and resistance. Intervention with young people has increasingly come to terms with the fact that kids offend in groups and need to be worked with in group contexts. This is reinforced by the realisation that for many young people offending behaviour is a maturational phenomenon: most 'kids' stop being criminal when they stop being 'kids'. In criminological theory, neighbourhood-based peer groups formed the basis for juvenile gangs, many of which were transient vehicles for male rights of passage before most 'drifted' back and developed their – however meagre – stake in conformity, leaving only a core of career delinquents to keep the justice system in business.

Aboriginal youth rarely form gangs in the traditional sense. There social groupings are based on connections with extended family and classificatory kin – often referred to as brother, sister, or cousin. These groups are only loosely formulated around matu-rational peers. They tend to range from as young as seven (sometimes younger) up to mid- or late-20s. This means that they come to the attention of the authorities earlier and stay connected much longer than in the profile of the juvenile offender in classic criminology. They tend not to try and pin down territory (Aboriginal people used guerrilla tactics in their struggle with the colonisers) instead they roam traditional places and sites, usually staying with family. Nyoongars call these connecting paths that once traversed sacred sites, their 'runs', and young men were initiated through their journey with older men through their clan's runs.

Much of the rivalry with other groups does not take place on the basis of ethnic rivalry or different youth styles but represents the continuation of traditional clan and family rivalries and feuds. They are also rarely over 'territory' but range across a diversity of site. Young Aboriginal girls are also active in feuding (Crime Research Centre and Donovan Research 1999):

> Family feuds exist and it is often the adults who pursue arguments however, it is common to find that despite their age, children from the families in question possess knowledge of the arguments as well and will continue the arguments at school with other Aboriginal students. (Kickett-Tucker 1998: 4)

The situation of Aboriginal youth is different and requires an alternative framework to make sense of behaviour. Tatz's (2001a) study of Aboriginal youth suicide addresses this point, and he maintains that Aboriginal youth are at risk of suffering more from social disorder rather than from mental disorder. For Tatz, the issue is existential, not psychological, it is a story of a world 'out of joint':

> Suicide for Indigenous youth is an oppositional act. The point is, that most Aboriginal kids hang themselves, and hanging themselves is very significant because hanging is dramatic, it's confronting, it's a statement to white society, it's a statement that incorporates notions of pathos, notions of injustice, notions of capital punishment, it's confronting. (Tatz 2001b: 43)

The post-colonial critique

Cunneen (2011) suggests that a post-colonial perspective is helpful in bringing to criminology an acknowledgement of the 'long-term impact of colonization and imperialism' and invites us to begin an 'analysis of the structures of sentiment and ideology that determine the intersections of race, crime and punishment' (Cunneen, 2011, 252). As noted earlier, post-colonial perspectives articulate and privilege the subjugated knowledge of colonised peoples and identifying the ways colonial structures of domination are negotiated and subverted by the colonised (Bhaba, 1994; Moore-Gilbert, 1997). It also places stress on the extent to which colonisation takes place in the realms of culture and knowledge. Gayatri Chakravorty Spivak (1996) talks, for example, of the 'epistemological violence' of colonisation, and colonisation as a process of 'worlding' where the colonised space is inscribed by the worldview of the coloniser. If nations are 'imagined communities' (Anderson 1983); then de-colonisation involves a 're-imagining' and re-mapping of place, time and space (Spivak 1996; Said 1993, 2003; Young 1990; Ashcroft Griffiths and Tiffin H 1998).

An Aboriginal re-imagining and re-mapping of youth justice space shifts the focus from mainstream institutions (courts, detention centres, community-based offices) to sites of ritual and symbolic significance to Aboriginal people. 'On-country' work with young people has taken on special significance for Indigenous organisations, they see a reconfigured and re-imagined youth justice system firmly anchored in Indigenous land. Land is becoming what Canadian First Nations critic and activist Greg Cauthold calls a 'site of resurgence' for Indigenous cultures globally (2014). Working on-country constitutes a powerfully decolonising turn, that inevitably re-shapes relationships between Indigenous people and mainstream structures. After decades of repressive policies intended to fragment Indigenous family structures, on-country initiatives reaffirm the importance of traditional authority and knowledge.

Aboriginal elders in the Kimberley still talk of the damage created when the old, draconian, administrative mechanisms of control that had kept Aboriginal people in check (government and religious missions, feeding stations, etc) suddenly withdrew in the 1960s. It led to a rapid movement into regional towns and an impoverished existence as 'fringe dwellers' on the margins of white society. It would be simplistic to see this sudden withdrawal as an act of de-colonisation. Rather it represented a shift in governmental strategies regarding the management of Aboriginal affairs, from overt paternalism to one of governing from a distance. Aboriginal elders see decolonisation in terms of creating a new relationship with the white mainstream, not being abandoned by it.

'On-country' initiatives in the Kimberley region of Western Australia have been nurtured by elders groups, such as Kimberley Law and Culture (KALACC). KALACC's has created a community-owned and controlled initiative, the *Yiriman* Project, which provides an intensive cultural immersion and 'healing' experience on traditional lands for at risk young people. The project has been created by Cultural Bosses in the Kimberley to help young people at risk reconnect with law and culture. Its prime means of engaging with youth is through intensive, 'on-country cultural camps' run by Cultural Bosses. The bosses are supported by a *Yiriman* youth workers (a mix of Aboriginal and non-Aboriginal workers who case-work young people, provide the interface with the justice and other systems and offer longer-term mentoring to young people who have been on the camps). This hybrid mix of intensive cultural work and systems intervention is intended to bridge the gap between state and community structures.

Aboriginal people call this 'working both ways' standing in both Aboriginal and non-Aboriginal worlds, creating a new 'engagement space', where Aboriginal cultural values and processes can be translated into non-Indigenous social capital (employment, education and training). The project, as is often the case in community owned initiatives, crosses boundaries: having 'variously been described as a youth diversionary program, a cultural maintenance project and a way to heal young people, heal country and heal community' (Palmer 2010: 10). This is because Aboriginal people rarely discriminate between young people in trouble with the law and those harming themselves in other ways. They believe that 'returning to country' helps to 'build stories, strength and resilience in young people' (Palmer 2010: 10). *Yiriman* Women's Project also runs a number of 'Back to Country' trips initiated and designed by young women, in consultation with senior women cultural leaders, such as a 2010 'Fitzroy Valley Women's Bush Meeting' and a *Wangkajungka Walmajarri* Bush Medicine Camp.

The camps focus on preparing young people to become rangers, and participate in the hybrid economy. Returning to country is central to the project. The elders 'share stories around campfires about their skin, their history and heritage, and their country' (Palmer 2010: 23). Cultural bosses said that 'kids come good' on the camps, they 'learned rain dance, how to make campfire, hunt Kangaroo, make damper'. As a result, one cultural boss said, 'around 40 younger men are taking control of their lives'.

Two intensive cultural camps were undertaken in 2009 and 2010 and directly focused on young people in trouble with the law. The first involved 10 young men who had admitted to breaking and entering houses, the second involved six boys involved in a spate of offending: there were also 12 others, including young women, referred by community members because they were believed to be at risk. The sentencing process was run as an 'Aboriginal Court', where cultural elders sit with the magistrate (Marchetti and Daly 2004). At the request of the elders the youths were referred to *Yiriman* and sentencing was deferred. Both camps were held at *Jilji Bore* on remote *Wangkajungka* country. The magistrate was impressed by the process and by the ways the young men responded, most had greatly reduced sentences. Several had been at risk of being sentenced to periods of detention in Perth, over 2000km away.

Contestations: culturally secure and on country

Yiriman became a site of contestation between KALACC and State government. Local Youth Justice workers respected *Yiriman* and genuinely wanted to place young people on community-based orders and provide some funding for vehicles, and equipment, but, in return, wanted a big say in how 'programs' were 'delivered' and wanted a degree of control over activities, places and duration of programs, to fit with their own governance requirements. Badging *Yiriman* as a 'program' immediately brought it within the domain of mainstream governmentality and subject to its regulations, especially around 'individualized risk management'. The cultural bosses resisted any attempt by Youth Justice to define *Yiriman* as a 'justice program', fearing this would mean the end of it as a community-owned initiative – Youth Justice workers were welcome to participate in cultural camps but 'justice must not be the bosses of the bush trips', one Cultural Boss said. Furthermore, justice could not dictate where the camps took place, or how long they would last. Justice workers also complained that the sites, such as *Jilgi Bore*, were 'too remote': a *Yiriman* worker responded 'that's the crux of it, its law-country, the camps won't work anywhere else. It might be remote for them, but it's the centre of the world for our people'.

One justice worker said, 'we were ready to put money into *Yiriman* but did not receive assurances that the kids would be safe. They take them a long way out bush, and it's tough going for them. We feared someone would die.' The response of KALACC and other Kimberley leaders was revealing. They reflected on the high rate of youth suicide in Kimberley communities (11 between January and March 2011 alone) and other 'multiple and compound' life risks facing their youth on a daily basis – could the risks be any greater? They added that the risks of perishing in the desert compare favourably with the risks of deaths in custody, sexual and physical abuse and damage to mental health that face Indigenous youth in the lock-up and prison regimes. One said that white institutions 'have never made our kids physically or culturally secure' and historically have been 'factories for destroying Indigenous culture'. Robyn William's description of a culturally secure environment as one that is 'spiritually, socially and emotionally safe, as well as physically safe for people' (Williams 2009: 553) has been widely adopted by Aboriginal organisations in their debates with government. The construct has been applied to argue for specifically Aboriginal-run and managed processes. KALAAC is seeking funding for four new '*Yiriman*' style projects in different parts of the Kimberley, to be the hub for a diversity of Aboriginal-managed local youth diversion projects.

In the Kimberly region of Western Australia Aboriginal organisations are claiming cultural rights to manage and control their own youth justice related initiatives. The approach is part of a broader strategy of building a specifically Aboriginal form of 'cultural capital'. The white mainstream has enormous power at its disposal to deflect the reforming thrust of these initiatives, colonising and absorbing them, turning on-country cultural camps into new sites of discipline, control and punishment. There are pressures to 're-brand' them as 'justice programs' and their duration, intent, practices and activities standardised and routinised to fit into the knowledge frames of the mainstream justice system: demonstrating the state's respect for 'cultural rights' while, Aboriginal people fear, perpetuating practices of colonial subordination. This may be the price tag for government support and finance. KALACC are well aware of the dangers of cultural appropriation, but they are keen, nonetheless, to pursue a creative, 'hybrid' compromise with youth justice that does not violate core beliefs. They want mainstream Australia to know that their law, land and culture are strong and alive, and a sound platform for building a future for their young people.

Notes

1   The 2008 inquest was held to explore the reasons for a large number of deaths of Aboriginal persons in the Kimberley 'whose deaths appeared to have been caused or contributed to by alcohol abuse or cannabis use and also, if possible, to identify reasons for an alarming increase in suicide rates' <http://www.safetyandquality.health.wa.gov.au/docs/mortality_review/inquest_finding/Kimberley_Coronial_Report_Findings>.

4

Restorative Justice: A Good Idea Whose Time has Gone?

Aboriginal people may find much to agree with in Nils Christies' (1986) well-travelled assertion that the state has a tendency to 'steel' conflict. The colonisation of Australia, and the creation of the Australian state, began with the theft of land and the deliberate destruction of existing forms of law and mechanisms of conflict resolution. There are a number of key questions to be answered: can restorative justice help Aboriginal people reclaim the capacity to resolve conflict? Does it offer a set of philosophies and practices, and a dialogic space, where Aboriginal and non-Aboriginal notions of law and justice can meet? Are the structures of restorative justice sufficiently 'liminal' to accommodate Aboriginal narratives?

On the face of it restorative justice would seem a natural component of any strategy designed to enhance Aboriginal involvement in the criminal justice process, and construct alternative justice mechanisms more in tune with the cultural practices of Indigenous people. The image of the Indigene liberally adorns many restorative justice texts, particularly where this involves reference to 'face to face' mediation as an alternative to the suffocating interference of judicial bureaucracy and the dead hand of the formal law. I want to argue in this chapter that, whereas restorative justice has generally had a largely energising effect on debates about the justice system, of itself it has little to add to justice reform strategies for Aboriginal people. Indeed, I will maintain that, in relation to justice reform for Aboriginal people, the restorative justice moment may have passed and been superseded by a renascent Aboriginal customary law which, while sharing some common features with restorative justice, has elements of practice that do not fit into existing models of restorative justice. Aboriginal customary law cannot simply be collapsed into restorative justice. Restorative justice articulates a range of popular feelings of alienation from impersonalised justice *institutions*: for colonised peoples the sense of estrangement is deeper and extends not just to social institutions but to underlying *social structures*.

State-initiated restorative justice, I want to suggest, reflects a Eurocentric imaginary of its Indigenous Other, assuming that a few concessions to Indigenous 'culture' (such as having Indigenous elders present at diversionary conferences) can sugar the bitter pill of Indigenous dispossession. Elizabeth Povinelli (2002) refers to such strategies as 'cunning' recognition: accepting a degree of cultural difference as long as it does not constitute a *radical alterity* that threatens white supremacy, particularly where this includes claims to land. However, it is land (or 'country' for Australia's Aboriginal people) that remains at the centre of Indigenous cosmology, as Aileen Moreton-Robinson suggests, 'the inalienable nature of our (Aboriginal people's) relationship to land, marks a radical, indeed incommensurable, difference between us and the non-Indigenous' (Moreton-Robinson 2003: 45).

Restorative justice: some key themes in the debate

Reviewing the now voluminous literature on restorative justice has become a daunting task and I do not intend to repeat what many others have accomplished. While restorative justice as a 'social movement' (Braithwaite 1999) has only been around for the past 20 or so years, many of its fundamental principles and beliefs had already been mapped out by those involved in innovatory work around informal justice in the 1980s in the United States and the United Kingdom. These encapsulated victim/offender mediation and reparation schemes positioned either at the pre-court or court stage, and a loose variety of neighbourhood-based programs, intended to work on the social causes of conflict at the grass roots level.

The definition established by Tony Marshall describes the aims of restorative justice:

> Restorative justice is a process whereby all the parties with a stake in a particular offence come together to resolve collectively how to deal with the aftermath of the offence and its implications for the future. (Marshall 1996: 37)

This definition has been criticised as too narrow (Braithwaite 1999) and because it restricts restorative processes to face-to-face meetings. Bazemore and Walgrave (1999) prefer a notion of restorative justice encapsulating actions which repair the harms caused by crime. The scope of restorative justice has widened considerably since its introduction as a concept in the early 1990s and it is no longer possible – or even desirable – to attempt a simple definition. Roche suggests that restorative justice 'became a unifying banner "sweeping up" a number of informal traditions of justice and capturing the imagination of many of those interested in reforming the criminal justice system', (Roche 2004: 7).

Interest in restorative justice was boosted by the emergence of family conferencing in New Zealand, as a vehicle for restorative solutions: conferencing lay at the centre of a raft of radical reforms to both justice and welfare services under the New Zealand *Children, Young Persons and their Families Act 1989*. According to Van Ness, Morris and Maxwell (2001), the strength of the conferencing process is that it:

> involves not only the primary victim and offender, but also secondary victims (such as family members or friends of the victim) as well as supporters of the offender (such as family members or friends). These people are involved because they have also been affected in some way by the offence, and because they care about one of the primary participants. They may also be involved in carrying out the final agreement. (Van Ness, Morris & Maxwell 2001: 7)

Restorative justice and the family group conference as a vehicle for making restorative justice happen were closely linked to diversionary approaches to youth offending. The attraction for policy makers, police and justice workers was that it had the potential to make diversion look less like a soft option. Diversion becomes not just a mechanism for re-routing individual cases away from contact with the existing criminal justice system but also a vehicle for directing cases into an alternative process of community-based justice. Diversionary conferencing seemed to suit the interests of a number of key players. The police might have increased confidence in cautioning juveniles when they know the young offender may have to face up to the victim, offer compensation and/or undertake some community task; while youth justice workers could feel they were removing the stigma associated with the courts, while providing a meaningful experience to young people and an opportunity for genuine community involvement. The emergence of interest in Braithwaite's thesis of 'reintegrative shaming' provided further evidence that conferencing was a valid method: indeed, it reinforced the belief that conferencing was a better method than existing models of justice (Moore 1993; Moore & McDonald 1995, O'Connell 1992). 'Reintegrative shaming' was a term coined by John Braithwaite to describe a form of shaming ceremony in which offenders are reintegrated into the fold through strategies of disapproval, in a way that condemns the offence but does not denigrate the offender (Braithwaite 1989; Braithwaite & Mugford 1994).

The theme of reintegration became a dominant one in restorative justice since Braithwaite's intervention. In Australia, Rob White has consistently asked the question: 'reintegration into what?' (White 2003), and he mounts a persuasive argument for developing forms of restorative justice which enhance social justice and community capital, particularly in relation to resources for marginal young people, and criticises the tendency to reduce restorative practices simply to youth conferencing (White 2003). A number of the cherished principles have been challenged on the basis of research with participants in restorative justice processes. Daly (2002) presents what she calls four myths about restorative justice circulated by advocates of restorative justice:

> (1) restorative justice is the opposite of retributive justice; (2) restorative justice uses indigenous justice practices and was the dominant form of pre-modern justice; (3) restorative justice is a 'care' (or feminine) response to crime in comparison to a 'justice' (or masculine) response; and (4) restorative justice can be expected to produce major changes in people. (Daly 2002: 55)

Daly is also critical of the view that restorative justice is an Indigenous practice, and here she is in company with other critics (Blagg 1997; Cunneen 1997; Polk, Adler, Muller & Rechtman 2001).

Indigenous perspectives

Any examination of the links between restorative justice and Indigenous people needs to begin with a process of demystification. There are a number of levels upon which a critique of restorative justice from an Aboriginal justice perspective could be mounted. A critique from a post-colonial perspective would focus attention on a number of dimensions: the 'Orientalist'-style appropriation of traditional Indigenous dispute resolution mechanisms and their repackaging to suit the needs of the non-Indigenous world, perpetuating processes of cultural colonisation; the post-modern kitsch involved in creaming off elements of Indigenous culture to shore up our need for meaning in an era of pessimism and melancholy. The use of Said's construct of Orientalism in the context of a restorative justice innovation may appear unnecessarily exotic. One can, however, mount a strong case for interrogating the relationship between restorative justice and Indigenous people in just such a way. Restorative justice advocates have been criticised for a tendency to construct a homogenised Aboriginality, extrapolating the warm and fuzzy elements and leaving aside the aspects of Indigenous penalty which rested on ritualised violence (Tauri 1999).

A post-colonial critique might also focus on the ways the ideals and purposes of conferencing were redefined by hegemonically powerful groups to meet their own interest and policy agendas. Indigenous processes can be appropriated, denuded of context and employed to meet the interests of the status quo. The conferencing model employed in New Zealand – developed as a forum for Maori decision-making and family empowerment – was dismantled, repackaged and represented as a 'shaming' ceremony by Australian criminologists, police and policy-makers in the early 1990s (Blagg 1997). The Wagga Wagga model of police conferencing, instituted in New South Wales in the early 1990s, borrowed elements of the New Zealand model and grafted them onto an unreformed policing system in a way that simply extended and supplemented already wide police discretionary powers in relation to young people. The police retained – and in many Australian jurisdictions still retain – control of the crucial gate-keeping processes that determine whether young people are warned, cautioned or charged and whether they will be eligible for family conferencing. In New Zealand, reform of the gate-keeping process was a core component of reform; police powers to approach, question, detain and prosecute youth were radically curtailed; a fact systematically excluded from debates about the conferencing model in Australia which focused on the capacity it offered for an expanded police role. Advocates suggested that the police were the natural conference convenors, and the police station a 'neutral' zone – a statement that, in the context of Aboriginal/police relations at least, is manifestly absurd.

Australian – and international – attention on New Zealand's system of family conferencing tended to focus on the conference as a site of reintegrative shaming. The Indigenous dimension provided a wholesome adornment to the nourishing imagery of restorative justice: redolent with images of peace-pipes, desiderata, the creator spirit and mother earth. Restorative justice has been criticised for its New Age connotations (Blagg 1998a). Recently Kelly Richards has suggested that restorative justice has become fashionable because it is influenced by 'a number of 'therapeutic' concepts and practices that have gained some currency in contemporary culture during the past quarter-century: namely, 'self-help', 'New Age', 'therapy' and 'recovery' (Richards 2005: 384). Restorative justice condenses themes typical of contemporary discourse: it plays on contemporary sensitivities about victimhood (victimhood having become an inclusive construct); encourages expressing emotions and 'being heard', and the 'New Age rhetoric of seeking "healing" and "closure"' (Richards 2005: 384).

It did not focus on issues of colonialism, nor the wholesale dismantling of Indigenous worlds through rapacious annexation of the Indigenous landscape; nor of the role that justice processes – and particularly the police – played in the dismantling of extant law and culture. Increasingly, and in classical Orientalist style, the New Zealand system was 'read through' the works of John Braithwaite and colleagues, in much the same way as the 'east' was constructed as an entity through the writings of Orientalists, explorers and diarists of the early colonial era (see the section on post-colonial studies above): producing a packaged Orient suitable for western consumption from which 'the actualities of the modern Orient were systematically excluded' (Said 2003: 177), and its 'actual identity withered away into a set of consecutive fragments' (Said 2003: 179).

The Wagga model has become a template for forms of youth conferencing globally. Its attraction – principally to justice authorities and the police – lies in the fact that it is heavily 'scripted', is run and organised by the police as a form of 'cautioning plus' (a kind of police caution with attitude), and operates on the lines of Braithwaite's (1999) theory of reintegrative shaming (Daly 2002; Young 2001). The power given to the police in this model has been heavily criticised (Blagg 1997; Blagg & Wilkie 1995; Cunneen 1997; Polk et al 2001; Sandor 1994), police dominance can lead to them being 'first among unequals' (Young 2001). Police control of the conferencing process received particular criticism in Australia in relation to Indigenous children (Human Rights and Equal Opportunity Commission and the Australian Law Reform Commission 1997), given the extraordinary control and removal powers enjoyed historically by the police, the *Stolen Children report,* argued that, 'the conferencing process has particular significance for Indigenous communities given the history of removals and prior police intervention (Human Rights and Equal Opportunity Commission 1997: 525). As Polk at al suggest, this 'raises questions about the extension of police powers in areas with few account-ability mechanisms. The police are not necessarily going to be considered supportive and cooperative, given the long history of friction between police and Indigenous communities (Polk et al 2001: 6).

A modified version of the Wagga model has become the norm in Australian youth conferencing and in jurisdictions in the United States and the United Kingdom. While schemes much of the conferencing process is now administered by the justice system – New South Wales, Queensland, South Australia and Western Australia (Polk et al 2001; Daly 2002) – the police retain their powerful gate-keeping function even where they share the family conferencing process with other agencies. Victoria stands out because referrals to conferences only come from the Children's Court at the pre-sentencing phase.

Restorative youth conferencing in States where rates of Aboriginal youth involve-ment is high tends to be heavily gate-kept by the police. In regional towns where relationships between police and Aboriginal youth are poor, cautioning is often used less as a diversionary option and more as a means of marking off Aboriginal youth and placing them within the system of controls that will inevitably lead in, rather than out, of the system. One justice worker interviewed during a field trip to Carnarvon in Western Australia in 2006 said in relation to Aboriginal youth and diversion, 'when the police have solid evidence they charge, when the evidence is poor they refer to the juvenile justice team (for group conferencing), when there is no evidence at all they caution'.

Aboriginal people and community

A fundamental error is to impose Eurocentric images of community on to Indigenous social structure. Those communitarian belief systems inform the simplistic dualism of restorative justice – establishing the state as bad and bureaucratic and the community as good and informal – are positively dangerous when imposed on to the Indigenous context. The appeal of the restorative approach lies in its promise to humanise what appears to be an impersonal, bureaucratised and dehumanising justice system. The warm and fuzzy imagery of community has not gone uncriticised; Bauman dryly castigates the communitarian lobby for promoting a naïve view of communal life, as the 'true home of humanity':

> Come back community, from the exile to which the modern state confined you; all is forgiven and forgotten – the oppressiveness of parochiality, the genocidal propensity of collective narcissism, the tyranny of communal pressures and the pugnacity and despotism of communal discipline. (Bauman 1997: 31)

Once again I want to introduce a contrapuntal dynamic into this discussion about restorative justice. The communitarian thread in restorative justice creates a dichotomy between the state and the community, with the latter representing good and the state bad. Colonialism entailed far more than just the imposition of an alien system of laws; it constituted the wholesale dismantling of one social formation and the implantation of another. The binary opposition of state versus community, or state versus civil society in the Gramscian sense, have little relevance to Aboriginal people, who stand outside both the Australian state and Australian community/civil society. The epistemic violence of colonisation involved the deliberate dismantling of Aboriginal community and attempted to wipe out Aboriginal people's symbolic, religious and proprietorial relationships with land. Aboriginal people were dispossessed in order to establish white 'community'. They represented the dangerous other, the background against which community had to be constructed. Colonised people are colonised not just by an alien state and an alien administration of justice but by alien 'settlers'. There is no refuge for Aboriginal people in the bosom of the community – harsh laws are enacted precisely to 'reassure' the community and, as we have seen, Aboriginal people often feel safer in prison than in the community. This problematises a key trope in restorative justice practice – and advocates of restorative justice are increasingly aware of the need to prevent community members from dominating meetings (Roche 2004).

The binary oppositions underpinning restorative justice philosophy and practice fail scrutiny in other respects. Restorative justice advocates identify a sharp distinction between social *relationships* and legal *rules* which may not fit in with Aboriginal world views. Zeher and Mika (1998) outline this philosophy in their 1998 article on the *Fundamental Concepts of Restorative Justice*. They argue that crime is fundamentally violation of people and personal relationships before it is a violation of laws. Restorative programs must focus on the harm caused by crime rather than on the rules that are broken. These principles do not simply match up with the ways Aboriginal people conceive of justice within customary law. As we shall see when discussing Aboriginal law, while Aboriginal customary law *is* concerned with re-establishing relationships, *does* include victims, offenders and the broader community, it is also meticulously and fastidiously concerned with the *rules that are broken* (not just relationships between people) particularly those governing avoidance relationships, ceremony, access to ceremonial spaces, men and women's business and so on. Traditionally the disclosure of sacred objects to those not entitled to see them, or the public utterance of words associated with secret ceremony was – and still is – taken very seriously by Aboriginal people

(Toohey 2006). It can, in this respect, be highly impersonal and focus heavily on the 'rules that are broken'. Moreover, traditional practices do not distinguish between legal rules and relationships between people, as is the fashion in restorative justice, they are intricately interwoven within the Aboriginal cosmology. The highly structured nature of Aboriginal law was acknowledged by Justice Blackburn in *Milirrpum v Nabalco* when he argued that 'if ever a system could be called a "government of laws, and not of men", it is that shown in the evidence before me' ((1971) FLR 141 at 267-68).

Aboriginal forms of conflict resolution have traditionally employed quite retributive mechanisms for ensuring that the over-arching system of law is repaired. Aboriginal forms of conflict resolution might not conform to those images of Indigenous 'peace-making' found in many restorative justice texts, there might be shouting, hitting and other forms of physical pay-back, fighting, cursing, sorcery or 'singing' a law breaker.

Deliberative accountability

Declan Roche (2004) promotes a process of 'deliberative accountability' as a means both of extending the promise inherent in restorative justice, while also ensuring restorative processes themselves remain transparent and accountable. Roche describes the process of deliberative accountability thus:

> A type of mutual accountability is built into meetings where participants provide verbal accounts which are scrutinized and assessed by participants, whose own accounts are in turn scrutinized. (Roche 2004: 80)

Roche acknowledges that communication in conferences can be undermined by underlying inequalities – Roche does not fall into assumption that conferences magically stimulate warmth and equality – and power differences do work to 'affect the communicative ability of whole groups and communities' (Roche 2004: 84). In relation to Aboriginal people, Roche acknowledges a number of inherent problems; including the legacy of colonial oppression and domination, and Aboriginal people's tendency towards gratuitous concurrence as a defensive mechanism in encounters with white authority, creating barriers to the kind of open dialogue required for deliberative accountability to occur. Beyond acknowledging this he does little to suggest how this problem may be overcome within the construct of deliberative accountability democracy, given the massive gulf in power between Indigenous people and mainstream agencies and communities.

Is the cultural and structural divide between Indigenous and non-Indigenous domains too wide to be bridged by deliberative processes of this nature? One problem is the language and narrative threads inherent in the deliberative process do not necessarily reflect those of Indigenous people, particularly when involved with white authority in processes that remain largely the property of white society. However, deliberative accountability presupposes that, despite real inequalities in society, there is still a common language: a set of commensurate meanings that can be voiced and understood. It is questionable whether these currently exist, or that restorative justice practices can create the space for generating commensurate dialogue. For deliberative accountability to work, it has to be as part of a dialogue between Indigenous and non-Indigenous domains. Can this take place within the confines of restorative justice?

Roche (2004) also raises the vexed question of who within the Aboriginal community should speak on its behalf.

The role of elders

Roche raises the important matter of the role of elders in restorative conferencing – noting that many schemes make provision for the involvement of elders:

> in the hope that some form of symbiosis will occur, that elders will make a contribution to restorative justice meetings while ... meetings will provide a forum for re-establishing the authority of elders and the traditional cultural values of which they are the custodian. (Roche 2004: 100)

Roche goes on to raise a number of caveats: what degree of control should elders exert? Particularly given widely voiced concerns regarding the legitimacy of some claims to elder authority, and who has the right to speak on behalf of whom. Also, there is the vexing issue of elders themselves who, exploiting the destruction of traditional authority structures, have set themselves up in positions of power, and have used this power to exploit and abuse their own communities. Roche suggests that a form of deliberative accountability be established where elders are 'invited' to participate, but are, in the process, open to accountability (Roche 2004: 100). This begs the question: who gives the 'invitation'? And another: how are these elders identified as elders in the first place? The issue of elder involvement in any process designed to improve justice for Indigenous people is a crucial one. Roche's assessment appears unnecessarily bleak: as we shall see, processes such as Circle Sentencing Courts and Koori Courts are founded upon elder participation in the process and have been extremely successful in identifying – through organisations such as State and regional Aboriginal justice councils – networks of respected male and female elders. Indeed, it is impossible to see how any process that intends to empower Aboriginal communities could be feasible without elder involvement. Elders should be identified and supported through processes of deliberation within the Indigenous community.

Hitherto, it has been possible for Aboriginal leaders who do not necessarily possess the necessary cultural authority within Aboriginal communities to become spokespeople for Aboriginal people, because they can speak the language of government. The structures of governance imposed on Aboriginal people – such as community councils and government-appointed liaison bodies – as a means of creating parallel structures to those of the white domain, have distorted Aboriginal forms of authority. Those with traditional authority may not be recognisable to the non-Aboriginal domain intent on identifying 'leaders' with whom it can conduct business. Rarely are elders able to speak with authority for a whole group of people, power being circumscribed by kin affiliation, and those with the cultural and ceremonial authority may not be able to – or may be unwilling to – play a role as communal leaders in the western sense of the term.

Consultations for the Law Reform Commission of Western Australia Customary Law initiative found that, in general, Aboriginal people wanted to see elders play a prominent role in justice issues. In the more urbanised areas there were concerns that many elders were not trusted. Young people, in particularly do not always respect 'elders', people who may themselves have done 'bad things' in the community (Perth

Consultations). In Carnarvon, a town with a history of systemic racism and deep divisions within the Aboriginal community that frequently spilled over into bitter feuding, one local Aboriginal person said:

> It is difficult to identify who the elders are. We can't define them easily. There is no interest from community in identifying who they are.
>
> There is no Indigenous leadership, how can there be when they are all fighting each other?
>
> Many elders have no right to call themselves elders: how do we define who they are anymore? We have no ceremonies for this anymore.
>
> There has been a serious breakdown of links between old and younger generations. Elders aren't respected'. (Perth consultations)[1]

In sharp contrast to this picture, consultations in the Pilbara region found this:

> It was explained to the Commission that Elders are law people and they are like the judge, lawyers for prosecution and defence (all in one). Elders will talk to the families involved and the community and decide on the dispute … White man cannot elect Elders. Each person from each area knows who the Elders are. Within the Aboriginal communities there is respect for Elders and they 'carry our law and culture very strongly'. (Pilbara consultations)

On the whole though, elders were looked on as a positive source of advice and support, often recognised through lineage (linkages through family trees), through earning community respect or through knowledge of law. As one person put it, Elders have 'knowledge, culture and respect and lead by example'.

Restorative justice will also need to come to terms with Aboriginal people's increasing demands for the acceptance of Aboriginal law as a solution to many of the problems existing in Aboriginal communities. Aboriginal law, as lived and practiced by Indigenous people, may not necessarily correspond to those highly derivative and sanitised representations of traditional dispute resolution practices found in many restorative justice texts. A great deal of effort is being exerted on finding ways to engage with Aboriginal families and make the process more culturally appropriate, through having designated Aboriginal liaison officers attached to conference teams and using Aboriginal workers to convene meetings. In some remote areas of Western Australia the police are being encouraged to allow elders to run conferences, as a way of increasing the currently pitifully low rates of diversion in rural and remote areas of the State.

Restorative justice, to be relevant, must at least come to terms with, and enter into, the debate about Aboriginal law. While restorative justice may claim lineage with Aboriginal culture it has been noticeably absent from key debates about law and culture in Australia, having become largely the captive of mainstream justice mechanisms. Restorative justice is something that arrives in Aboriginal communities in the back of a familiar wagon train of government initiatives, brought in from the outside to resolve crime problems, rather than having been nurtured from within. We could also critique the fact that, despite the radical rhetoric about working *outside* the system, it has tended to colonise conservative institutional spaces *within* a largely unreformed criminal justice system, having become synonymous with forms of diversionary youth conferencing, strongly influenced by, and in some instances controlled by, the police.

In Canada, restorative justice has emerged in partnership with a number of strategies designed to enhance Indigenous involvement. Canadian scholars have been aware for some time of the dangers inherent in simply 'Indigenizing' non-Aboriginal programs, or cramming Indigenous people in programs and practices designed solely for non-Aboriginal people. 'Indigenization' was the term coined by Paul Haverman to describe the practice of inserting Aboriginal people piecemeal into existing structures as a means of making them more culturally appropriate without having to radically decolonise the system as a whole. Indeed, the aim of Indigenisation has been to shore up the dominant system while seeming to respond positively to criticisms from within the Aboriginal community. Elements of traditional culture may be incorporated into mainstream models to mask the fundamentally Eurocentric structures 'despite its appearance as more benign than the model of pure imposition, the integration or indigenised model is one in which the coloniser preserves aspects of the Indigenous social control system, primarily in order to utilise its authority to support the new pattern of domination' (Haverman 1992: 113).

In Canada, restorative justice seemed to offer a viable alternative, both a panacea for the diverse array of problems Indigenous people experienced in the criminal justice system and a vehicle for transforming communities themselves. Perhaps because the underpinning philosophy of restorative justice appeared sensitive to traditional Indigenous practices: there was a firm belief that it could achieve what previous reforms could not. Restorative justice ran in unison with circle sentencing and healing programs: forming what Dickson-Gilmore and La Prairie (2005) have called the 'holy trinity' of Indigenous justice reform.

Dickson-Gilmore and La Prairie's gloss on the Canadian experience of the 'holy trinity' is that the commitment to evaluation has not matched the enthusiasm for establishing such initiatives. The research that does exist raises as many questions as it answers – are the needs of Aboriginal victims being bargained off in the name of community empowerment? Are restorative solutions simply ensuring second-class justice for Aboriginal people?

They form this sombre conclusion:

> We have appointed Aboriginal Justices of the Peace and judges, recruited Aboriginal police and pressed for band policing and created 'healing lodges' to replace prisons – and nearly three decades later we still have not managed to reduce over-representation. Providing for Aboriginal people to be arrested by Aboriginal cops, defended by Aboriginal lawyers before Aboriginal judges, and sent to places of healing rather than correction did not reduce the sheer numbers of them in the system, or improve their risk factors for recidivism; if anything the number continued to climb. (Dickson-Gilmore & La Prairie 2005: 229)

The implications of Dickson-Gilmore and La Prairie's (2005) work are bleak indeed. Reform has made the existing machinery simply more effective and efficient in its business of incarcerating Aboriginal people. What's more, tinkering with institutional reform has been a distraction from the main game, because the reasons for Aboriginal over-representation are not institutional but systemic. The focus on Aboriginal 'culture' as means of reducing over-representation has been misguided, ignoring the matrix of socio-economic and social justice issues which underpins First Nation over-representation. The focus on culture, however, appealed to the mainstream (and some Aboriginal leaders) because it diverts attention away from the unpalatable truth: many Aboriginal communities exist in states of endemic crisis; meaningful reform will be long-term and costly.

All the reforms noted in the quote above 'Indigenise' a system that remains fundamentally white. Dickson-Gilmore and La Prairie (2005) offer a stark warning to those offering restorative justice as a simplistic solution to the issue of over-representation in the criminal justice system. A focus on 'cultural appropriateness' and a willingness to try alternatives to the present system of justice cannot themselves transform the underlying situation. There has to be parallel commitment to addressing questions of sustainable governance, economic marginalisation and so on. It is difficult to find fault with the general thrust of this argument. Critics in Australia since the Royal Commission into Aboriginal Deaths in Custody, and similar processes in Canada, have agreed on the need to tackle the underlying systemic issues, which ensure enmeshment in the system. Nevertheless, there are a number of problems with Dickson-Gilmore and La Prairie's interpretation of developments: including a tendency to accept a limited definition of what 'culturally appropriate' means. While healing lodges do have a powerful resonance with traditional First Nation culture, how close to traditional culture is it to have Aboriginal cops, Aboriginal lawyers and Aboriginal judges? There has been a tendency in Canada and the United States to see progress for Indigenous people in terms of establishing stand-alone justice systems (police, courts) that in many respects mirror those of the dominant culture. Why would being arrested by Aboriginal police and being defended by an Aboriginal lawyer before Aboriginal judges reduce recidivism? Is it sufficient to simply replicate western forms of justice and policing, add a few cultural adornments, and employ more Indigenous people?

One difficulty – and this is an especially difficult issue to unravel, and we should not pretend there is a simple way either of demarcating or resolving the issue – lies in the way we have handled the notion of culture in relation to our dealings with the Aboriginal domain. Strategies aimed at improving the lives of Aboriginal people across a diversity of sites (health, education, childcare, justice) attempt to be culturally relevant. The Overcoming Indigenous Disadvantage process focuses on the effects of 'cultural loss' as part of a cascading series of negative events: the response is to reinforce positive social and environmental factors; strengthening culture is seen as a crucial step in building resilience and developing protective factors. The focus on, and respect for, culture represents one way in which we can distinguish ourselves from the assimilationist strategies of previous generations. The justice system, however, remains the property of the non-Aboriginal domain, irrespective of how it is presented and glossed over with 'culturally relevant' strategies: and it remains so no matter how many Aboriginal police, corrections officers, judges we employ. Aileen Moreton-Robinson's assessment is that the cultural turn has become another technique of control, part of the regime of power through which whites possess Aboriginal people (Moreton-Robinson 2002). The discourse of culture opens up space for technologies of control to be deployed: for where there is culture, there is also cultural dysfunction and cultural maladjustment, constructs that permit the deployment of control strategies. The weakness of Moreton-Robinson's Foucauldian analysis here is one generic to Foucault's approach to questions of power: techniques of power are granted absolutist status and alternative strategies are doomed to become simple nodes of resistance to these discursive practices.

Returning to Dickson-Gilmore and La Prairie's (2005) argument that we should focus greater attention on the economic and social justice deficit in Indigenous communities, rather than on cultural reform within the justice arena as the principle target, there are a few points that need to be raised. Shifting attention to economic and social justice issues does not resolve the problem of culture; it simply moves it somewhere else. Issues of poverty, unemployment, sound governance and economic sustainability have all become discussed within cultural terms of reference – for good or ill – and it has become difficult to have a discussion about economic governance or social inequalities and human rights without the issue of culture being raised. Despite the misgivings of scholars, and the very real problems associated with the deployment of culture in reform strategies, Aboriginal people see the cultural dimension as a crucial element in any process of reform. Socio-economic conditions and inequalities alone cannot account for the higher rates of Aboriginal offending and for the hyper-incarceration of Australian Aboriginal people (Cunneen 2006). In Australia the issue of Aboriginal culture is increasingly being embedded in debates about the continuing relevance of Aboriginal law as the essential anchor for discussions about culture.

Restorative justice is often viewed by Indigenous activists, when it is viewed at all, as just another globalised and de-territorialised 'method' circulating in the reified ether of international policy transfer through the medium of western NGOs. Embedded in a northern epistemology and philosophy, restorative justice is focused on individual as opposed to collective rights, and individual 'victims' and 'offenders' as, autonomous agents, each with responsibility for his/her own actions: notions at odds with Indigenous epistemologies. A more 'critical' form of restorative justice might be capable of moving beyond these Eurocentric constructs of 'responsibilisation' and forge alliances with Indigenous peoples in a non-colonising way.

While both critics and supporters of restorative justice recognise that it should not put its faith in conferencing as the principle vehicle for restorative practices to flourish, the question needs to be asked, in relation to the criminal justice system at least, without conferencing, what does restorative justice have going for it? Specifically, in relation to Indigenous Australians, while there are areas of good practice in Aboriginal-related restorative justice, these practices alone cannot form the basis for a 'restorative vision': by which I mean a set of practices informed by an imperative to decolonise the criminal justice and related systems through processes promoting self-determination and respect for Aboriginal law and culture. The question then becomes where and how does restorative justice fit in to this decolonising process? There is a real danger of restorative justice being left behind as debate (as is increasingly becoming the case) shifts towards processes concerned with the renewal of Aboriginal law. Such processes demand more from all of us (criminologists, police, lawyers, judges, magistrates, social workers) than convening conferences. A thorough exploration of the issue by the Law Reform Commission of Western Australia – the most in-depth exegesis of the issue of Aboriginal customary law since the ground-breaking study by the Australian Law Reform Commission in 1986 – points to a need for multiple and multi-faceted solutions and a commitment to resourcing 'Aboriginal-owned' community justice mechanisms (Law Reform Commission of Western Australia 2006b). Decolonising justice also implies a restructuring of relationships between Aboriginal people and policing.

Notes

1   Law Reform Commission of Western Australia, Thematic Summaries of Consultations, at <www.lrc.justice.wa.gov.au>.

5

Aboriginal People and Policing

Brendan Behan's celebrated aphorism, that there is no situation already so calamitous that police intervention can't make considerably worse, could have been coined with specific reference to contact between the police and Aboriginal people in Australia. The statistics are truly alarming. Aboriginal people in Western Australia are roughly 12 times more likely to be arrested by the police than non-Aboriginal people. It gets worse when we look at particular sub-groups. Aboriginal women are arrested at 47 times the rate of non-Aboriginal women and Aboriginal young people. Increased rates of arrest inevitably lead to higher rates of incarceration. As we have noted, around 40% of prisoners in the States' prisons are Aboriginal – it bears repetition that Aboriginal people represent less than 4% of the State's population.

Yet, 'policing' (in some form) remains critical to any strategy intended to reduce levels of violence in Indigenous communities. Indigenous people want to see police on communities – provided they respect local customs and norms, and prioritise issues of importance to the community (Pilkington 2009; Anthony & Blagg 2013). Aboriginal people deserve the same levels of security as anyone else, what remains at issue is the way this security is provided: how it is structured and administered; how it is embedded culturally; how, and to whom, it is made open and accountable? How are policing priorities defined: and by who? In light of the historically complex and emotionally charged relationship between the police and Aboriginal people, is it naïve to assume that there can have been at some obscure point in the recent past a rupture with previous patterns of sentiment and attitude towards Aboriginal people on behalf of the police and a transformation in the nature of Aboriginal/police relations?

Certainly, the police as an agency have grappled with the problem and most police services in Australia have an Aboriginal policy framework, through which they attempt to build better relationships with the Aboriginal community. On the other hand, I will suggest, there are also some pervasive continuities in policing practices towards Indigenous people which, while regally glossed over with appropriate references to improved relationships, inevitably continue to exacerbate tensions. It has been *the Aboriginal problem*, rather than *Aboriginal people's problems*, that has been the focus for policing historically. Can the terms upon which the policing of Indigenous people are undertaken shift to such an extent that the police are viewed as a service for, as opposed to a force over, Aboriginal people?

As noted in Chapter 1, there is evidence that, on a local level in particular, good relationships between Indigenous communities and police can be fostered. Any place-based analysis of relationships between the police and Indigenous people would uncover significant variations across regions and towns, depending on host of historical and cultural factors. In towns where Indigenous people have come to 'constitute the public' and where there are robust Indigenous organisations and structures capable of articulating their demands, relationships with the police tend to be constructive. Towns such as Fitzroy Crossing, in the Kimberley region of Western Australia, with its dense network of Indigenous structures and consultative bodies, now enjoy good working relationships with the police, who, particularly where young offenders are concerned, go out of their way to avoid prosecution. Such arrangements are, however, tenuous and unstable, and, as senior police officers and station sergeants readily admit, may not survive the rotation of key personnel. Currently, the police in key towns in the Kimberley (Derby, Fitzroy Crossing and Halls Creek) are managed by experienced sergeants who have painstakingly built close links with Indigenous organisations and elders and police through consent and negotiation. However, these experienced sergeants and district superintendents will be moved on after a brief tenure.

In this and the next chapter I want to suggest that such a shift is only possible within a framework of a radically new partnership between Aboriginal communities and the police. I want to look closely at two dimensions of the debate about Aboriginal/police relations: the first involves a brief review of these relations since the Royal Commission into Aboriginal Deaths in Custody (RCIADIC); the second involves an examination not of *the police* themselves, but of *policing* as a broader range of activities, and how current trends towards what Bayley and Shearing (2001) have called 'multilateral policing' can have positive outcomes for Aboriginal people.

Policing remains a controversial and sensitive topic for Aboriginal people. Cunneen (2001b) maintains that the policing of Indigenous Australians is inextricably bound up with the issue of colonialism. He argues that the Australian police force in its dealings with Aboriginal people has tended to be an oppressive instrument of state policy whether involved in pacification, regulating movement, or removing children in the name of protection. The process of nation building required the establishment of policing systems that became intimately involved in the dispossession of Aboriginal people and the remaking of Aboriginal society. Policing ensured that Aboriginal people remained dominated by, but excluded from participation in, the nation state through a diversity of strategies. While these may have changed over time – from so-called protection to contemporary practices of 'criminalisation' – they have been essentially products of a colonial 'mentality' (Cunneen 2001b: 3). The colonial construction of Aboriginal people as a breed of criminals nourished a set of images and stereotypes of Aboriginal people that persist in many forms today. It is as a policing problem, as a problem of order, that Aboriginal people become visible to the Australian mainstream.

A brief excursus through colonial history

Reviewing the history of colonial policing in Australia suggests that policing was an important instrument in the forcible removal of Aboriginal people from traditional lands and the legitimation of this land theft (Finnane 1994). Moreover – and this is a crucial fact that has had long-term repercussions – the police were to act as the 'consistent point of contact with colonial power' (Cunneen 2001b: 49), a process which embedded a set of images and ideas about the nature and intent of policing that has informed the thinking both of the police and the Aboriginal domain.

The police were – and remain – bearers of a particular culture, not just mindless instruments of colonial power. They brought and disseminated this culture wherever they went, and they developed relationships with Indigenous Australians premised on a particular set of beliefs and sentiments about their rights, duties and responsibilities and about the nature and value of the land and people they were policing. Gayatri Chakravorty Spivak expresses this kind of cultural practice wonderfully well in her notion of 'worlding' which describes a complex set of practices designed to obscure the 'epistemic violence' of the colonial project, while making western dominance and geographic possession appear somehow given or natural, as subject peoples, were exploitatively absorbed into the Imperial system (Spivak 1996). Spivak does not see 'worlding' as simply the prerogative of the rich and powerful, or some abstract entity such as the colonial state, rather the process is also performed by what criminologists would call, after Howard Becker (1963), 'low level functionaries'. Spivak uses the example of the British soldier marching through India, consolidating the space as a European enclave, forcing the native to 'experience his home ground as an imperial space' (cited in Ashcroft, Griffiths & Tiffin 1998: 241-42). The police in Australia played a role similar to the army in India. Policing as a practice represented a technique by which Indigenous people were rendered knowable to colonial authorities.

The police were not immune to framing their activities within a colonial discourse of a kind, which legitimated their work and helped assemble a set of images and forms of knowledge about the Aboriginal Other. E Morrow's text, *The Law Provides* (1984), recalls his life as a trooper in the north-west Australian Mounted Police in the early 1920s. Of significance is how Morrow 'imagined' the country, his role as a white man of British stock and his task as a police officer on the frontier. His biography reflected a number of themes of colonial discourse. Significant also is that Morrow joined the West Australian police four years after serving in the army: his war-time experience had taken him to Egypt and other parts of the 'Orient': an experience which shaped his sentiments and attitudes. Morrow writes that the posting 'appealed to me as a place of romance and adventure. It was in the North-West and the North-West was full of wonderful possibilities' (Morrow 1984: 1). On his journey north into 'the strange unknown' we become acquainted with his views on Aboriginal people:

> [T]hree natives who had been brought to Perth, as witnesses in a trial, were being sent back to Broome. They were put in my charge, and the responsibility made me feel important. I was conscientious in my desire for their welfare, for I looked upon them then – as I do now – as children. (Morrow 1984: 22)

This is hardly a journey these Aboriginal people would have undertaken willingly. It was a 2000 kilometre journey, far away from kin and country – they might just as well have been taken to the moon. Aboriginal witnesses were routinely chained together by the neck – a practice that did not die out until the 1960s in the Kimberly region, due to their tendency to run away at any opportunity.

We are struck by two realities here. In the 1920s, police powers over Aboriginal people has been consolidated into a series of regulations and laws which gave individual police officers extraordinary powers. These covered a range of issues because the police had been designated protectors of Aboriginal people, distributors of rations, and instruments for imposing the Draconian regulations which excluded Aboriginal people from white towns and settlements. The police did not simply police the frontier, they constituted the frontier in everyday life; contact between Aboriginal people and white society was frequently mediated through contact with the police. So what kinds of power might Morrow have wielded vis-à-vis these Aboriginal people? Before examining them and assessing whether such power relationships between Aboriginal people and the police exist today, it is worth pausing momentarily to consider the other dimension of the work of the police on the Australian frontier: a frontier that faced two ways, inwards to surrounds and fence the 'outback' and outwards, to defend the colony against the dangers poses by proximity to the Orient. An Australian collective consciousness was framed by a double anxiety: the Other within (Aboriginal people) and the Other without (the Asiatic). A double anxiety that has contemporary resonance, as the settler state in Australia's far north attempts to deter 'boat people' from outside, while increasing controls over the colonised Other within, through the appropriation of Indigenous land, increased policing and imposition of white governance following the 2007 Northern Territory Intervention.

Jensen (2005) describes the patrolling of the far north of Australia in the early part of the 20th century as partially concerned with halting long-standing contact between Macassan traders and Aboriginal people. The evidence of sophisticated trade-links between Asians and what Australian's believed to be a primitive and nomadic people potentially de-legitimated the possession of the continent and had to be stopped. Policing represented a mechanism through which territory could be fixed, the Oriental firmly put in his place and the Aborigine coerced into fulfilling his/her role as a doomed race. In Morrow's book, the Asiatic has an unsettling presence, but what is also interesting is that – the further north he travels – the way these anxieties are projected onto the terrain itself:

> A strange, yet almost familiar smell permeated the boat. I wondered where I had known it before. It was cloying and unpleasant. Thoughts of Turkish Delight flashed through my mind, but were dismissed. It was not salt, nor fish, nor putrefaction, nor even body odour. I knew it, but could not place it. The crew began to haul up, the anchor. As they pulled they chanted in a low, monotonous tone. Immediately I knew where I had experienced the smell before. In Egypt! That strange mysterious smell which cannot be located as belonging to any other thing. It was ages old; had been built up and acquired through countless years; it was the East. (Morrow 1984: 26)

Classic Orientalism. Morrow's 'journey' recalls elements of journey into the heart of darkness. When Morrow arrives at his destination, the pearling town of Broome in the West Kimberley region of Western Australia, these anxieties persist. So many are olfactory, the strange smells etc, 'I was conscious of a strange, unpleasant smell. It seemed to me a mixture of heat, salt water, mud, and decomposing vegetable matter. Later, I learned that what I had smelled was only the mangrove swamp and gambling dens' (Morrow 1984: 27).

One does not need to labour the conscious linkages between mangrove 'swamps' and 'gambling dens' the home of the Asiatic. The mango 'swamp' somehow symbolises European anxiety: a landscape that transgresses established principles, bushes in salt water, no clear distinction between land and sea. How can such a landscape be mapped, made solid, predictable, defensible? Morrow's colonial anxieties only increase when he conducts a patrol in Broome's 'China town':

> Down the narrow, smelly lanes between the flimsy buildings we forced our way through Chinese, Japanese, Malays, Koepangers, Ambonese and occasional Cingalee. They dodged away from our horses' feet into their dimly lighted dens, and sometime we glimpsed a scowling yellow face peering from a latticed window. (Morrow 1984: 29)

Policing has been instrumental in fixing and establishing the northern frontier as a permanent aspect of Australian territory and in keeping the potentially hostile and treacherous oriental in his place.

Policing, power and control

Since the early days of colonisation the police had controlled Aboriginal access to towns under colonial ordinances; establishing a form of apartheid that many Aboriginal people see as surviving to this day. In Western Australia, following the 1905 Roth Royal Commission into the Condition of the Natives which identified widespread abuse and exploitation of Aboriginal people, legislation was enacted that granted statutory powers to the Chief Protector of Aborigines to develop measures for the relief, protection and control of Aboriginal people: relief, protection and control were the domain of the police. Roth's Commission had established the basis for a major extension in police powers in some areas, while being aware of the capacity for abuse inherent in such, largely unchecked, powers. The Commission heard evidence of police chaining together large groups of Aboriginal men and women (the latter chained by the ankles even though they were witnesses) and habitual sexual assaults against Aboriginal women.

Roth recommended the abolition of the Prisoner's Meal Allowance system, which empowered police sergeants in rural and remote areas to provide prisoner's meals in police lockups and then charge the government. Roth recognised that this scheme provided an incentive to detain Aboriginal people – police witnesses at the inquiry saw making a profit in this way as entirely acceptable. The scheme was not abolished until the mid-1990s – a 90-year lag between recommendation and implementation! The police exercised awesome powers over the daily lives of Aboriginal people and cemented the subordination of Aboriginal people to a range of processes, such as rationing, and to welfare organisations and the ubiquitous missions.

These must have appeared as powers over life and death – there have been persistent claims of police involvement in massacres of Aboriginal people (Green 1995), and the fact that Aboriginal people were rarely informed of their legal rights and the limitations of police powers under white man's law until the development of dedicated legal services in the 1970s. As Tonkinson recalls:

> [I]n the early 1960s, older Martu believed the killing of Aborigines by the policemen to be as legally permissible as the terrifying dawn raids aimed at shooting camp dogs ... I will never forget the palpable fear of the police that obtained back then, before the advent of the Aboriginal Legal Service brought a much needed and more

accurate understanding of where the police officer stood in the legal hierarchy. (Tonkinson 2006: 4)

During the years when the police were the protectors, Aboriginal people had a clear understanding of the powers of the police. The police tended to use their powers to advance white vested interests, and the protection role of the police was employed to further the policing goals. Anna Haebich maintains that there was nothing in the police culture that would reward a 'welfare' approach to Aboriginal people, whereas it did reward activities focused on controlling the Aboriginal problem; the police displayed, 'high levels of prejudice and discriminatory behaviour, including the condoning of unlawful killings of Aboriginal people in the Kimberley in the 1920s' (Haebich 2000: 221).

Aboriginal people gained the clear impression that the police were the law in a real and direct sense in everyday life, as well as the 'boss of the courts' (Dodson 1991), running the criminal justice system for their own ends. Were these practices occurring in Europe we would be using language such as police state, totalitarianism, Stalinism. One lawyer, working on a history of police controls over Aboriginal people, described the process of reading police files on Aboriginal people talks as akin to reading 'Statzi' files from the old soviet bloc.

RH Pilmer served with the West Australian Police from 1892 to 1919. His views about Aboriginal people are couched in similar terms to those of Morrow. He finds Aboriginal people to be a 'swiftly diminishing people ... much to the discredit of the white population, from south to north' (Pilmer 1998: 152). His sympathy for Aboriginal people has to be set against a fundamental belief in the need to make them 'amenable to the white man's law' (Pilmer 1998: 152). He is able to make a distinction between 'deliberate cruelty' to Aboriginal people and the need for firm controls over them, which included flogging (at a time when the practice had been banned for white people):

> Flogging was gazetted as punishment ... When I first saw a native flogged, I could have smashed the man who did it, but later I accepted it as part of my duties. We received an allowance of 10/- for every native flogged to engage a man to administer the punishment, and, according to the letter of the law, a justice of the peace must be present at the flogging. We used an improvised cat of plaited greenhide. It was soft and did not cut, it was painful but humane. (Pilmer 1998: 152)

Pilmer then goes on to describe instances where pastoralists almost killed Aboriginal people by 'brutal' floggings. He notes that it was difficult to 'secure a verdict against a white man for an offence against the black' (Pilmer 1998: 152) and that native evidence was usually unreliable. However, in his role as Protector of Aborigines he was able to cancel permits to employ Aboriginal people. Pilmer believed that Aboriginal people needed to be protected against the oppressive and exploitive tendencies of white people, but he does not question the overall framework of controls and the necessity of white law and justice to control the lives of Aboriginal people. As we have seen in relation to young Aboriginal people, scholars and a number of inquiries have drawn parallels between these practices and contemporary policing of young Indigenous people (Human Rights and Equal Opportunity Commission 1997; Cunneen 1994).

Moving them on in the 21st century

For many Aboriginal people, a number of contemporary 'zero tolerance' policing initiatives simply perpetuate colonial control practices. I regularly meet Nyungar people who can clearly recall the activities of the 'bashing squad' from the 1960s who made sure that Aboriginal people left the city of Perth by nightfall. While the discriminatory legislative controls over Aboriginal movement have fallen away, there are continuities of practice, only these are presented in terms of public order. In Cunneen's (2001b) terminology, the criminalisation of Aboriginal people – particularly youth – has acted as a bridge connecting old policies concerned with restricting movement to new practices of social exclusion.

Across Australia there has been a new wave of legislative change, which has increased police powers to move young people on from public space, particularly in the Northern Territory, Queensland and Western Australia. A report on the impact of police move-on powers on homeless people in Brisbane (Taylor & Walsh 2007) found that current powers disproportionately affected young and/or Indigenous homeless people, and that police use of powers was influenced by a person's appearance rather than behaviour and were not always being used in instances where there was a real threat to public safety. A survey of homeless people, many of whom were Indigenous, found high levels of police contact, and a tendency to use the legislation to exclude homeless people from public space. The report recommended better data collection to monitor the use of the laws, including a person's age, housing status, whether they are of Aboriginal or Torres Strait Islander descent, and the location, timeframe and reason provided for the move-on direction.

In Western Australia, amendments to the *Police Act 1892* have enabled the police to issue individuals with notices ordering them to leave a public place and not to return for 24 hours; if they do not comply they risk being breached and are open to 12-months imprisonment or a $12,000 fine. The police need only to 'reasonably suspect' that the person is about to commit an offence for the powers to be triggered. Aboriginal people have been the main target of these powers. How could it be otherwise? In a submission to the Human Rights and Equal Opportunity Commission, the Aboriginal Legal Service of Western Australia (ALS) insists that the laws are 'criminalising an already over policed Aboriginal population' (ALS 2006: 4). The ALS goes on to draw parallels between the new legislation and the old 'prohibited areas' legislation of the early 20th century, in that the new legislation is essentially concerned with penalising someone for being in a defined area (2006: 15). The Goldfields town of Kalgoorlie was identified by the ALS as having the highest rate of move-on orders against Aboriginal people of any region in Western Australia.

Systemic racism: a Kalgoorlie vignette

The public realm has been a traditional site for the construction and defence of frontier between Aboriginal and non-Aboriginal society. The very presence of Aboriginal people evokes fear and loathing: their 'difference', their social etiquettes (moving around in a loose mob, sitting in groups in parks) offends white sensibilities. Aboriginal people report being discriminated against in public places (Law Reform Commission of

Western Australia 2006b): examples abound of Aboriginal children being ejected from shopping malls for breaches of dress codes while white youths aren't, of adults being refused service in pubs (Law Reform Commission of Western Australia 2006b).

In talking to Aboriginal people, they report that what amazes (and scares) them is how mundane and normalised racism is. An Aboriginal woman in Derby told me of an incident with a new police officer from Perth:

> I look sort of white: I told him I was Aboriginal, he said, 'You must be one of the good ones then'. I thought about it and wondered, 'Is he being racist?' He just said it so matter of fact, with a smile on his face, like it was okay to talk to me like that, that I wouldn't be offended, he couldn't see anything wrong. (Perth consultations)

In August 2006, the first person in Western Australia to be tried under the State's new racial vilification laws was an Aboriginal teenager.. The 'offence' occurred in the mining town of Kalgoorlie. The 14-year-old Aboriginal girl was alleged to have been part of a group of people who repeatedly kicked a 19-year-old Caucasian woman in the head and racially abused her. Alongside assault charges, police initially charged the teenager with engaging in conduct likely to incite racial harassment and animosity, later scaled back to the lesser charge of racial vilification. The ABC News reported that the WA police believed the case would set a legal precedent because it is the first time a racial vilification charge had been tested in court. The case of racial vilification was dismissed by the Kalgoorlie magistrates as an unnecessary criminalisation of common street language – the Aboriginal girl called the white girl a 'white slut' (ABC Radio 2006b).

No-one can condone the alleged violent behaviour, however, what is at issue here is the way that an Aboriginal girl's language was conceptualised as racist. The rules of the game highlight individual acts of criminality by Indigenous people, but excluded the systemic and structural effects of everyday racism in towns like Kalgoorlie – including police racism. There is a profound irony in the fact that the police in Kalgoorlie brought racial vilification charges against an Aboriginal person. Kalgoorlie had the highest numbers of deaths in custody (five) assessed by the RCIADIC, and Commissioner O'Dea noted problems associated with 'the use of racist language by the police and allegations by Aboriginal people of mistreatment by the police':

> Evidence I heard in Kalgoorlie caused me grave concerns about the level of racism that existed in the police force. Many Aboriginal witnesses told me about police officers using offensive and provocative language towards them. Two former senior police aides (both with ten years duty in the force) gave evidence that the police at Kalgoorlie used racist terms such as 'Nigger', 'Coon', 'Boong', and 'Rock Ape' to describe Aboriginal people. Other terms Aboriginal people complained of were 'black bastard' and 'black cunt'. (O'Dea 1991: 599)

In a telling passage O'Dea reports that, 'One officer expressed the view that the term "Nigger" was not offensive. The Aboriginal witnesses conveyed a very different perspective to me' (O'Dea 1991).

Asked about steps the police were taking, the Commissioner of Police said:

> On our interpretation of the evidence in the Kalgoorlie cases, the use of derogatory and racist terms was not widespread and did not reflect a systematic practice. Individual officers on occasions may use such terms and they may swear and utter

profanities. None of this conduct is necessarily evident of discriminatory attitudes that require a firmer response. (cited in O'Dea 1991: 601)

To which O'Dea responds:

I find this response of the Department illustrative of a general lack of preparedness to accept the evidence of witnesses other than the police and to respond in a positive way to criticism. This attitude has coloured the police response throughout the life of my commission in Western Australia. (O'Dea 1991: 601)

Throughout the 1990s, the peak body responsible for monitoring the implementation of the RCIADIC voiced concern about the ongoing levels of racism in Kalgoorlie and the practices of the police (Aboriginal Justice Council 1999). There were complaints of heavy-handed policing in public space. There are high levels of contact between Aboriginal people – particularly young people – and the police, and rates of arrest are extremely high.

Royal Commission into Aboriginal Deaths in Custody and policing

The Royal Commission into Aboriginal Deaths in Custody (RCIADIC) was established in 1987 to inquire into the reasons why Aboriginal people were dying in prison – 99 between January 1980 and May 1989. Not surprisingly, the incident that sparked the inquiry took place in Western Australia: the killing of John Pat in the Roebourne Lock-Up. The RCIADIC did not deliver the prosecution of individual police and prison offices desired by many Aboriginal people, and there were – and still are – those who believed that the process let down those who died under murky circumstances in custody: , no individuals were brought to account for the deaths and no police officer was brought to trial for the killing of John Pat.

In the words of Commissioner Elliot Johnson:

The conclusions reached in this report will not accord with the expectations of those who anticipated that findings of foul play would be inevitable and frequent … Commissioners did not find that the deaths were the product of deliberate violence or brutality by police or prison officers. (Johnson 1991: 2.2)

What the commission did uncover was systemic racism, often manifest in an indifference to Aboriginal suffering and a refusal to accept a duty of care; the sloppy, careless supervision; the stigmatisation of Aboriginal people, for whom imprisonment was considered a normal condition of existence. The systemic indifference to the needs of Aboriginal people reflected the extent to which their Aboriginality placed them outside the boundaries of moral responsibility. The RCIADIC, whatever its faults and limitations, represents a watershed in terms of awareness of how how Indigenous people viewed the justice system. The commission also uncovered a deep-seated sense of alienation and a cynicism among Aboriginal people about the criminal justice system, informed largely by their contact with the police as gate-keepers of the system. Commissioner Patrick Dodson recalled:

> What became apparent during consultations, was that Aboriginal people felt power-less to change the situation, felt that the police, the courts, the inquiry processes were not just inadequate, but were in direct conflict with, or in opposition to, Aboriginal people. They felt there was no justice anywhere and the police, being the first wave of interaction with the criminal justice system, were very much to blame for this situation. (Dodson 1991: 215)

The commission has left an indelible mark on the way Indigenous justice issues are discussed and debated, because, while the commission did not make individuals accountable for the individual deaths, it made the structures and systems that recruited, managed supported, trained and empowered these individuals accountable. The RCIADIC found that the majority of deaths (63) were associated with police custody, 33 were in the adult prison system and three were in juvenile detention. Importantly, the commission established that Aboriginal people in custody did not die at a greater rate than non-Aboriginal people in custody. What was overwhelmingly different was the rate at which Aboriginal people come into custody, compared with the rate of the general community.

> Aboriginal people die in custody at a rate relative to their proportion of the whole population which is totally unacceptable and which would not be tolerated if it occurred in the non-Aboriginal community. But this occurs not because Aboriginal people in custody are more likely to die than others in custody but because the Aboriginal population is grossly over-represented in custody. Too many Aboriginal people are in custody too often. (Johnson 1991: 46, 69)

The commission concluded that there were two levels on which the problem of the disproportionate numbers of Aboriginal people in the criminal justice system and in custody could be tackled. The first, and, the commission suggested, 'in many ways least difficult', was 'at the level of the criminal justice system itself'. The second was the far more challenging task of altering the 'fundamental factors, which bring Aboriginal people into contact with the criminal justice system' (Johnson 1991: 1.6.1).

Stripped down to the core, the commission's key areas for intervention can be grouped into three areas: diversion from arrest and detention, diversion from custody, and the underlying issues (Cunneen 2001b). Diversion involves re-routing cases away from the criminal justice system, either by doing nothing, or by shunting offenders into some alternative, hopefully less intrusive, mechanism. It can take place at numerous points in the system, from first contact through to custody.

The RCIADIC noted two key points: first, the point of first contact, before a defend-ant gets before the court, covering 'the interaction with police, the arrest or charge on summons, the questions of bail', examples of the kinds of innovation needed included 'Notices to Attend', summons, cautions, warnings, diversion to a sobering-up facility; secondly, post-sentence:

> where a defendant found guilty can be directed ... away from the prison system as opposed to into it, examples of this included, 'community service orders, conditional release orders, intensive supervision orders, deferred sentences'. (Johnson 1991: 73)

The commission also stressed the need to develop diversionary mechanisms for those breaching non-custodial orders, 'which often place Indigenous people in prison for rela-tively minor offences'. The commission wanted to see increased 'input from Aboriginal communities, and particularly discrete communities, as to their views on penalty and the role that they may play in supervising non-custodial options' and for fresh initiatives around community-based custodial options and parole.

This interconnected suite of diversionary options established the framework for reforms in the RCIADIC era. It acknowledged the extent to which the criminal justice system needed to be viewed in systemic terms, where decisions made at one stage had consequences for decision-making at later stages. Unjust, capricious and arbitrary decision-making in one arena – particularly at the point of contact with the system's gate-keepers (the police) – had consequences further down the judicial track. It therefore opened up the whole question of discretionary decision-making by policing and judicial officers and whether decisions were being made on the basis of racist stereotypes of Aboriginal offenders. A number of key recommendations involved influencing police practices to ensure that they used arrest as a sanction of last resort, particularly in relation to juvenile offenders (Recommendation 239). The main finding of the RCIADIC, however, was that the major factors which brought so many Aboriginal people into conflict with the criminal justice system lay outside the system and were rooted in their 'unequal position'– 'socially, economically and culturally' (Johnson 1991: 1.7.1).

Policing communities and community policing

Aboriginal people consulted as part of the Law Reform Commission of Western Australia's Aboriginal Customary Law Project expressed some concerns that they had little say on how policing is practised and are unable to set priorities and goals. Aboriginal communities want to see a police presence to halt the violence and disorder and break the cycle of crime in communities that ensured high levels of contact with the system (family violence; grog running; out of control petrol sniffers; young people 'humbugging' and running amok on communities). When the police arrive, however, they bring with them a whole suite of white law (the *Criminal Code*, the *Police Act*, the *Road Traffic Act*, etc). While they may exercise some discretion over which laws they will impose there are a number of core responsibilities associated with doing police work which are difficult to shift.

What alarmed remote Aboriginal communities was that the police seemed to focus on what were perceived by the community to be relatively minor, *non-destructive* acts, and infringement of law that were essential and largely unavoidable given the realities of Aboriginal life on remote communities, where there was no public and very little private transport: driving with no licence and unroadworthy vehicles. In one western desert community the Law Reform Commission of Western Australia visited, there were 2000 people, many vehicles and not one valid driving licence. The police were increasing their presence on the community, at the request of the community.

The police – from their perspective – simply policed vehicles and licensing issues as they would anywhere else – without fear or favour, as the saying goes. Members of the community complained that this policing was seriously disruptive of life on the community. There were responsibilities, such as attending funerals, taking people to a clinic or to ceremony, which individual Aboriginal people simply could not shirk – being 'bound' by Aboriginal law meant they had no discretion in the matter, they could not choose whether to obey its dictates or not. Community members who welcomed the police on the community to deal with violence found themselves fined, even jailed, for traffic-related offences and punished for obeying Aboriginal law (Blagg 2005).

Roadworthy? Where are the roads?

Below are some typical examples from the consultations:[1]

It is the case that many Aboriginal people do not have driver's licences, however they are not driving on main roads or in towns. A lot of Aboriginal people were jailed for driving without a licence or for travelling between communities but not on a gazetted road ('back roads').

Aboriginal people in the communities without a driver's licence may still have to travel to Court and there is usually no other option but to drive.

Funeral business is very important business, people have to go and have no choice. The police know this and wait for you up the roads, check vehicle and licenses. Put the people in gaol.

The meeting voiced considerable criticism of police behaviour at funerals and their tendency to lie in wait for Aboriginal people driving to them. There was also some anger that the police treated driving conditions in the area as similar to urban areas, imposing standards of road worthiness inappropriate in places where there were no roads. (Perth consultations)

Research by Anthony and Blagg (2012, 2013) in the wake of the Intervention in the Northern Territory provides further evidence that simply dropping mainstream polic- ing practices onto remote communities can have negative outcomes. The police 'surge' in remote Indigenous communities of the Northern Territory saw the deployment of local and federal police and army officers, the installation of 18 police stations, the broadening of police powers and the establishment of crime intelligence taskforces.[2] The police surge was given legislative backing by the *Northern Territory National Emergency Response Act 2007* (Cth) (the Emergency legislation)[3] and related administrative meas- ures, which were collectively known as 'the Intervention'. The federal government was responding to a moral panic over Indigenous child sexual abuse and family violence in remote Northern Territory communities.

The 'intervention' led to the takeover of Aboriginal-owned governance structures, welfare income management and alcohol bans and prohibitions. Anthony and Blagg concluded, following Jonathan Simon (2007), that the regulation of Indigenous land and mobility, constituted an attempt to 'govern through crime' (Anthony & Blagg 2013). This governance saw the settler state seek to normalise the 'outback', assimilate its space into the Australian mainstream, and eradicate Indigenous difference (Anthony & Blagg 2012, 2013). These draconian options may have been justifiable had they led to greater safety for victims of family violence and child abuse. However, there was no increase either in prosecutions for intimate partner violence or notifications for child abuse. Instead Anthony and Blagg found a massive increase in Indigenous prison rates,[4] includ- ing the rate of prosecutions for minor driving-related offending across the Northern Territory, (Anthony & Blagg 2012). Police processing of charges of unlicensed driving, unregistered driving, driving unroadworthy vehicles and driving uninsured increased by 250% in the five years following the *Northern Territory Emergency Response Act*.

The problem in relation to policing remote communities is the tendency for the police (although this applies equally to other agencies engaged with communities on issues as diverse as health, mental health, education and family violence) to arrive with a predetermined formula, devised for a non-Indigenous context and simply impose it on the community. McNamara (1995), for example, provides evidence from Canada where Native Constable programs were established on Aboriginal lands, operating on a traditional incident-driven model of policing. The underpinning approach was to impose 'law and order' on communities, without reference to the impact this may have on other important strategies around reducing over-representation and increasing self-determination:

> Native Constable programmes were primarily concerned with making policing more effective. They were not fundamentally concerned with reducing incarceration rates of Aboriginal people, though supporters of the programme would likely prefer this to happen. If it didn't, however, the programme would not be seen to have failed. Social control, not self-determination, was the main concern. (Harding, cited in McNamara 1995: 3)

Strategies in the post-Royal Commission era

The reform agenda in the aftermath of the Royal Commission into Aboriginal Deaths in Custody has been dominated by strategies aimed at transforming Aboriginal/police relations by making policing more accountable and transparent, eliminating discriminatory practices, enhancing the procedural and human rights of suspects and increasing levels of Aboriginal recruitment into the existing police service, either as fully designated officers or as police auxiliaries. Significant amounts were expended on building and refurbishing police facilities (see Cunneen 2006). The strengths and weaknesses of these various strategies have received considerable critical attention (Harding, Broadhurst, Ferrante & Loh 1995; Cunneen 2006b; Cunneen & McDonald 1996; Cunneen 2001b; Broadhurst 1999). The focus of attention – and policy – has been on making the system effective in diverting Aboriginal people from custody. One noteworthy development was the role assigned to Aboriginal people, terms of providing a community resource for those diverted from custody. However, less attention was given to involving Aboriginal communities in the diversion process.

Many of the core themes in these debates were developed at a time when the State police monopolised policing. Discussions of policing in relation to Aboriginal people need to be broadened to take in to account two new factors: first, the police have lost their monopoly on policing and, secondly, Aboriginal people have become players in relation to the provision of policing services.

Diversified policing and community justice

Increasingly, policing is being carried out by a plurality of organisations – some public, some private – offering forms of policing adapted to the specific needs of particular localities – for example, shopping malls, central business districts, residential or 'gated' communities and public transport. The contours of the new policing environment have been exhaustively debated (Bayley & Shearing 2001; Shearing 1994, 2001; Shearing & Stenning 1981; Johnston & Shearing 2003; Rigakos 2003). An inquiry in Canada describes the process as one in which policing services are:

> provided by a complex network of overlapping public and private policing bodies. Clearly, public police are the primary service providers, but they no longer have a monopoly on the provision of policing services. (Law Commission of Canada 2002: 3)

The genuine extent to which the new era represents a genuine break with the past, however, has been hotly debated. Jones and Newburn (2002), for example, maintain that there has been too much focus on the 'epochal' nature of these shifts, gliding over deeper continuity in the organisation of policing, while Lucia Zedner maintains that:

> It now appears increasingly possible that this model of the police may come to be seen as a historical blip in a more enduring schema of policing as an array of activities undertaken by multiple private and public agencies, and individual and communal endeavours ... To this extent, to speak of 'the police' looks increasingly like a reference to a distinct historical period, with particular characteristics, practices, orientations, values and goal. (Zedner 2006: 269)

Zedner suggests we ask a number of questions, including: 'Who ought to have responsibility for policing? What ethical issues arise where policing is pursued by agents outside the criminal justice state?' These questions have relevance to the issue of policing of, and by, Aboriginal communities: furthermore, her conclusion that the '[a]nswers to these questions depend not least upon our conception of the good society and the proper role of policing within it' (Zedner 2006: 27) are also of importance. The question then, is how, and by whom, is the notion of the 'good society' defined? Is there a space within the notion of the 'good society' for explicitly *Indigenous* concerns, given that the good society has overwhelmingly been defined by Australian governments in Eurocentric terms and Indigenous people expected to fit in to it: that is, of course, when they have not been deliberately excluded from it?

The next questions become: how is the role of Aboriginal people in policing to be defined? Should we simply see Indigenous people as consumers of police services, or objects of police intervention? Should Aboriginal involvement in policing be viewed as a marker of Aboriginal progress in regards long-term equality and, hopefully, reduced levels of contact with the system? If so, what kind of involvement should it be? Should Indigenous people be encouraged to become police officers? Or police auxiliaries, exercising some reduced police powers in discrete 'tribal' or community environments, operationally subordinate to the State police? Should there be a stand-alone police service separate from the main police and exercising similar powers but within the Indigenous domain? Or should Indigenous policing set out from an alternative value base, avoiding vexed questions of formal 'power' in the non-Indigenous meaning of the term, and attempt to construct forms of policing in-keeping with Indigenous notions of cultural authority, with its own ethical and moral precepts?

The area of citizen policing has historically been the source of controversy, raising fears of vigilantism. Nonetheless, citizen involvement in policing is a fact of life in many parts of the world, where policing is increasingly being viewed as a multi-layered practice involving communities and a range of agencies, rather than simply the domain of the police; this is occurring not simply in relation to low-level order maintenance policing but includes the management of sensitive and potentially combustible situations such as sectarian parades and marches in Northern Ireland (Jarman 2007). Of particular interest to those concerned with strategies for empowering the truly disadvantaged and marginalised, are the various linked debates underway in post-colonial societies regarding the potential for alternative forms of governance linked to 'local capacity policing' (Wood & Font 2003; Leach 2003; Shearing 1994; Johnston & Shearing 2003). In Australia, Aboriginal Community Patrols represent one of the most developed and widely dispersed forms of community driven policing. Let us examine the origins and current status of Aboriginal patrols.

Notes

1   The consultation examples (Law Reform Commission of Western Australia 2006b) can be found in the regional and prison consultations at <www.lrc.justice.wa.gov.au>.

2   Northern Territory 2008 *Police Annual Report* p 3.

3   The Emergency legislation, in the main, was transferred to the *Stronger Futures Act 2012* (Cth) and has a sunset provision of 10 years (s 118).

4   The Northern Territory prison rate has increased faster than any other State or Territory since the Intervention, with a 52% increase between 2006-12 (ABS 2006:14, ABS 2012: 27). The Indigenous population constitutes 86% of the total prison population of the Northern Territory – an increase from 82% in 2006 (ABS 2006: 5, ABS 2013). This was the highest Indigenous prison population of any Australian jurisdiction.

6

Aboriginal Self-policing Initiatives

Aboriginal Community Patrols are local initiatives evolved to intervene in situations where Indigenous people are at risk of enmeshment in the criminal justice system, or where they face multiple hazards associated with community disorder, alcohol, drugs and violence. Aboriginal Community Patrols are found in urban, rural and remote parts of Australia, making them the most flexible and adaptable model of non-government policing in Australia. Begun as Night Patrols in the Northern Territory, they have increasingly been referred to as Community Patrols, due largely to the fact that many work day shifts and have extended their activities beyond those limited to night-time issues around drinking and fighting to encapsulate a range of social problems experienced by Aboriginal people. Blagg and Valuri (2003) identified in excess of 100 patrol schemes across Australia. Two-thirds of the respondent patrols were in rural and remote parts of Western Australia and the Northern Territory. The remainder were in urban centres, with a scattering of patrols in remote areas of Queensland and South Australia and rural New South Wales and Victoria. Recent estimates suggest anywhere upwards of 130, with new patrol initiatives being rolled out in Victoria (under the Victorian Aboriginal Justice Agreement) which has seen the number of patrols rise from four in 2000 to 15 in 2006; and new initiatives in Queensland and the Northern Territory. In Western Australia there are currently 21 Community Patrols.

The Royal Commission into Aboriginal Deaths in Custody (RCIADIC) made positive reference to successful Aboriginal Night Patrol initiatives in the Northern Territory – particularly the Julalikari Night Patrol in Tennant Creek (Johnson 1991; see also Langton 1992; Curtis 1993): the RCIADIC praised the Julalikari patrol's 'attempt to reinforce Indigenous mechanisms for preserving law and order and resolving disputes at the point of initial contact' (Johnson 1991: Vol 4: 29.2.25) and recommended that patrols be:

> examined with a view to introducing similar schemes into Aboriginal communities that are willing to operate them because they have the potential to improve policing and to improve relations between police and Aboriginal people rapidly and to substantially lower crime rates. (Royal Commission into Aboriginal Deaths in Custody 1991: 118, Recommendation 220)

The context in which discussion of patrols took place in the Royal Commission was varied – but inadequate policing services featured prominently as a reason for their emergence. The background to the Royal Commission report, *Too Much Sorry Business* (by the Aboriginal Issues Unit of the Northern Territory), said of the Julalikari Night Patrol:

> The involvement of Aboriginal Councillors in voluntary policing ... and their preparedness to use their own vehicles and money to patrol the streets and camps every night, points to their dissatisfaction with policing in their communities. (Report of the Aboriginal Issues Unit of the Northern Territory 1991: 439)

Curtis (1993), in his assessment of Julalikari, puts matters more bluntly. He said that the Julalikari Patrol began, because there was nothing else:

> While it was not obvious to government agencies, it was tragically clear to the Julalikari community that something had to be done if the escalating violence, trauma and deaths in the town-camps were to be halted. (Curtis 1993: 2)

The strength of the patrol, according to the Aboriginal Issues Unit, lay in its capacity to resolve conflicts between Aboriginal people in an 'Aboriginal way'. Their use of Aboriginal language made an enormous difference to their success (Report of the Aboriginal Issues Unit of the Northern Territory 1991: 439). The Aboriginal Issues Unit saw Aboriginal offending linked to alcohol, disrespect for Aboriginal law (by both Indigenous youth and non-Indigenous people), the inadequacy of existing services attempting to deal with the multiple problems of the community, and poverty. The patrol did not simply police the community, but became actively involved in trying to resolve underlying disputes. The reports also pointed to an emerging concern with Aboriginal family violence – presenting police figures showing that 50% of disturbances attended by police in Tennant Creek involved domestic violence, and 95% of these involved alcohol (Report of the Aboriginal Issues Unit of the Northern Territory 1991: 440).

The literature from the Northern Territory reveals some examples of fruitful partnership between the Night Patrol at Julalikari and the police. On the other hand, there were also signs of tension as competing definitions of the role and purposes of patrols began to surface. These concerns pre-figure differences alive today. Curtis (1993), for example, rejects the police description of the purpose of Night Patrols, as simply 'assisting in removing intoxicated persons from the streets'. He suggests this is a misrepresentation of patrol work:

> [T]he object of the patrol is not to assist in removing intoxicated persons from the streets. This is a frequent case of misunderstanding for the police and the general public. The object is to resolve problems in the town camps and special purpose leases; to settle disputes when they begin and not after the have exploded, drawing in extended families or entire tribal groups. (Curtis 1993: 75)

Curtis also maintains that the patrol was able to function successfully because it was strongly embedded in the Aboriginal community structures.

The Royal Commission saw self-policing initiatives as enhancing the quality of community policing and building up resilient community structures. In Recommendations 214-19 (devoted to 'community policing') the commissioners stress the importance of employing Aboriginal people in a liaison role between Indigenous communities and the justice system and the importance of building sustainable community justice mechanisms. Night Patrols, and initiatives such as community-based corrections, were being viewed as playing a positive role in increasing Aboriginal involvement in the justice system and 'reducing rates of criminalisation' in the Northern Territory (Tyler 1995: 128).

Aboriginal self-policing initiatives of various kinds have a history pre-dating the Northern Territory initiatives identified by the RCIADIC. In its ground-breaking review of customary law, the Australian Law Reform Commission discussed policing and self-policing in some depth: the initiatives they came across were functioning in the 1970s. They found some warden and security schemes in remote South Australia, and several in the Northern Territory including the 'security men' patrol at Roper River, representing the four skin groups on the community, and the Lajamanu Council's night watchman scheme of older men who patrolled the community (a forerunner of the current Lajamanu Night Patrol), and the Pilbara-based 'Ten Man Committee' (discussed later). They also uncovered a number of urban initiatives, including a scheme in Redfern (Sydney) started in 1980, involving community liaison officers who patrolled Aboriginal Housing Company areas to check on anti-social behaviour, vandalism and drinking (Australian Law Reform Commission 1986: 103-5).

The Commission went on to discuss the strengths and weaknesses of self-policing and concluded that it 'advantages both communities and the State and Territory police forces' (Australian Law Reform Commission 1986: 105). In relation to communities, the commission argued that self-policing could ensure that communities were able to 'deal with trouble makers in a more flexible manner ... more appropriate to circumstances and more in accord with local customary law'. While the police might benefit because of reduced demands on their time, the commission also maintained that self-policing, as in the Redfern case, could be of value in urban areas. The risks included unreliable services and the danger of partiality (Australian Law Reform Commission 1986: 105).

The Ten Man Committee

The story surrounding the rise and fall of the 'Ten Man Committee' is illustrative of a number of the issues involved in Aboriginal self-policing. This committee operated in Western Australia from the early 1970s until sometime in the mid-1980s (Australian Law Reform 1986: 105). These senior men from the Strelley Aboriginal Community picked up drunken, rowdy people from Hedland and Roebourne and transported them back to Strelley to face a community meeting and punishment consistent with Aboriginal law:

> [T]he community selects what is called the 'ten-man' committee. The committee's function is to apprehend and bring wrong-doers before a community meeting. The meeting will ... determine an appropriate punishment. (Australian Law Reform Commission 1986: 27)

During consultations for the Law Reform Commission of Western Australia's Customary Law Project in 2002-03, I was able to interview elders in the remote Pilbara region who could recall the 'Ten Strong Men' or 'Ten Man' Committee. The consultations also found that a variant of committees also operated out of the Jigalong community (covering the town of Newman). The elders regretted that the scheme ceased operating because of complaints about the use of coercion and violence used to apprehend drinkers and return them to the community – this was aside from any physical punishment meted out on the community. They said it was the loss of police support (the police had initially backed the scheme) which fatally weakened the scheme, as they were then liable for prosecution if found to be unlawfully detaining and assaulting people. Interestingly, consultations also found that many Aboriginal people, as well as the non-Aboriginal legal system and the welfare sector, would not support the levels of force used to 'apprehend' and 'punish' wrongdoers.

Many Aboriginal people who had migrated to the town of Hedland insisted that this kind of highly coercive intervention could not be tolerated in towns: they could no longer force people to come back to the community, as they did in the 'old times'. A number of respected elders in Hedland said that practices – such as forcibly detaining people against their will, public shaming and even flogging – were acceptable in remote communities where the legal jurisdiction of Aboriginal law was almost absolute, but not in towns where Aboriginal law had to coexist with non-Aboriginal law. It was acceptable to make someone attend a community meeting when that person was on a community but not when that person was in town, even when that person intended to return to the community at some stage and had not severed connections. The Ten Man Committee were also accused of 'kidnapping' by church and welfare groups.

On the other hand, elders from Jigalong and Kunawaradji in the remote East Pilbara said that the Ten Man Committee had been effective and that the situation in regards to alcohol and violent behaviour had worsened in its absence. What powers should a community have to make its members return? Should communities have police powers? A group at a meeting at one remote community said:

> Attempts to bring people back to the community for their benefit have been thwarted by the government and the town. This has been particularly felt in the case of attempts to bring children back to get them away from difficult social environments. This represents a case of the enforcement of traditional law incurring liability for contravention of European law. (Pilbara consultations)

There was dissonance between an emerging body of individual rights – around arbitrary detention, deprivation of liberty – and the collective rights of Aboriginal people to police their community members, both on and off the community. In fact, the debate was more complex than that. There were those who maintained that under Aboriginal law – not just Gadiya law – it was unacceptable for one group (even if they were elders) to coerce people in this way, as it interfered with Aboriginal notions of autonomy. In an intervention in the debate over the death in custody of an Aboriginal man on Palm Island, Noel Pearson has suggested that elders be empowered to intervene with drunken people and coerce them in to sober-up facilities (Pearson 2006). Noel Pearson is motivated by a profound concern that there are currently no reliable or consistent patterns of traditional authority remaining in some Aboriginal communities. There are, though, success stories, where Aboriginal people working from within traditional cultural authority have been able to persuade drinkers to attend sober-up facilities. I want to examine the nature of this cultural authority and identify how it informs the practices of Aboriginal patrols.

The role and function of Community Patrols

Patrols fulfil a diversity of functions, largely determined from within Aboriginal communities. A review of Night Patrols in the Northern Territory by the Tangentyere

Remote Area Night Patrol Unit (Walker & Forrester 2002), for example, found a diversity of activity typical of Indigenous patrols:

> Night Patrols perform a huge range of functions, according to the needs of their communities and the resources they have available. They act as a nexus to connect people and services such as clinics, courts, police, community government councils, and family. They mediate disputes, remove people from danger, keep the peace at events such as sports carnivals, are consulted by agencies such as courts for input into sentencing, and play a crucial role in the development of community justice groups. (Walker & Forrester 2002: 4)

In their review of Aboriginal Patrols across Australia, Blagg and Valuri (2003) describe them as providing a range of order maintenance services, designed to prevent or stop harm, and maintain community peace, security and safety. Patrols carry out a form of community-based policing, but they should not be confused with the police or private security. Nor should patrols be viewed as police auxiliaries or simply there to fill gaps in services (although they do provide the latter service): rather they reflect the extent to which Aboriginal communities still exist at some distance both from non-Indigenous government structures and, to a large extent, from non-Indigenous 'civil society'. They are best located within the orbit of the Aboriginal domain, occupying a space within what Rowse (2002) calls the Indigenous sector. This sector provides a degree of 'choice' for Aboriginal people and therefore a degree of autonomy from non-Indigenous systems.

Rowse (2002) views the Aboriginal sector as offering Aboriginal people a degree of structural distance from non-Aboriginal institutions:

> The Indigenous Sector is neither the 'state' (though it is almost entirely publicly funded), nor is it 'civil society' (though its organizations are mostly private concerns in their legal status). Rather the Indigenous Sector is a third thing created out of the interaction – sometimes, but not always, frictional – of government and the Indigenous domain. The Indigenous sector is an important source of Indigenous choice. (Rowse 2002: 72)

Patrols provide other options, in cases where contact with the non-Indigenous welfare and justice systems may be unwelcome. As commentators have observed (Blagg 2000a; Cunneen 2001b) many Indigenous people – including Indigenous victims of family violence – do not always look to agencies, such as the police, as 'service providers'.

Acting as a 'link' while providing a 'buffer'

Patrols, therefore, do not simply act as a link, or conduit, between Aboriginal people and government services. Indeed, in some instances patrols do quite the opposite. They also function as a *buffer* between Indigenous people and government agencies, in instances where such contacts may result in unnecessary enmeshment in the criminal justice, or, occasionally, in the mental health system. As with other parts of the Indigenous Sector, patrols derive their status and authority from their links within the Aboriginal community. Tyler (1995) refers to a 'unique kind of ambiguity' in the status of Night Patrols due to the fact they may be 'trained by government agencies, funded and supported by a mix of public and private interests, but, at the same time, remain accountable to community organisations' (Tyler 1995: 137).

This 'ambiguity' may be a source of resilience for patrols, rather than a problem to be resolved by assimilating them further into governmental structures. The Cape York Justice Study (Fitzgerald 2001) sees initiatives such as patrols, community-controlled diversionary programs and crime prevention initiatives as part of a new 'sub-contract' with Indigenous communities with, 'central government deferring to local institutions to organize local life to the greatest extent possible' (Fitzgerald 2001: 113). In this vision, patrols would constitute elements of what he terms 'pods of justice' where authority is 'devolved to Aboriginal communities'. While Cunneen (2001b), sees patrols forming part of an expanding Indigenous 'social space' (2001b: 196), and, in a review of Aboriginal community crime prevention, one of the 'major and longest running crime prevention programs in Indigenous communities' (Cunneen 2002: 50). He argues that local evaluations of patrol programs have been 'positive', showing reduced levels of juvenile offending (including criminal damage, motor vehicle theft and street offences), reduced fear of crime, and reductions in drug and alcohol-related problems (Cunneen 2002: 50). In their major review of violence in Aboriginal communities, Memmott, Stacy, Chambers and Keys (2001) argue that patrols are effective on a local level in reducing crime and anti-social behaviour by 'intervention, mediation and dispute resolution between people in conflict, and the removal of potentially violent persons from public or private social environments' (Memmott et al 2001: 67).

Memmott et al argue that the idea has enormous potential:

> Its capacity as a self-controlled volunteer community intervention program with a relatively low budget has great utility and potential ... Properly managed, such programs also have great potential to build cooperation and mutual respect and support with local police. Night patrols are a tried and proven program type. (Memmott et al 2001: 68)

An inquiry into violence in Indigenous communities in Western Australia heard evidence from Aboriginal communities praising patrols as 'essential to the operation of their communities' (Gordon, Hallam & Henry 2002: 199). The inquiry concluded that patrols had a role to play beyond simple order maintenance and needed to be viewed as essential elements in community capacity building.

Patrols make a significant contribution to crime reduction and community safety strategies. A number of evaluations have been extremely favourable, showing reduced levels of juvenile offending (including criminal damage, motor vehicle theft and street offences), reduced fear of crime, and reductions in drug and alcohol-related problems (Cunneen 2001b). Evaluations by the National Drug Research Institute of patrols in the Kimberley region of Western Australia, for example, found that patrols were successfully diverting intoxicated people from the lock-ups as well as providing support to women and children 'at risk' (National Drug Research Institute 2000).

Patrols and police

The police are the agency with most to gain from the presence of an Aboriginal patrol. In the post-RCIADIC era, police have pursued a strategy of reducing numbers of Aboriginal people detained for drunkenness and patrols offer a ready-made diversionary mechanism, particularly when they work with sober-up facilities. Problems can begin, however, when police believe they have the authority to dictate the working practices of patrols, or simply see them as a vehicle for law and order policing (Blagg & Valuri 2004a, 2004b).

Aboriginal women

One interesting feature of patrols is the high level of involvement of Aboriginal women, who are well represented as patrol workers. Women have often been at the forefront of initiatives to establish patrols in their communities and long-running women's patrols are found in the Northern Territory and Queensland. Well-established patrols such as Yuendumu, Ali-Curung and Lajamanu in the Northern Territory were instigated by women tired of the alcohol-related violence. They have also established their own women's safe houses on the communities.

In their study, Blagg and Valuri (2003) found that roughly 50% of patrollers were women, and women also make up around half of clients. Perhaps as a consequence of being women's initiatives or having women strongly represented on patrols – patrols reported seeing their work in terms of mediation and persuasion rather than force, and fulfilling a preventive/welfare role, rather than a reactive/controlling one (Blagg & Valuri 2003). Patrollers have not nurtured those elements of a masculine culture historically associated with the police and private security organisations, or attempted to mimic them in their dress and presentation, which tends to be casual with only a distinctive shirt or T-shirt displaying their particular emblem.

From remote to urban contexts

I have suggested so far that the Community Patrol model is highly adaptable and flexible and patrols have become embedded in urban as well as rural and remote contexts, taking on a variety of issues – including intervention with young people and itinerancy. The Aboriginal Justice Council of New South Wales supports the NSW patrol initiatives, which operate in urban Sydney and rural regions, describing the Aboriginal Community Patrols program thus:

> Under the Aboriginal Community Patrols program, volunteers provide a protective presence while transporting young indigenous people and others to their homes or another safe place. The key goal of the patrols is to reduce the involvement of young people in unlawful and anti-social behaviour by intervening before police action is required. (Aboriginal Justice Advisory Council New South Wales 2002: 2)

Most of the 15 Community Patrols in New South Wales are resourced through the Attorney-General's Department as part of the State's crime prevention strategy and deal largely with youth anti-social behaviour.

Services to clients

What services do patrols offer their clients? In most instances in Western Australia the service offered involves a 'safe transportation' away from trouble spots to some place of safety, this can include a sobering-up shelter, a refuge, accommodation for the homeless, hospital, home, or to kin.

Community Patrols tend to patrol by vehicle or on foot and:

- check on at-risk groups;
- intervene in family violence situations and take victim, or potential victims, to a safe place and offenders to a cooling off place, as well as link victims with advocacy services;
- conduct truancy patrols, transporting children to school;
- patrol known 'hot spots' to deter anti-social behaviour and head off problems;
- divert intoxicated people from police lock-ups by taking them home or to a sobering-up facility;
- mediate between Indigenous groups (when feuding);
- mediate between Indigenous people and the police. Patrols divert Indigenous people from unnecessary contact with the criminal justice system;
- work in partnership with police by alerting them to incidents and give early warning;
- monitor behaviour in public places;
- ensure safe levels of drinking around licensed premises, or on drinking grounds; and
- act as a referral on service for itinerant and homeless Indigenous people in Perth and other large towns. (Blagg & Valuri 2003)

Patrols surveyed by Blagg and Valuri (2003) found alcohol to be the major issue faced by most patrols, followed by anti-social behaviour, family violence and drugs and other substances. The field work component of the research found that patrols were also involved with issues linked to homelessness and mental health issues, preventive intervention with children at risk and a range of other concerns.

Many patrols work in with – some even work out of – sobering-up facilities. As we shall see in relation to a number of patrols, there have been assumptions made in some areas that the major function of a patrol should be to take drunks to a sobering- up facility. This is not necessarily how patrols see the purpose of their work from within Indigenous terms of reference. Nevertheless, sobering-up facilities have become a fixture of the diversionary landscape in the post-RCIADIC era (see Memmott & Fantin 2001). Brady, Nichols, Henderson and Byrne (2006) describe their role thus:

> Sobering-up centre do not pretend to solve the problems of alcohol abuse in the community. A sobering-up centre is not a detoxification centre, nor is it geared towards long term rehabilitation. Its role is to keep people out of police custody, to reduce alcohol related harm and to offer practical care in a safe environment for a limited time, providing protection, shelter and food. (Brady et al 2006: 201)

While this portrait of the work of sobering-up facilities is generally accurate (and the author's research is based on South Australia) there are discussions within Aboriginal organisations running sobering-up shelters in Western Australia to use shelters as a means of delivering programs and building relationships with clients that may lead to longer term treatment. A shelter in Port Hedland, Western Australia, runs a family violence program from within the shelter and is developing a scheme in conjunction with other agencies to work with Aboriginal people from remote communities – known locally as 'trenchies' – who live rough on the edge of town. The sobering-up centre in Derby, Western Australia, has been involved from its inception in early intervention work with young drinkers in the town and is a key partner in the local family violence prevention program.

The role of Community Patrols in dealing with homeless and itinerant Aboriginal people has been a source of conflict in the Northern Territory where concerns about the anti-social behaviour of the 'long grassers' – Aboriginal people, reputedly from remote communities, living rough in Darwin. It became the centre of a moral panic in the run up to the 2004 election in the Northern Territory. There were deep concerns that the existing Community Patrols were being forced into becoming a quasi-police organisation.

Itinerancy, 'homelessness' and law and order

Memmott and Fantin (2001) illustrate the dangers of patrols being forced into a 'para-policing' role in their study of policies in Darwin. The Darwin and Palmerstone Aboriginal Night Patrol has been given the task of removing itinerants, and Memmott and Fantin compare the patrol unfavourably with the Julalikari 'model' which they describe as a the 'reference point' for a successful Night Patrol. At the core of the Julalikari model, they suggest, is a commitment to 'strengthening community processes and facilitating dispute resolution' through culturally appropriate methods and patterns of authority. The authority must rise out of Aboriginal culture and not be 'the product of an external agenda (such as the Police or Government)' (Memmott & Fantin 2001: 74-5).

They go on to recommend that the patrol adopt a pro-active, harm reduction strategy, including a commitment to, 'broader community-based objectives ... than night-watch' and be involved in 'education, case management, community capacity building, liaison with other agencies, referral and coordination with DCC (community services) and Police Patrol' (Memmott & Fantin 2001: 78). Two key themes emerge here that have vital relevance to the work of patrols across Australia. First, the requirement not to place patrols in an enforcement role – they are not 'para police'. Secondly, the need to think outside of a box, not fixing patrols in a 'night watchman' role, and realise the potential inherent in patrols to act as facilitators of services. The politicisation of the issue of 'Long Grassers' in the run-up to the 2004 election in the Northern Territory led to the collapse of the Aboriginal patrol – forced to adopt a coercive approach and coerce people into the 'spin dryer' (Darwin's sober-up facility) as part of a strategy of making itinerant Indigenous people leave Darwin and return to their communities.

Another relevant theme emerging from the 'Long Grassers' report is the relevance of the very notion of 'homelessness' to Indigenous people, who may not make a self-reference as homeless, particularly where they have a long-standing cultural attachment to a place and see the place as 'home'. 'Homeless' people, by definition, have no attachment to a place, cannot stake a claim to belonging and tend only to be targeted by agencies intent on moving them on. Indigenous people, on the other hand, may have a *long-term attachment to a place*, even when this is not presented in the trappings of residence, and tend not to self-refer as homeless: referring to themselves as 'parkies', 'goomies', 'long grassers', 'river campers' (Memmott & Fantin 2001: 24), or 'rough sleepers' and 'beachies' (Blagg & Valuri 2004a), depending on the locality.

An innovative project in Brisbane developed to meet the needs of itinerant Indigenous women at risk of being arrested, moved on by the police and a host of security guards, as well as subject to ongoing violence in inner-city Brisbane (see Coleman 2002), adds value to an already existing patrol service, the Community Access Support Service (CASS). CASS provides an outreach service to Aboriginal people in Brisbane (mainly women), monitors the safety of vulnerable people in public places, offers assistance and transport (or pays bus/train fares), maintains a client database and undertakes individual and systemic advocacy (Blagg & Valuri 2003).

According to Coleman (2002), CASS directly empowers Indigenous women who live out, or rough, in public space and links them with a 'healing framework'. Rather than dealing with their homelessness as *the problem*, they work with these women acknowledging that, 'in these spaces, they (are) part of a community ... and accepted as part of that community' (Coleman 2002: 8). Coleman notes:

> The majority of CASS clients are Indigenous women, who experience significant problems in accessing accommodation and a range of other services ... CASS demonstrates the effectiveness of outreach as a service model in working with Indigenous women in the inner city, and the importance of relationships based work. (Coleman 2002: 15)

Encouraging patrols to act as enforcers and exclude what non-Indigenous agencies consider to be 'itinerant' and 'homeless' people from public space (such as Fortitude Valley, Darwin streets, or Northbridge) does not solve the problem. Such exclusionary strategies are only successful in removing Aboriginal people in the short term and ultimately fail because they fail to take into account Aboriginal attachment to place, which is not transient and contingent, but is strongly held and deeply embedded (Coleman 2002; Memmott & Fantin 2001).

Perhaps the greatest challenged faced by Community Patrols in the longer term – besides the constant struggle for resources and recognition – lies in retaining ownership of the role and purpose of a patrol from an Indigenous perspective. It bears repetition that there will be considerable pressures placed on patrols to fulfil mainstream expectations concerning the role of policing in relation to the Aboriginal problem: to move it on, keep it out of site, make it disappear. Ryan (2005) expresses concern that the preoccupation of much research on patrols – focused on 'non-Indigenous concepts such as funding, reporting, management, training, outcomes, and administration' (Ryan 2005) – will act to obscure the 'purpose and function of patrols' within Aboriginal communities, which 'remain an enigma' to most people (Ryan 2005: 3). Ryan sees the main challenge in terms of integrating patrols into existing mechanisms for conflict resolution and social control on communities, and operates in ways that support these mechanisms.

The kinds of pressures exerted on patrols to conform to non-Indigenous definitions of their roles and functions are present in the following case studies from Western Australia. They reveal both the risks and potential for Aboriginal Community Patrols involved in local strategies.[1]

Competing expectation: two case studies from Western Australia

(1)   The Nyoongar Patrol in the Northbridge Area of Perth

Nyoongar Patrol started out because of concerns within the Aboriginal community about a host of issues linked to Aboriginal people at risk in the Northbridge area of Perth. This included concerns about anti-social behaviour by young people, but there was also considerable concern about young Aboriginal people in Northbridge becoming vulnerable to drugs, violence and involvement in the sex industry; as well as concerns about older 'rough sleepers', and other itinerant Indigenous people, becoming dangerously intoxicated and subjected to violence and/or being arrested by the police. As with other forms of Indigenous itinerancy, Aboriginal women are over-represented and are frequently targets of sexual and other forms of violence, many are escaping family violence (Blagg & Valuri 2004a; Coleman 2002).

Nyoongar operates a foot patrol in the Northbridge area and works closely with the police Juvenile Aid Group and community services to identify Indigenous people at risk in the area, and also operates a safe transportation service that takes young people without transport home. Nyoongar has representatives of the various Nyoongar family groups on the Patrol, ensuring there are usually pre-existing relationships between Patrollers and the client group. Patrollers quickly identify people at risk, and those likely to be a risk to others. The close relationships also ensure that patrollers get to know where the hot-spots and hot-times are likely to be and can head off trouble before things get out of hand.

Overwhelmingly, the media and political focus on Northbridge has been on only one dimension of the Northbridge issue – the Aboriginal juvenile crime 'problem'. Northbridge, and adjacent areas such as Perth Railway Station, have become synonymous with Aboriginal youth crime and disorder. The Aboriginal community was placed under a spotlight for an inability to control and discipline its young people. Northbridge has been tagged as a 'landscape of fear' and patronage of its cafés and restaurants has declined. Local retailers blame Aboriginal people but the broader realties are more complex. Women, in particular, are turned off by Northbridge's increasing air of sleaze (it is home to a number of sex shops and brothels), its reputation as a haunt for drug users, panics about 'drink-spiking', well-publicised feuds between rival 'Asian' gangs, and the number of aggressive drunken (non-Indigenous) youths spilling out of the bars and clubs in the area.

In keeping with present trends in networked security, a number of multi-agency committees were formed, including a host of government agencies, local stakeholders, Indigenous peak bodies and community-based organisations. Nyoongar Patrol became actively involved with a number of linked forums on Northbridge 'issues'. A State government inquiry into the future of Northbridge (Busch 2002: 17) was supportive of the Nyoongar Patrol's role of 'providing culturally based early intervention and mediation on the streets of Northbridge'. So too was a visiting inquiry from Victoria (Parliament of Victoria Drugs and Crime Prevention Committee 2001).

However, the Northbridge Retailers Association, the Perth City Council and the state's peak crime prevention body (Safer WA) had other ambitions for Nyoongar

– solving the 'problem' of Aboriginal youth by removing them from the streets and, hopefully, luring nervous punters back to enjoy uninhibited *al fresco* dinning. Nyoongar has consistently refused to fulfil this role and the disappointed retailers concluded that it had 'failed' (at a task it never set itself). Nyoongar sees itself as existing to do more than simply meet the interests of the Northbridge business community. Business people want Nyoongar to be publicly funded security officers' and execute a night time curfew for Aboriginal youth in Northbridge, while Nyoongar themselves see their role as providing a 'support service'. In April 2003, under pressure from retailers, the State government announced a 'curfew' for Aboriginal youth in Northbridge, to be implemented by the police, using existing powers under s 138B of the *Child Welfare Act 1947* (WA), to clear the streets.[2] This instrumentality has been employed a number of times during moral panics about Indigenous youth in the area (Blagg & Wilkie 1995).

For Nyoongar, the cost of membership of the local security network was steep. It has had to conduct a continuous struggle to retain its integrity as an agency working for Aboriginal people, rather than simply another instrument of social exclusion. This has included having to exchange its very recognisable yellow T-shirts for conservative blue shirts, the yellow ones were considered to be too Aboriginal and made them look scruffy according to critics within the Perth City Council.

(2)   Marrala Patrol: diversion and customary law

The second case study also focuses on differences between local security networks and Indigenous organisations, this time involving issues related to Aboriginal Customary Law and its influence on the work of one Aboriginal Community Patrol. The Marrala Patrol has operated in the remote town of Fitzroy Crossing in the East Kimberley region of Western Australia since the mid 1990s. Fitzroy Crossing is over 90% Aboriginal and is linked by culture and language to a number of small Indigenous communities along the Fitzroy Valley. Like many towns of its kind it is beset with problems linked to alcohol abuse. The communities in and adjacent to the town have had a long history of conflict with the police who, locals believe, are racist and insensitive to Aboriginal cultural issues.

Marrala was established chiefly to provide a safe transportation service back to the Aboriginal communities from the Crossing Inn (Fitzroy's 'Aboriginal' pub). Aboriginal people were being detained in large numbers by the police or, even more problematically, were being killed and injured on the roads while intoxicated. Marrala has elders from the five language groups in the area on the Patrol vehicle, each deals with its own language group and, crucially, has knowledge of the complex 'skin' relationships which proscribe social and physical contact between certain individuals of the 'wrong skin'. These elders sanction and give 'cultural authority' to the work of the patrol. Their *local Aboriginal knowledge* underpins its operation.

In 1998 a new sobering-up shelter was established in Fitzroy by the Western Australia Drug Abuse Strategy Office (WADASO), as part of an unfolding process established after the 1991 Royal Commission into Aboriginal Deaths in Custody to divert Aboriginal people from police detention and, hence, reduce the possibility of deaths in custody. The problem was, that neither WADASO nor the police had followed appropriate cultural protocols and sat down with Aboriginal elders and the Marrala

Patrol to agree on who would be responsible for taking intoxicated people to the facility. In many parts of Western Australia, and other States, patrols work out of, or in close partnership with, sobering-up facilities (Blagg & Valuri 2003). Not surprisingly, there was a powerful common sense in play among the agencies that the task of the patrol, indeed its *core function*, was to service the sobering-up shelter.

Fitzroy, however, has its own cultural peculiarities, which make this difficult. The patrol does not believe it is its responsibility to take drunken people to the shelter, arguing that they would require the consent of an Aboriginal person before they could transport them, and that those sober enough to consent would tend to want to go home rather than spend the night in the 'spin dryer'. When they come across someone too intoxicated to consent, they call the police to take them to the sobering-up shelter. Should they move someone without consent and that person dies later in the shelter, the patroller would, *under Aboriginal law*, be held responsible and would become the target of a 'pay back', such as a spearing or 'flogging'.

Local Aboriginal people insist that the police and WADASO have ridden rough-shod over Aboriginal law and culture, while, for their part police and WADASO believe they are simply implementing a diversionary strategy. Moreover, there was a clear danger of the expensive sobering-up shelter becoming a 'white elephant' (no pun intended), as Aboriginal people avoided using the facility. Marrala rarely transported Aboriginal people to the shelter (at most one or two each shift). Vigorous lobbying of government by the police and WADASO led to Marrala – a patrol well embedded in the local community and with an exemplary record in terms of reducing the incarceration of Indigenous people – being de-funded in 2003 and attempts made to establish a new patrol, run by the police, with the explicit function of taking drunks to the shelter.

The two brief case studies reveal, in differing ways, how cooption occurs. In the case of Nyoongar in Perth, a moral panic about Aboriginal youth on the streets of Northbridge generated demands for a curfew and tough action by the authorities. The competency of the patrol was increasingly judged in relation to the numbers of Indigenous youth on the street, rather than according to the health and safety of vulnerable Indigenous people using the area. In the case of Marrala Patrol, more complex issues (which can only be touched on briefly here) emerge. While Nyoongar operates in a liminal environment, including both Indigenous and non-Indigenous social space, Marrala operates within an overwhelmingly Indigenous 'domain'. Remaining embedded within this domain means operating within Aboriginal law, with all its attendant proscription, penalties and forms of censure. The demands of this law dramatically disrupted the logic underpinning liberal post-RCIADIC reforms involving diversion to sober-up facilities, where this involved the patrol in prohibited forms of inter-personal contact. Worse still, under forms of Aboriginal law operating in the Fitzroy area, a patrol worker may be held responsible for the death of an inebriated person they transported to the shelter without that person's consent, even if the death was in no-way related to the negligence of the patrol.

The decision to disband Marrala Patrol needs to be set within an emerging consciousness within the leadership in Fitzroy Crossing that the existing matrix of community-based services were failing to halt the rise in alcohol violence and social disorder in the town and surrounding communities. A new generation of strong women leaders, particularly June Oscar, Maureen Carter and Emily Carter, backed by key community elders from their base in Kimberley Aboriginal Law and Culture, were influential in shaping a new strategy in Fitzroy Crossing. These women had been responsible for developing a number of new structures in the town able to work 'both ways': that is embedded in Indigenous culture and law while partnering with a mix of mainstream agencies to create new 'hybrid' systems. Nindilingarri Cultural Health services and Marninwarnintikurna Women's Resource Centre, respectively, were to transform the policy context by agitating for new restrictions on the sale and availability of alcohol, rather than manage the consequences through the patrol and the sober up shelter, neither of which now exist. New strategies have emerged focused on cultural healing in partnership with focused multi-agency partnerships around core concerns, often involving intervention in the damaging legacy of unrestrained drinking, such as Foetal Alcohol Spectrum Disorders. Recent discussions with some Indigenous people previously involved with Marrala revealed no interest in recreating a patrol of a similar kind, although there has been talk of creating some kind of youth focused patrol that might work in, in some way, with the school and on-country diversionary projects such as the Yiriman project (discussed in Chapter 3).

Crime prevention and community justice

Community Patrols represent a distinct form of policing, as they fit neither in the public police nor private security. The public police act with the authority of the law and as its agents, while private security agencies tend to act as agents of business. Community Patrols, on the other hand, operate in the interests of a particular community or constituency. As such they represent a radically different alternative to both the state and private paradigms of policing.

There are dangers, however, of Indigenous initiatives being co-opted as subordinate instrumentalities of new security 'networks' – meeting the security needs of non-Indigenous players, rather than the needs of Indigenous people. Patrols can be vulnerable to being colonised, appropriated and co-opted as junior partners by more powerful agencies, business and government. Their position 'at the bottom of the foot-chain' (as one sympathetic senior police officer in Perth eloquently expressed it in relation to Nyoongar Patrol) makes them vulnerable to appropriation. Nyoongar, while it has survived the cut and thrust of policy change in Perth now has to contend with a more neo-liberal funding framework. Patrol 'services' have become subject to government tendering processes, and Nyoongar, like many Indigenous community-owned entities, increasingly have to compete with other agencies to run their service (NGOs such as Mission Australia have become particularly active in terms of bidding to run services once considered to be part of the Indigenous 'sector' – such as youth and health services, family violence services, hostels etc), with 'efficiency' and 'value for money' becoming key factors.

In relation to work with young people, while not uncovering any extremes of vigilante justice and violence found by Leach (2003) in her study of community self-policing, studies have unearthed some hostility between the patrol and young people.

The kinship links between some patrollers and young Aboriginal people sometimes increased tensions due to a strict 'guardianship' relationship, which frequently over-rode the patrol's principle of only working through consensus, leading sometimes to a 'heavy-handed approach' (Sputore, Gray, Bourbon & Baird 1998: 57). There were also some criticisms by youth advocates in Perth about Nyoongar Patrol's surveillance role over Aboriginal youth (Blagg & Valuri 2003). These issues aside (and certainly in these examples, critical comments were more than balanced by positive accounts by youth workers and advocates for the diversionary and social support work of these patrols), patrols have received considerable support from within the Aboriginal community.

The Northern Territory: addressing the cycle of failure

Aboriginal Night Patrols have been a feature of life on remote communities in the Northern Territory for some time. A report by Higgens in 1997 found that out of 53 patrols said to be operative in the Territory, only 25 were functional, a similar conclusion was reached in Blagg and Valuri research (2003). There is a remarkably swift turnover in the patrols in the Northern Territory, due to a host of factors, including poor and inadequate funding and what Ryan and Antoun (2001) refer to as the 'cycle of failure'. Looking back over the period since the RCIADIC it is impossible to identify some consistent patterns in terms of the life histories of patrols and government and agency attitudes towards them. Despite a steadily mounting literature extolling the work of patrols they have remained inadequately funded and neglected by government in the Northern Territory until very recently.

In one of the first attempts to identify the structures necessary to establish a remote area patrol, Mosey (1994) argued that, initially at least, little is required to set up a Night Patrol, and that infrastructure such as vehicles, radios and other supports are not always essential – they may even undermine an initiative when they are appropriated for wrong purposes – subject to resource capture (Mosey 1994: 9). Mosey identified a number of pre-requisites for successful implementation of a Night Patrol initiative including community consultation, establishing protocols with local police, clear task descriptions for patrollers, and a sound administrative base. She argues that patrollers should not be drinkers, there needs to be a willing pool of volunteers, and traditional owners and elders need to endorse the patrol.

Higgens (1997) reviewed seven projects in Alice Springs, Darwin, Daguragu/Kalkaringi, Ngukurr, Katherine, Tennant Creek, Yirrkala and Yuendumu. The Higgens Report addressed five evaluation criteria: community input and control structures; administrative and management structures; resource structures; linkages and network structures; and monitoring and evaluation structures. Higgens concluded that the initiatives enjoyed universal support; the authority and power of patrols was vested in their 'Aboriginality, and from their strength of character and practice of cultural protocols'; the symbols of patrols (such as badges, uniforms) were respected by communities; and the patrols fulfilled multiple roles of care and protection, acting as a buffer between the community and the police and an early warning of trouble.

Higgens also identified two different models: first, the traditional model, emerging from within communities themselves; and, secondly, government initiatives funded largely through a levy on cask wine (such as the Tangentyere Council's warden schemes). Higgens concluded that these urban schemes tend to be more operationally diverse and less certain about their core functions. Higgens also recognised that there is – and should be – a clear separation of roles and responsibility between Night Patrols and the police, and that Aboriginal communities supported a police presence to maintain law and order. Higgens concluded that government needs to nurture and support Night Patrols while maintaining a watching brief which:

> ensures schemes are not ignored or abandoned by government, but are not subject to undue controls either. … this should involve addressing the funding of schemes on their merit, rather than applying a proscriptive funding formula. (Higgens 1997: 45)

The Higgens Report sets out some best practice guidelines for patrols. Essentially they establish what he calls authenticating structures for setting up and developing Night Patrols involving processes, procedures and methodology for development, implementation and funding (Ryan 2001: 45). Ryan (2001) and Ryan and Antoun (2001) have further highlighted the problems associated with implementing and sustaining a Night Patrol service in remote communities. Reviewing problems of establishing and maintaining a patrol in Lajamanu, Ryan notes:

> A cycle of failure with Aboriginal community night patrols is extremely common. The reasons for this situation are complex and include a range of social and cultural issues. Some of these are the failure of traditional social management and control structures under the impact of social change, alcohol related issues, generational conflict between older and more traditionally orientated people, community youth, and conflict between families and residents in the community. (Ryan 2001: 2)

Ryan notes that although the Lajamanu community has attempted to grapple with these issues, they lie 'beyond the capacity of the local community to resolve', attributing failure to poor establishment practices (Ryan 2001: 2). Factors common to failed initiatives in these communities included:

- initiatives being established by a select few influential people in isolation from the community and most of the community being excluded;
- clan ownership of the patrol (including vehicles);
- poor governance and ineffective administration;
- lack of clear rules and guidelines for operation; and
- high turnover of vehicles and no accountability for usage; and insufficient linkages between Night Patrols and other support agencies. (Ryan 2001: 3)

To break the cycle of failure, Ryan (2001) recommends a 'phased process of support' for remote communities wanting to establish patrols (2001: 5), designed to assist the community in assessing its preparedness (culturally and structurally) for the patrol, and then to assist them in setting up community support structures and operational support mechanisms. These principles have informed a number of successful 'Law and Justice' initiatives on communities in the Northern Territory (such as Lajamanu and Ali-Curung) where women's patrols and safe houses work with traditional 'elders' committees and a community 'Law and Order' council to police 'dry community' policies and prevent family violence. No 'quick fix': the strategies may take up to two years to mature.

Ryan also summarises a number of critical issues in an (undated) paper on Aboriginal Law and Justice Strategy, including the lessons from some 30 Law and Justice workshops,[3] called 'Community Safety and Justice Planning Workshops', kindred processes to the 'Negotiating Table' proposed in the Kimberley Region (discussed below) and the 'round table' approach currently being adopted in Far North Queensland as part of the government response to the Cape York Justice Study.

Ryan notes the importance of 'workshopping' issues over a period of time, to 'identifying community capacity, and the likely strengths and impediments that may affect the process. These can vary from community to community' (Ryan undated: 3). The workshops included a number of separate male and female sessions, followed by joint meetings. This culturally appropriate process was necessary so that the divergent views of men and women could be identified – they often defined the issues in different ways and had different priorities; men saw alcohol and women saw family violence as the main problem.

The policing surge in the Northern Territory that accompanied the 2007 'Intervention' brought with it a greater focus on the work of Night Patrols, and greater investment them. However, it was not accompanied by the kinds of careful and respectful dialogue with communities recommended by Ryan and others. Instead, Night Patrol policy was resolutely top down and imposed without much negotiation with communities. The significant increase in police resources was complemented by the creation of 50 'new' Night Patrols – bringing the full complement to over 80 with over 350 paid positions (Blagg & Anthony 2014). The patrols, with a few exceptions, were to be administered by NT 'Shire Councils'. The effect was the immediate disempowering of local communities that had tended to administer patrols through their own local councils (Blagg & Anthony 2014). Patrols do need support from government to buy vehicles, uniforms, radios, and to pay patrollers and run a base on the community. The Australian Commonwealth government has provided these things and has recently pledged to maintain funding for them as part of its *Stronger Futures* policy (Australian Government 2014) that replaced the formal Intervention. For the first time nearly every remote community and town in the Northern Territory has an Indigenous Night Patrol. However, greater security of Australian government funding has come at a price: an increasingly more restrictive regulatory environment that, while seeking to protect the safety of patrollers and ensure some degree of consistency in role and remuneration, has reduced local control and responsiveness.

For example, as Anthony and Blagg (2013) observe, patrols are restricted from working off community; meaning they may cease to perform the kinds of functions (looking for people lost in the bush, helping drinkers outside the community, taking elderly people to the clinic, and people to court) that ensured they had legitimacy within Indigenous rules of reciprocity. Turning them into instruments of law and order, despite additional funding, may create another potential pathway to failure. The issue of policing in Aboriginal communities is of major concern to Aboriginal people. They also have an increasing stake in the ways the court system deals with issues of Aboriginal culture.

Notes

1   The case studies are derived from field work undertaken for the two reports, *An Overview of Night Patrols in Australia* (Blagg & Valuri 2004a) and *Evaluating Community Patrols in Western Australia* (Blagg & Valuri 2002). The field work in Fitzroy Crossing was undertaken in three stages, during the dry seasons of 2001-02, the Northbridge case studies were undertaken over a two-year period, from 2001-02. Both involved interviews with key participants, patrollers, police, Indigenous Affairs, ATSIC and Indigenous community organisations, sitting in on local networking groups (such as the Northbridge Priority Project Steering Group, an inter-agency liaison group) and going out with the Patrols.

2   The *West Australian* ran a series of articles on the proposed curfew, and the Northbridge 'problem' from late-May 2003, in lead up to the curfew announcement, see article 12 June; the ABC ran a number of stories on reactions to the curfew <www.abc.net.au/perth/stories/s833642. htm>; so too did Perth's *Sunday Times,* see 'Curfew Bites', 3 July.

3   The remote communities involved included: Ali-Curung, Ngukurr, Numbulwar, Port Keats, Lajamanu, Yuendumu and Willowra.

7

Silenced in Court? Aboriginal People and Court Innovations

Innovation in the 1990s, in the wake of the Royal Commission into Aboriginal Deaths in Custody, tended to focus on the 'front end' of the criminal justice system through the creation of diversionary options for juvenile offenders, such as police cautioning and family conferencing. These were very successful in taking out of the system a population of first and minor offenders and increasing the opportunities for families and victims to participate in the justice process. One reason for these initiatives was a belief that they would increase Indigenous involvement in the justice process: although success rates have been greater for non-Aboriginal young offenders – the main beneficiaries of diversionary mechanisms, as we have seen.

Less attention was paid to the courts themselves as the site for reform. The courts were comprehensively condemned as the problem by some in the restorative justice movement, and often believed to be responsible for high rates of Indigenous imprisonment. Yet, as we have seen, it is the courts rather than agencies such as the police or justice, who have been the most ambitious in terms of referring cases for family conferencing in Western Australia. The much maligned court system has shown itself to be more flexible and more able to accommodate alternative strategies for dealing with offending than was assumed to be the case. Indeed, justice innovation internationally has been led by a new generation of courts.

There has been a growing interest in recent years, particularly in the United States, the United Kingdom and a number of Commonwealth countries such as Australia, Canada and New Zealand, in the potential for developing less adversarial approaches to court-based justice and a greater focus on fixing the underlying issues that ensure repeated contact with the justice system for particular groups. The influential Centre for Court Innovation in New York[1] has provided a vibrant focal point for research and policy debate focused on the twin pillars of current court reform: the practices of the problem-oriented court and the philosophy of therapeutic jurisprudence. What King et al (2009) describe as 'non-adversarial' justice creates new pathways into treatment and support for those who, by dint of some disability or extreme marginalisation, find themselves enmeshed in the justice system and ensuring just outcomes for offenders and victims alike. It may also offer ideas for imagining new, 'networked' forms of justice where courts become nodal points in the creation of local, decentred justice systems.

The non-adversarial approach may increase the role of restorative solutions while not abandoning the safeguards provided by courts for offenders and victims alike in regards to due process and fundamental legal safeguards (Ashworth 2003: 427). I have already suggested that an increased role for 'communities' may not necessarily improve justice for Aboriginal people who have been excluded from the public and communal realms as a necessary aspect of nation building. The New Zealand youth court system reveals that courts are able to relinquish control over parts of the process – to the Family Group Conference – while retaining overall responsibility for the justice process: as McElrea suggests, the youth court 'acts as both a backstop (where Family Group Conference plans break down) and a filter (for patently unsatisfactory recommendations)' (McElrea 1996: 71). The approach has some support from scholars, who maintain that the Westminster system, and its system of common law, is sufficiently robust and flexible to accommodate a diversity of customary rules (McIntyre 2005: 6).

The 1990s saw the emergence of an Australian judiciary more willing to grasp progressive ideas – such as therapeutic jurisprudence, drug courts, problem-oriented courts and similar mechanisms. In relation to Indigenous offenders, two particular innovations have attracted attention: Aboriginal Courts and Circle Sentencing Courts. These practices give space for the participation of Aboriginal elders in the court process. It needs to be stressed at the outset that Aboriginal Courts and Circle Sentencing Courts do not operate on the basis of Aboriginal law. But they do, Circle Sentencing Courts in particular, open up a new hybrid space, break down some of the barriers preventing dialogue between Indigenous and non-Indigenous people on justice issues, and provide a vehicle for renewing Indigenous eldership. Where restorative justice philosophy and practice has been of importance is in supporting initiatives seeking to relax the rigid uniformity of legal process, and in encouraging a relative plurality of justice mechanisms to flourish.

While the involvement of Indigenous people in sentencing has taken place on a local level for a considerable length of time, arrangements have tended to be relatively *ad hoc* and dependent upon the energies and commitment of local magistrates, prosecutory authorities and senior members of the Indigenous community. Recently, however, there have been moves to give these proceedings greater formal recognition in some States and link them to broader Aboriginal justice strategies designed to increase Indigenous involvement in the criminal justice system. There are Aboriginal Courts operating in South Australia (the Nunga Court), Queensland (Murri Courts), the Northern Territory (Community Courts – which, while open to all are clearly modelled on the principles of the Aboriginal Court) and, most recently, Aboriginal Community Courts in Western Australia. Victoria has been perhaps the most innovatory. Koori Courts operate in Melbourne, Shepparton, Broadmeadows and Warrnambool with others planned in Mildura. There is also an innovative Koori Children's Court (launched in 2006). The Koori Court initiative has been driven by the Aboriginal Justice Forum and Regional Aboriginal Justice Councils, and is a key plank of the Aboriginal Justice Agreement: it is also enthusiastically – passionately would not be an overstatement – championed by Attorney-General Rob Hulls. The importance of the justice agreement and the support of the Koori community (both inside and outside of government) in nurturing the courts should not be underestimated (Blagg, Morgan, Cuneen & Ferrante 2004). It is also interesting that, of all States and Territories, Victoria has demonstrated less enthusiasm for developing police conferencing as a vehicle for diversion for juveniles.

Aboriginal people from urban, rural and remote communities consulted by the Law Reform Commission of Western Australia (2006b) as part of its Inquiry into Aboriginal law expressed a sense of alienation from the criminal justice system. Many believe that the present system has failed them and does not understand them. A summary of consultations in the Murchison area is typical:

> The white system has failed traditional peoples. Even well-meaning judicial officers do not understand. [T]hey (Aboriginal people) plead guilty too readily. The solution may lie in Aboriginal courts that parallel the existing ones. The Koori Court in Victoria is of interest, particularly to the extent it is different from any of the WA arrangements. (Community consultations, Murchison region)

The commission's consultations identified a desire for a greater role for Indigenous people in the court process, and for a reconfiguration of the layout of the court itself to make it more accessible and comprehensible to Indigenous people.

Aboriginal Courts operate within the framework of the general law; which is not to say that Aboriginal values and principles are necessarily excluded from the process. These courts may reduce the sense of estrangement many Aboriginal people feel when confronted by the non-Aboriginal system. Lack of understanding of cultural issues in courts raises some considerable difficulties for Aboriginal people, as one Aboriginal person told the Law Reform Commission of Western Australia (2006b):

> White man doesn't understand the black man law. There is no understanding of Customary Law protocols. Pre-sentence and Court reports should include cultural matters, such as the significance of avoidance relationships. Lack of understanding of these avoidance principles sometimes causes Aboriginal people to break their law and get punished when they return to the community and even while a trial is going on. The trial itself creates situations where law is broken. For example, where a mother-in-law testifies about a son-in-law, people coming into Court who have avoidance relationships and are forced to sit or stand with each other. (Community consultation, Pilbara)

Furthermore, as they are currently configured, courtrooms are spatially, culturally and linguistically non-Indigenous – there are no Indigenous cultural points of reference, and they are presided over by authority figures to whom Indigenous people usually cannot relate and with whom they have little or no connection. Aboriginal people maintain that the alienation many experience in the system is a factor in the high rates of repeat contact with the system, failure to attend court, and failure to comply with court orders.

Multiple influences have contributed to the emergence of Aboriginal Courts. They include a number of factors discussed already, such as the continuing over-representation of Indigenous people in the criminal justice system and the failure of the established system to deal with Indigenous offenders. This has encouraged the search for alternative solutions to the problem. Some working close to the problem, such as magistrates, have been keen to implement key recommendations of the Royal Commission into Aboriginal Deaths in Custody, including those focusing on Indigenous involvement in the justice process (Marchetti & Daly 2004; Harris 2004). The interest in Aboriginal Courts comes along at the same time as other initiatives such as 'therapeutic jurisprudence', which attempt to make the court process more sensitive to particular problems or issues – such as offending linked to drug use. However, Marchetti and Daly reject claims that Aboriginal Courts are simply another variant of therapeutic jurisprudence, arguing that they exist in a category of their own 'due to the greater role played by the Indigenous community in the process, and the changes they bring to the ways business is conducted' (Marchetti & Daly 2004: 5). They suggest an increasing synergy between Indigenous and non-Indigenous values, 'the black robe appears to be deferring to the black face, at the same time, Indigenous people are embracing portions of white law' (Marchetti & Daly 2004: 5).

Aboriginal Courts and Circle Sentencing Courts share similar objectives, such as reducing Aboriginal over-representation in the prison system, providing credible alternatives to imprisonment, reducing failure to appear rate in court and reducing the rates at which court orders are breached (for a full review, see Harris 2004; Marchetti & Daly 2004). At the community level they may empower Aboriginal communities and overcome some of the alienation many experience (Briggs & Auty 2005).

Circle Sentencing Courts also provide a valuable means of involving Indigenous people more directly in the justice process. Having evolved in Canada to suit conditions in remote communities, this model may well be appropriate to conditions in outlying areas, because the model is more 'portable' – requiring only basis infrastructure. New South Wales has vigorously pursued the *Circle Sentencing* option, with strong backing from the State's Aboriginal Justice Advisory Council.[2] The initial scheme was piloted in Nowra and is being rolled out in other parts of the State. Lilles (2001) offers this description of the circle:

> It engages the community and the criminal justice system as partners, and to lesser extent victims and offenders in the resolution of criminal justice disputes ... It is not a panacea and its use should be restricted to motivated offenders who have the support of the community. (Lilles 2001: 167)

In New South Wales, Circle Courts are designed for more serious or repeat offenders and aim to achieve full community involvement in the sentencing process. Circle Sentencing Courts were established in Nowra (2002) Dubbo (2003), Brewarrina (2004), Walgett (2004), Bourke (2005), Armidale (2005), Lismore (2005), Mount Druitt (2006) and Kempsey (2006). Selection of the sites was based on the number of eligible Aboriginal defendants appearing in the Local Court, the number of Aboriginal defendants being sentenced to a term of imprisonment, Aboriginal community support for the program, and local service infrastructure. The aim is to broaden the sentencing phase so that it can fully examine the underlying issues of offending behaviour and examine the needs of victims of crime. The experience of Circle Courts in New South Wales reveals them as more labour intensive than Aboriginal Courts: requiring anything up to three hours to complete, plus a follow-up meeting to determine whether the plan worked up in the Circle Court has been completed. Circle Courts are similar in some respects to the Family Group Conferencing process.

The focus in the process is on informality. The Circle Court, as the term implies, breaks up the hierarchical model of the court and established a circle, which includes the presiding judicial officer, the offender and the other participants. The defence council sits with the offenders and his/her family or support people. Others participating in the sentencing are free to sit anywhere in the circle. The discussion that follows would then focus on a broad range is issues, often of a nature considered irrelevant in criminal procedure, such as the role of the community in preventing further offending and the extent of similar crimes in the community. The circle is reconvened several months later and the court hears from the support group about the offender's progress. If the offender has successfully met the conditions these conditions may be extended or modified as probation conditions. If the offender has shown no willingness to meet the conditions, then the circle may be abandoned and the offender sentenced in a regular court. There is considerable support for the process among the NSW Aboriginal community.[3] Many Aboriginal offenders would prefer to see an Aboriginal person when they attend court, as Lawrie found in her interviews with Aboriginal women prisoners in New South Wales:

> The women who participated in this study clearly stated that they would be respon-sive to community based justice mechanisms. Many said that their own elders should be involved in their sentencing, and that having their own people involved would make sentences have a greater impact on them and be more relevant to their circumstances. (Lawrie 2002: 3)

The rationale for the Darwin Community Court is typical. The Guidelines for the court suggest the court recognises that:

> in some cases community, cultural or other factors play a significant role in reaching a sentencing outcome which is beneficial to the community The concept for the Community Court grew out of discussions between the court and the Yilli Rreung (Aboriginal) Council in 2004 but the court is not restricted to Indigenous offenders. (Bradley 2007: 1)

While the court is not restricted to Aboriginal offenders it is clear that the system was developed with Aboriginal people in mind, and following discussion with a distinct Aboriginal entity the Yilli Rreung Aboriginal Council, the peak body for the Darwin area. The court was established in recognition of the fact that the Northern Territory has problems associated with different languages as well as different cultures, and anticipates that Indigenous offenders will make up the bulk of its client base. It is intended that at least one community member will sit with a magistrate. The role of the community member is to:

> discuss aspects related to the offence and background of the offender and victim/s (if present), explain how the offending behaviour has breached the community code of conduct and ... consider an appropriate sentence. (Bradley 2007: 3)

The insertion here of 'community code', rather than just breach of the law, signals a shift in the ways courts involving Aboriginal community members see the purpose of process, clearly there is an appeal to cultural values rather than simply legal principles. The Kalgoorlie-Boulder Community Court was established in 2006 on the recommen-dation of the Law Reform Commission of Western Australia, and has been designed to ensure 'Indigenous values and cultural input' in the sentencing process.

The changes to the court included:

- selected elders and respected people would advise the magistrate and speak directly to the offenders;
- all court participants, including the magistrate, would sit at a special table;
- legal jargon would be replaced with everyday language;
- Aboriginal artwork and flags would be prominent in the court; and

- elders and respected people from the local Aboriginal community would sit alongside the magistrate during hearings.

A total of 15 Aboriginal court members, nominated by the local community, had been trained in court procedures, conflict resolution, juvenile justice and other matters. The court opened on 21 November 2006, presided over by Magistrate Kate Auty, who had been the magistrate of the first Koori Court in Shepparton ,Victoria. She told the ABC that similar courts in other States had seen reduced offending and:

> fewer bench warrants, a greater capacity for magistrates courts to do their business efficiently and effectively and we're also seeing Aboriginal people having greater commitment to what takes place in court – all of which leads to a safer community for all of us. (ABC News Online 2006)

Koori Courts in Victoria

The Koori Court is an initiative of the Victorian Aboriginal Justice Agreement and was developed in collaboration with the State's Regional Aboriginal Justice Coordinating Committees. The Koori Court is enabled under the *Magistrates' Court (Koori Court) Act 2002*, which establishes a Koori Court Division of the Magistrates' Court. The legislation has the objective of:

> ensuring greater participation of the Aboriginal community in the sentencing process ... through the role to be played in that process by the Aboriginal elder or respected person and others. (*Magistrates' Court (Koori Court) Act 2002* at s 1)

The Act goes on to define a family member, an elder and an Aborigine for purposes of the Act, and sets out the kinds of offences that can be dealt with and those proscribed (sexual offences, family violence). The defendant must enter a guilty plea and consent to involvement in a diversionary program.

The Department of Justice's Indigenous Issues Unit has responsibility for the development of the courts. The first court was established in the rural town of Shepparton in 2002 followed by metropolitan Broadmeadows in late 2003 and, in the rural town of Warrnambool in 2004; there are now six Koori Courts in Victoria since Bairnsdale, Le Trobe Vally and Mildura were added to the list. In 2005 a Children's Koori Court was established in Melbourne. Business is conducted at an oval table rather than from the bench. The offender sits at the table beside his or her solicitor and is permitted to have a support person. Once the charges have been read and the defence counsel has responded, the offender and the support person are invited to speak directly to the magistrate about the offender's behaviour. Others in the spectators' area may also be asked to speak.

One long-serving elder of the Shepparton Koori Court insisted that 'the elders are the court' (Blagg et al 2004). Active participation by elders is essential if the court is to be an Aboriginal Court – as opposed to simply a court with Aboriginal elders' participation. The Koori Justice Workers (Justice Department employees) play a pivotal role in the process, acting as the link with the Koori community and giving advice to the Magistrate.

The system rests on close partnership between the presiding magistrate and elders: active participation by elders is essential if the court is to be an Aboriginal Court – as opposed to simply being a court with Aboriginal elders' present but playing a minor role. Within a properly developed Aboriginal court system, elders play a prominent role and introduce an additional dimension to the proceedings, articulating a set of Aboriginal values and principles. It was clear from discussions with Koori prisoners and workers (Blagg et al 2004) that, while some offenders may successfully 'neutralise' censure by 'white-fella' law, they may be less successful in neutralising the 'big shame' of censure by Indigenous elders.

The court process is firmly geared towards involving Koori people. There is a focus on reintegration with the Koori community and family support as the key to change. Considerable time is spent on each case, often including rich detail (of a nature and degree that would not normally emerge in court) of the life and family history of the defendant. This contextual material can place a different framework around dealing with the person. Emphasis is placed on linking Aboriginal offenders with Aboriginal community programs, employment services and drug and alcohol services.

Aboriginal people interviewed by Blagg et al (2004), were extremely positive about the fundamental philosophy and underlying principles of the Koori court, and criticisms were reserved for what some perceived as limitations in the scope of the court (discussed below). A representative from an Aboriginal Corporation, who regularly attends court to offer support services to Indigenous offenders, observed that:

> It has credibility because it is taken seriously, we don't feel we are being patronised by it. Sentences are worked out carefully. More information about individuals and their circumstances are available then in court. A person's true circumstances come out (and this) can influence sentencing in both directions.
>
> Many Kooris never had a chance before, because they had been sent straight to jail. Aboriginal people with long records never had a chance. Things need to be addressed such as homelessness and violence before some can move forward. (Blagg et al 2004: 167)

Male and female prisoners interviewed in a number of Victoria jails were also positive and reflected such views, one male prisoner said, 'It's not a soft option, should be in every area, you have more respect for the court, seeing elders' (Blagg et al 2004).

Criticisms and limitations of the Koori Courts from an Aboriginal perspective

Some respondents contacted by Blagg et al (2004) expressed concern that the Koori Court might have a net widening effect; and that its processes may end up being more punitive and intrusive than the general courts. One senior member of the Victorian bar reputedly suggested that the Koori Court 'tipped the scales' and provided 'luxury' or 'special' courts and some ill-defined special regime of sentencing options. The senior member – obviously concerned to halt the march of political correctness – also compared the establishment of the Koori Court initiative with the banning of Father Christmas from child-minding centres (Briggs & Auty 2005). One (non-Koori) observer, with many years' experience in the justice area, believed that, on the day he had observed the Shepparton court, some offenders had been sentenced to intrusive supervisory orders for offences that might generally have been fined. This view did not appear to be shared by the Kooris to whom we spoke. However, it has been an issue with the introduction of alternative to imprisonment in many jurisdictions; and has also emerged as an issue with respect to 'specialist courts' in other jurisdictions (see Indermaur & Roberts (2003) on Western Australia's Drug Court). It is therefore a matter that requires careful monitoring.

The degree of credibility, in spite of the likelihood of being dealt with more severely, was reflected in the fact that, some prisoners told us of occasions, of people pretending to be from a Koori Court catchment area, in an effort to have their cases dealt with through that process. Other criticisms of the scheme were that it only applies to Magistrates Court matters and can only be accessed on a guilty plea. The jurisdictional limitation was accepted as inevitable at the current time; but the necessity to plead guilty was a major source of dissatisfaction. Koori people, it was said, want to go to a Koori court because they want to be judged by their elders and to have access to culturally appropriate treatment options – there is a wide belief that the court is not a soft option but is willing to address the cultural, health and welfare needs of offenders. We were told on many occasions and by different sources, that this has led to some Koori offenders pleading guilty to charges they might otherwise have challenged (or which they said they had not committed), in order to gain access to the court. As one expressed it: 'I wanted to turn my life around, only my own people could help me do that'.

Below are some typical comments made to Blagg et al (2004):

> Why do people need to plead guilty first, what is wrong with having elders involved in trials as well?

> Some people plead guilty just to get there. They can get access to services that way – also they get contact with elders and with Aboriginal law.

> The Koori court is good idea, but can't plead not guilty, some plead guilty to charges because they can see justice when elders are sitting round the table.

> They might not have done that crime but have numerous problems in their lives, elders might help and they might get the proper help for getting off drugs.

> They give you lots of support at the court, but people are pleading guilty to gain access, other give a false name and address. It just puts them on the carousel. (Prisoner consultations)

Elders

There was a strong belief among Kooris that the Koori Court model should be extended to other regions of the State, including Children's Courts; and that it should no longer be restricted to guilty pleas.

It was also felt that, although it is an important step in the right direction, but it should be taken further. Many prisoners suggested, for example, that the elders who are involved in the court should be given the necessary resources to extend their work into other parts of the criminal process, including coming into prison to talk to prisoners. Also, Indigenous support workers who develop good relationships with prisoners should be allowed to support them when they go to court, for example after remands, as one woman prisoners said: 'They can fully explain women's issues better than anyone else (particularly) for country women, they find it hard talking to people in the court' (Blagg et al 2004). Although issues of 'Aboriginal Customary Law' were not as dominant as they would be in some parts of Australia, many also believed that the court should hear evidence, and introduce Aboriginal customary law principles: 'Need to have black law as an option. Like to see more tribal law practised', one prisoner said.

The initiatives demonstrate that potential for systemic reform that increases levels of Aboriginal involvement. Over time it is possible to envisage a larger role for Aboriginal people in these processes, with elders being involved in the trial rather than just the sentencing stages.

Notes

1   See <http://www.courtinnovation.org/>.
2   The enabling legislation is the *Criminal Justice Interventions Act 2002*. Circle sentencing origi-
        nated in Canada – the first officially recorded case was in the Yukon Territorial Court (*R v Moses*
        (1992) 71 CCC (3d) 347 (Yukon Territorial Court)).
3   For more information, see the Aboriginal Justice Advisory Council website: <www.lawlink.nsw.
        gov.au>.

8

Family Violence

Unlike the notion of domestic violence, which has gathered greater specificity over recent years, the concept of Aboriginal family violence continues to evade conceptual capture and appears to become more diffuse and elusive the more vigorously it is pursued. While there have been attempts within official discourse to pin down the concept of family violence and link the construct more closely to that of domestic violence, its usage within Aboriginal communities remains variegated and localised; indicating, perhaps, that we are not dealing with a single construct but with a series of intersecting narrative strands requiring multiple and situated readings. It is not my purpose to reconcile the construct of family violence with domestic violence, indeed I believe there is good reason to retain a certain conceptual tension and a degree of theoretical distance between the two constructs. Too often, the kinds of conceptual certainty preferred by non-Indigenous discourse (and demanded by funding agencies) can operate to the detriment of Indigenous agency, 'discourse capture' ensures that concepts are refined, defined and encoded along lines strengthening the position of white bureaucracy and reducing the scope of Indigenous autonomy. There are a number of core continuities between discussions of family violence and other aspects of the 'Aboriginal problem'. These cohere around the idea that Aboriginal victims are helpless and hopeless.

It is my objective in this chapter to challenge these beliefs: in a number of crucial respects mainstream theory and practice around violence in Indigenous communities – highly reliant on feminist theory and zero tolerance policing – lags behind critical praxis within the Aboriginal domain itself. Many of the valuable initiatives developed by Indigenous people on a local level to tackle family violence remain invisible because they do not fit in with the established domestic violence paradigm and its systems and structures. The current dominance of the zero tolerance model, the focus on criminalisation, the refusal to look for causes outside the gendered victim/perpetrator dyad, the dominance of the male power model, a failure to accept causes outside of power relationships (alcohol for example), refusal to work with men and suspicion about alternative models of policing and justice, severely inhibit a dialogue between feminism and those Aboriginal organisations involved in the fight against family violence.

A context of difference

The question of whether non-Aboriginal women can, or should, speak on behalf of Aboriginal women on sensitive issues such as family violence has been the source of considerable – and sometimes bitter – controversy. Aboriginal scholar Aileen

Moreton-Robinson has criticised feminism's claim to speak on behalf of Indigenous women and articulate their experiences on the basis of the 'deracialised but gendered universal subject' (Moreton-Robinson 2002). Firmly rejecting the assumption of a necessary 'equivalence' between non-Aboriginal and Aboriginal women's experiences (the latter's being over-determined by relationships-based colonialism and racism), she argues that white women enjoy privilege associated with whiteness, and have, like white males, been beneficiaries of colonialism. The values of the feminist 'middle-class, white woman' are globalised to represent the interests of women everywhere (Moreton-Robinson 2002). Moreton-Robinson, along with other Indigenous women, questions the motives of feminist activists who seem most intent on 'helping' Aboriginal women. In contrast to the feminist focus on male oppression, Aboriginal women have developed their own agenda focusing on 'genocide, land and citizenship dispossession, stolen children, and mass imprisonment' (Haunani-Kay 2003).

It remains clear that there are considerable differences between the ways many Aboriginal women and non-Aboriginal feminists identify the causes of violence and seek solutions. Heather Nancarrow looked at the work of two task forces in Queensland concerned with violence against women, one composed entirely of Indigenous women (representing the spectrum of urban, rural and remote communities); the other composed entirely of urban non-Indigenous women. There were considerable differences between the ways the two groups wanted to see the issue of violence against women handled. The Indigenous women, Nancarrow reports:

> strongly rejected the criminal justice system as an appropriate and effective response to domestic and family violence, and non-Indigenous women embraced the criminal justice system as the best response to domestic and family violence, even though they recognised that it is largely ineffective in achieving key objectives. (Nancarrow 2006: 100)

The ways Indigenous women tend to think about violence issues is encapsulated in the preference for the term 'family' as opposed to 'domestic violence'. Aboriginal people employ the term 'family violence' to designate and diversity of aggressive, destructive and violent behaviours that continue to haunt family and communal life: it is of major concern for Indigenous people, unlike property crime which tends to obsess white society (Homel, Lincoln & Herd 1999: 192). The Aboriginal and Torres Strait Islander Women's Task Force on Violence Report (2000) found that 'deviance and atrocities have become accepted as normal behaviour and as such, form an integral part of the children's socialisation'. While the West Australian Gordon Inquiry (Gordon, Henry & Hallam 2002) found 'a frightening picture' of violence on Indigenous communities.

Aboriginal observers have suggested that to understand Aboriginal narratives on violence it is necessary to set them within a 'context of difference' (Jackson 1999), because these narratives condense a range of meanings at variance with mainstream narratives. The family violence paradigm stresses collective Indigenous experience of powerlessness. The forms of violence seen in Aboriginal communities is utterly different from the religiously sanctioned and highly ritualised violence of traditional punishment; it is distinctively post-colonial, in the sense that it was set in train by the 'founding violence' of colonialism, and has reverberated through Aboriginal society since.

A family violence approach

How do Aboriginal communities themselves define family violence? Let us dispense with the notion that there is, or can be, a unitary definition of family violence and explore the construct in its diversity. There is no settled, one-fits-all definition and the meanings associated with the term shift from region to region in the light of local history, circumstances and concerns. They can also shift over time as new issues emerge. In the family violence category generally belong issues related to violence against women and children, but the category tends to be variegated and capacious enough to contain room for:

- clan and family feuds;
- jealous fights and *jealousing up* behaviour,
- the bitterness and uncertainties left in the wake of 'wrong way' marriages (people marrying outside of 'skin' relationships);
- alcohol- and drug-fuelled violence;
- neglect of obligations around kin and country;
- the 'humbugging' of elderly relatives for food and money; and
- providing petrol to sniffers in return for sexual favours.

Family violence is not restricted to wife abuse; Memmott et al define it in terms of a 'range of violence forms occurring frequently between kinspeople in Indigenous communities' (Memmott 2001). Let us explore some of the definitions developed from within Aboriginal terms of reference: Mow's (1992) definition is a good starting point:

> [B]eating of a wife or other family members, homicide, suicide and other self-inflicted injury, rape, child abuse and child sexual abuse. When we talk of family violence we need to remember that we are not talking about serious physical injury alone but also verbal harassment, psychological and emotional abuse, and economic deprivation, which although as devastating are even more difficult to quantify than physical abuse. (Mow 1992: 10)

Researchers developing the Kimberley Regional Domestic Violence Plan were told by Aboriginal women in the West Kimberley region that:

> [F]amily violence is family fighting. It happens when someone uses violence or threats to have power and control over someone close to them. This can be a partner or involve other family members. It includes family feuding. (Clarke & Varos 1995: 2)

A number of the violence forms identified here fit in within the domestic violence framework, others don't, Clarke and Varos (1995) refer to the role of 'other family members', which could include elder abuse, child neglect, it implies a view of violence within the broad sphere of intimate relations and gives prominence to both issues related to children and young people. Stories of family violence narrated by Indigenous women, defy simple categorisation, take this one:

> If you are being abused in any of the following ways: family fighting, jealousy, physical abuse, emotional blackmail, racial or cultural abuse or have problems caused by too much alcohol, drugs or gambling, this is family violence. (Regional Domestic Violence Coordinating Committee 1997)

Condensed in this statement by the Kimberley women are a number of locally significant issues, it is worth pausing to consider their meanings. First, the references to alcohol, drugs and gambling:

- *alcohol* has had a devastating impact on Aboriginal communal, familial and spiritual life. It was acknowledged as the primary cause of Aboriginal contact with the criminal justice system and hence deaths in custody (Langton 1992; Johnson 1991). Sagger and Gray (1998) summarising a number of reports on the issue calculate the costs in terms of loss of income and employment, 'driving licences, family violence and breakdown, alcohol-related deaths of family members and friends, and lives which are totally fixed on "grog" and how to get it' (Sagger & Gray 1998: 18).
- *drugs* and poly-drugs are becoming a source of concern in places like the Kimberley, on top of existing problems of alcohol, the widespread availability of 'ganja' and amphetamines is said to be the cause of increased violence and youth suicide (Law Reform Commission of Western Australia Consultation 2006a).
- *gambling* is a cause of stress and anxiety in Aboriginal communities, the pressures include a distorted form of traditional 'demand sharing' (Macdonald 2002). Sharing is an obligation 'initiated by a demand from the intended recipient. It is not an act prompted by generosity or goodwill of the giver' (Macdonald 2002: 2), as gamblers try to recoup the money lost in gambling.
- *jealousy* – I discuss the issue of jealousy later. Aboriginal people rate jealousy and jealousing (a form of jealous fighting) as one of the biggest causes of family violence.

The women also identify 'racial and cultural abuse' as a form of family violence. This could include a range of concerns, including the impact of racism on family life. Caroline and Judy Atkinson, building on Judy Atkinson's definitive work in the area, maintain that 'the term family violence is more suitable (than domestic violence)' because it 'brings focus to the trauma of the interconnecting and trans-generational experiences of individuals within families' (cited in Aboriginal and Torres Strait Islander Social Justice Commissioner's Report 2004). Atkinson and Atkinson's thesis foregrounds the *relational* aspect of family violence. It has emerged as a consequence of colonial relationships and continues to impact on relationships within family incidence of physical, emotional, mental and physical distress, including self-harm and harm of others. Atkinson (1991) traces distinctive 'trauma lines' from first contact through to contemporary experiences of marginalisation and dispossession:

> Family violence ... can be directed towards an individual, family, community or particular group. Family violence is not limited to physical forms of abuse, and also includes cultural and spiritual abuse. There are interconnecting and trans-generational experiences of violence within Indigenous families and communities. (Atkinson & Atkinson, cited in Aboriginal and Torres Strait Islander Social Justice Commissioner's Report 2004: 11)

Aboriginal women place emphasis on racism rather than sexism when they consider questions of oppression, as the Aboriginal Social Justice Commissioner notes:

> Indigenous women's experience of discrimination and violence is bound up in the colour of their skin as well as their gender. The identity of many Indigenous women is bound to their experience as Indigenous people. Rather than sharing a common experience of sexism binding them with non-Indigenous women, this may bind them more to their community, including the men of the community. (Aboriginal and Torres Strait Islander Social Justice Commissioner 2004: 12)

Aboriginal narratives of family, therefore, tend to focus on collective loss. Blagg (1998b; 2000b) summarises these narratives of loss as including: loss of land and traditional culture; the breakdown of community; 'skin' and kinship systems and Aboriginal law; entrenched poverty; racism, alcohol and drug abuse; and the effects of institutionalisation and removal policies on the 'stolen generations'. A key narrative of loss focuses on the 'redundancy' of the Aboriginal male role and status, that is often compensated for by an aggressive assertion of male rights over women children (Blagg 1998b, 2000b; Aboriginal and Torres Strait Islander Women's Task force on Violence Report 2000).

One problem, for non-Aboriginal researchers at least, is that the family violence construct – as narrated by Aboriginal people – is both highly general and extremely local. It can represent an historical narrative about the collective suffering of a people and describe locally specific incidences of spouse abuse or the economic damage caused by gambling. Senior Aboriginal women when asked about family violence on their communities have talked about the disrespect shown to them by young people 'humbugging' them for food or money to buy alcohol – of particular concern was the fact that in many instances this demand-sharing broke avoidance rules governing contact between skin relatives. This may not appear to a non-Aboriginal gaze to fall within the sphere of violence, but to these women were outraged and affronted by this form of disrespect to law and culture (Crime Research Centre and Donovan Research 1999).

At the level of practice, the family violence approach leans towards finding pathways to family healing, rather than new routes into the criminal justice system. In this crucial respect it transgresses current orthodoxy around domestic violence intervention. None of this means that Aboriginal women do not hold offenders accountable or that the violence is culturally sanctioned. Emphasis is placed on the need to work constructively with Aboriginal men – acknowledging that they are 'hurting too' (Sam 1992); and need to link work with men to past and ongoing social, economic and cultural marginalisation rather than just 'pointing the finger and laying blame' (Sam 1992).

A forum hosted by the Ministerial Council for Aboriginal and Torres Strait Islander Affairs (MCATSIA) in 1999 (see Thompson 1999) established a number of the ground rules for future family violence strategies, including work with users of violence. The forum rejected 'mainstream models of domestic violence ... premised on feminist theories', offering, 'solely punitive responses' (Thompson 1999: 2). Among the forum's principle recommendations was a strong endorsement of the need to shift resources away from correctional strategies to those involving family healing.

The forum concluded:

> There is a critical need for a holistic health approach and for inter-agency co-operation and co-ordination in partnership with communities. Appropriate Australian models for prevention and intervention in our own Indigenous communities should

be developed rather than adapting European models or those from other Indigenous peoples. (Thompson 1999: 2)

The approach set out by the forum requires both a 'bottom-up' approach to the issue of family violence and improved local coordination and partnership between agencies and communities. The strategy is holistic, emphasising the interrelationship between violence and a constellation of problems within Indigenous communities and the need to link together primary prevention, crisis intervention and treatment strategies. A key concern raised at the women-only session of the forum – signalling an increased willingness by some Indigenous people to discuss the issue – was the problem of sexual abuse, as the 'hidden dimension' and 'a major contributing cause of family violence' (Thompson 1999: 3).

What does the research say?

Aboriginal women and children are probably the most repeatedly and multiply victimised section of Australian society. The profile of violence in Aboriginal communities challenges criminological orthodoxy: Aboriginal women are far more likely to be victims than men. A ground-breaking study by Ferrante, Morgan, Indermaur and Harding (1996) found that the risk of domestic violence is not spread equally throughout the population; some groups suffer much higher rates and are more vulnerable than others of being victims of crime. The study revealed that rates of intimate violence among Aboriginal women were staggering. Although these women made up only about 3% of the adult female population in Western Australia at the time, they accounted for half of all the domestic violence incidents reported to the police in 1994. Based on police figures, Aboriginal women are more than 45 times more likely than non-Aboriginal women to be a victim *of domestic violence*. Yet, we know that police statistics remain underestimates given Aboriginal people's unwillingness to report matters to the police. They were more likely to suffer serious injury than non-Aboriginal women – in 23.5% as opposed to 11.4% of reported cases (Ferrante et al 1996: 35, see also Atkinson 1990).

We also know that intimate homicide is twice as likely than any other kind (for example, by a stranger) and that victimisation generally is more likely to be by family. Small wonder that Aboriginal people talk about family violence as the main issue in their communities. Ferrante et al's (1996) work highlighted three main areas. First, better information on the extent and distribution of domestic and family violence – official data does not provide the full picture. Secondly, interventions need to be carefully designed and managed, and informed by a proper understanding of the dynamics of violence in hyper-marginalised groups. Thirdly, they need to be tailored to meet the needs of specific localities.

A study by the Australian Institute of Criminology (Mouzos 2001) found Indigenous homicides were more likely to involve a woman as either victim or offender than non-Indigenous homicides. One-fifth as opposed to one-tenth in non-Indigenous homicide. Three-quarters of killings involved a male-intimate partner, as opposed to 44% in non-Indigenous homicides. The study also found that Indigenous homicides tended to be sparked by 'domestic' altercations. Alcohol was as factor in the majority of cases – with both parties drinking, and knives were the weapon of choice.

Dealing with Aboriginal victims

Yet, from an Indigenous perspective, there is continuing alarm that policy-makers continue to place enormous faith in 'one-off' programs delivered on the whole by agencies that have no roots in the communities they service, and in the capacity of what is – from an Aboriginal perspective – a wholly alien system of justice, to resolve the problems: a system viewed as 'fatally flawed, ineffective and unable to meet the challenges currently being presented' by many Indigenous people (Aboriginal and Torres Strait Islander Women's Task Force on Violence Report 2000, xvii).

The mainstream criminal justice system has not dealt well with Aboriginal victims because of a diversity of structural factors. I want to briefly summarise these before looking at matters in detail. There are strands in current Australian policy which see solutions largely in terms of extending the reach of victim's policies in mainstream Australian to resolve violence issues. For example, the recommendations of the Gordon Inquiry into Sexual Abuse in the Indigenous Community included extending policing, victim services, and child witness services to the Aboriginal community as the solution to these problems along with improved agency partnership (Gordon, Henry & Hallam 2002).

Yet, there are numerous unresolved issues regarding existing victim services and the capacities of the criminal justice system to intervene in a way that does not re-victimise and behave in a culturally appropriate manner:

- First, research on victims of crime points to a tendency for the system to construct 'ideal victims' (Christie 1986) these excite empathy and engage the system: empathy for Aboriginal victims may be limited because they exist outside of culturally generated representations of the 'ideal victim'. Criminal justice systems are not simply mechanistic structures, they constitute what Raymond Williams (1976) called 'structures of feeling', or 'structures of sentiment and feeling' (Said 1993). Agencies dealing with victims may struggle to cathect emotionally with Aboriginal victims, there is only a shallow repository of positive images of Aboriginality to draw on – the face of criminality is so often an Aboriginal face (Sercombe 1995).
- Secondly, most victim services are only activated once a criminal offence has taken place and the matter has been reported to the police. Yet we know that Aboriginal victims massively under-report and Aboriginal victims do not always see the police as a service – the most victimised of Aboriginal women who experience violence in family life are also likely to be victims of institutional violence. Many see the criminal justice system – and particularly the police – as agents of oppression.
- Thirdly, there are profound problems of embedded systemic racism: whether deliberately or unwittingly, our processes and procedures remain stubbornly ethnocentric and frequently – if unintentionally – discriminate against Aboriginal people. There has been little investment in translator services which listen and validate the full experiences of Aboriginal victims, or attempts to gauge the meanings attached to victimisation from an Indigenous perspective, in particular to understand what aspects of a victimisation may cause

'shame' – it might have less to do, for example, with physical injury than with the transgression of skin or avoidance relationships.

- Lack of investment in appropriate forms of victim support and counselling, particularly outside major centres, services are *metro-centric* as well as *ethno-centric and Eurocentric*. There is a dearth of appropriately structured and funded community-based prevention, intervention and treatment programs capable of mobilising and engaging Aboriginal communities in the struggle against violence.

- Aboriginal victimisation patterns challenge the mentalities underpinning dominant forms of 'crisis intervention'. Aboriginal victims are more likely to exist in situations of 'multiple and compound crisis' (Blagg 2000a; 2000b) meaning that they may be victims of crime while having to contend with a host of daily crises: poor housing/homelessness, unemployment, alcohol, family conflict, prison, children, poverty, ill health, loss and bereavement and mental health.

Earning victim status

It is an accepted tenet of critical victimology that becoming a socially sanctioned victim requires that those claiming the 'legitimate status' of victim (Walklate 1989: 9) fulfil a number of criteria. The stereotypical domestic violence event takes place within the private domain of the family and, generally, has to be rendered public through the intervention of the authorities. The very concept of domestic violence rests on some kind of pre-figured distinction between domestic and public realms. These oppositional realms, public/private, are discursively Eurocentric and do not necessarily match up with the variegations and divisions operating in Aboriginal domains.

Aboriginal family violence flares up in 'public' as well as 'private' space, on drinking grounds, in parks, on ovals, on the street, in pubs, and Aboriginal victims may not present as vulnerable, docile and passive (like those 'real' victims on the television adds). The event might include a host of players and move across space, place and time. The principle victim might, herself, have committed acts of violence and be seriously inebriated. In one research visit to Broome in 2006, I talked to a young Aboriginal woman at the Miliya Rummurah Alcohol Rehabilitation Centre who had been charged with wounding her partner (she had stabbed him with a broken bottle in the neck because, she told me, simply hitting him over the head with a piece of wood had not stopped his aggressive behaviour). They had been in a drinking group and he had become jealous when another man spoke to her, he became, first verbally then physically, violent to her. They had been arrested, charged and placed before the court; she was diverted onto a rehabilitation program while he (having a previous record) was jailed. They both wanted to do an alcohol rehabilitation program and then resume their relationship back in their own community outside of Broome. There are a number of typical characteristics here: the drinking group, alcohol consumption, jealousy (and maybe a little 'jealousing' as well), verbal and physical violence, retaliation, 'fighting back', arrest by the police, court, jail, reconciliation. The key difference in this instance was the availability of a new court diversion project, which allowed the woman to be diverted to Miliya Rummurah to deal with her substance abuse.

Jealousing

I was introduced to the concept of *jealousing* when beginning research on Aboriginal violence in Derby in the West Kimberley region of Western Australia. Jealous fighting, between partners, between rivals, between interested observers, within and across family groups, often involving alcohol is a common occurrence in Derby, as it is across the Kimberley. It goes unreported to the police unless it leads to significant injury or death. It has led to the murder of women by their partners, as well as numerous minor acts of violence. It is linked to family feuds and family violence.

Very serious fights take place between girls because of jealousy over boys. Women often leave paid work because their husbands become aggressively jealous and fearful when they are around other men. Families sometimes 'jealous up' a family member by spreading stories of their partners behaviour. Jealousing behaviours are associated with young people self-harming to make partners feel responsible (Hunter 1993). It regulates social behaviour by ensuring people don't become more successful, beautiful and desirable than others around them. Men are said to bash young wives 'ugly' to relieve their anxieties of losing them.

Jealousing is employed as a test of a partner's commitment. Young women sometimes jealous up their boyfriends by flirting, to see if he cares enough to be angry. To understand jealousing requires an understanding of the context in which such processes occur:

> Relationships are one of the few commodities available to many Aboriginal people. The feared loss of a valued relationship is far more personally threatening in a context of on-going poverty and deprivation than it is for an individual who has access to other opportunities for self gratification and self-definition such as meaningful employment. (*Taking Control*, cited in Dodson 1991)

Insecurity about relationships is a fundamental feature of family violence in a time when Aboriginal people are having to negotiate forms of cultural change where old rules no longer apply, particularly those governing marriage and sexual relations, traditionally controlled through skin relationships and promised marriages (Blagg 1998b). Jealousing is one highly destructive outcome.

There had been a number of ongoing debates on Aboriginal culture which have primed the discussion and provided 'scientific' substance. These have centred on the nature of Aboriginal culture itself and whether, irrespective of the impact of colonisation, it is irredeemably misogynistic. One group of Aboriginal women consulted by the Law Reform Commission of Western Australia (2006a) in Bandyup Women's Prison (the majority of whom had histories of abuse, violence, abandonment and neglect) were asked whether they would report violence against them to the police. They said they would never 'go to the police for help … the police are not a service – the service is to lock you up' (Bandyup Prison Consultation). The Gordon Inquiry noted that 'distrust' of the police was a 'barrier' to reporting family violence (Gordon, Henry & Hallam 2002). Aboriginal women in Western Australia are almost 14 times more likely to be arrested by the police than non-Aboriginal women (Aboriginal Justice Council 1997). When police attend a disturbance in an Aboriginal community the line between victim and offender may be blurred. The picture presented may appear more like an all-out brawl than a domestic assault on a spouse or partner. Victims of violence in these situations – who are usually, but not exclusively, women – are not always likely to present as ideal victims (Blagg 2000).

Recent legislative change in Western Australia – designed to improve the police response to domestic violence, removes victim consent as grounds for the breach of a restraining order. Several Aboriginal women in the East Kimberley region have been arrested under these new powers when they have made or encouraged contact with the subject of the restraining order. Blagg (2002) found evidence of police indifference to Aboriginal women's demands for a safe house to be established close to the police station in Roebourne, Western Australia, in the wake of several horrific murders, on the grounds that they were not there to provide a security service to Aboriginal women.

Aboriginal women appear in the criminal justice system as both offenders and victims, and research with Aboriginal women in prison reveal histories of severe and repeated victimisation. Over 78% of Aboriginal women prisoners surveyed by Lawrie in New South Wales reported having been victims of violence as adults. Nearly one half had been victims of a sexual assault as an adult:

> Approximately four in five Aboriginal women have been victims of domestic/family violence, whilst 75% said they had experienced mental or psychological abuse. A significant 86% of Aboriginal women in custody experienced emotional abuse and 36% of women experienced systems abuse. Some women stated that they had experienced more than one type of abuse. (Lawrie 2002: 14)

The image of the crime victim has come to occupy a particularly constitutive place in the discursive arena; 'we' reflexively position ourselves as members of community on shared sentiments of being potential if not actual victims. The 'we' here is an important qualifier. The 'we' represents deserving victims, who correspond to certain expected criteria. Aboriginal women do not always fit the stereotype of the deserving victim.

Non-Indigenous 'Crisis Intervention' systems are viewed as part of the problem, not the solution

Many of the tools in the crisis intervention kit, developed in non-Indigenous situations, have been manufactured on the premise that a 'crisis' is a distinct event to be set against a background of relative stability and normality. This belief system also underpins orthodox restorative justice practices, where a one-off reintegration ceremony 'resolves' the crisis created by acts of delinquency, and then everyone gets on with their lives (Blagg 1997). Aboriginal families frequently exist in conditions of ongoing crisis; crisis events multiply and compact over time until it become impossible to disentangle one from another. The notion of a 'crisis' itself, therefore, need rethinking to accommodate the impact of a crisis event on people who may already to be gripped by manifold crises, relating to health, housing, employment, structural racism, poverty, bereavement and alcohol abuse. It is frequently said in the Perth Nyoongar community that by the time an Aboriginal child is 10 years old he/she will have been to at least 10 funerals; he/she may have also been in contact with the criminal justice system; have witnessed and/or been the direct victim of violence.

Victim's faith in the capacity of the criminal justice system to deal sympathetically and efficiently with their case may be misplaced. There is an abundance of literature detailing problems associated with *secondary* or *system's* victimisation of victims of intimate violence in Australia (Taylor 2004; Victorian Law Reform Commission 2006). Even credible white victims may have difficulty in persuading prosecutory authorities – let alone defence lawyers during trails – to 'believe' them: as the Falconio murder case in the Northern Territory illustrated, when Joanne Lees (the secondary victim in the case) felt she was 'disbelieved' by the NT Police and the international media.[1] Lees did not present as an ideal, deserving victim. The media coverage of her trial focused heavily on her dress and demeanour, the fact that she did not cry or seem to show emotion, and the fact that she had been involved in an affair.[2]

When the law gets it wrong

When the white legal system does intervene it does not always get it right. Occasionally it makes matters worse. This is not because the system is soft on Aboriginal culture but because of a profound systemic racism and cultural insensitivity operating at all levels of the system, often leading to negative outcomes for Aboriginal victims. Research with Aboriginal women in the remote Kimberley region by Wohlan found that Aboriginal women were less concerned with 'socially sanctioned Aboriginal law violence against Aboriginal women' (the dominant culture's view) than they were by a 'lack of control and a lack of justice for women when dealing with the state's legal system' (Wohlan 2005).

In one example described by Wohlan, a drunken Aboriginal man (Japurru) murdered an Aboriginal woman, but because video evidence of the police interview had to be deemed inadmissible by the magistrate, due to the fact that the police did not follow standard procedures for interviewing an Aboriginal person, the charge was reduced to manslaughter. Moreover, the police had intervened to arrest the offender before traditional punishment – which would probably have involved serious physical injury by spearing – could be carried out. The offender served 18 months, having already been remanded in custody for 18 months. On release he sees his victim's mother:

> When Japurru sees her, he taunts her, motioning for her to come over to him ... He has changed after the murder and his jail term. He seems to have an attitude of being bulletproof: nobody's law is controlling him anymore. (Wohlan 2005: 9)

This is not an example of customary law 'excusing' or 'justifying' violence, rather it is an example of Aboriginal law being refused jurisdiction, with devastating consequences. Because the legal system let Aboriginal victims down by failing to abide by its own rules of evidence and procedure, while simultaneously preventing Aboriginal law from taking its course, there was in fact *lawlessness*. Senior Aboriginal women interviewed by Wohlan did not see traditional Aboriginal culture as responsible for family violence, instead they pointed to alcohol abuse and community decay. Moreover, they wanted to see discussion of customary law decoupled from debates about family violence and attention given to reviving – not abolishing – Aboriginal cultures as a means of regenerating communities (Wohlan 2005).

Fighting women

Aboriginal women do not always behave according to dominant western gender stereotypes around femininity. The radical alterity of Aboriginal women's culture is demonstrated in their views concerning their own physicality, many fight, and are proud of their capacity to take and give out punishment. Aboriginal women in those Aboriginal domains where traditional law is particularly strong practice traditional punishment which can include the use of fighting sticks (Nulla Nullas) to 'flog' or 'give a hiding' to those who have broken law. Aboriginal women, particularly young women, are involved in family feuding and jealous fighting. But they distinguish between this from 'bull-shit' violence – where Aboriginal men claim 'traditional' rights to violence against women (Bolger 1991) – as well as alcohol-fuelled violence. It is not surprising to find that physical resistance to violence may be the only avenue open to Aboriginal women given the 'pressures ... against the involvement of the police' (Cunneen & Kerley 1994: 82-83; Dodson 1991). Resistance of this kind may also account, in part, for the alarmingly high rates of injury sustained by Aboriginal women in Western Australia in abuse cases. La Prairie (1989) and Langton (1992) suggest that Aboriginal women are often imprisoned because of their resistance to abuse where this leads to the death or injury of the abuser.

When they do access the domestic violence facilities such as refuges, Aboriginal women tend to use them as places of immediate safety and respite rather than as exit points from relationships (Blagg 2000b). The police, when they are contacted, may be called in as a 'crisis intervention tool, to stop the abuse at a critical stage' but women may not necessarily want to press charges (Aboriginal and Torres Strait Islander Women's Task Force on Violence Report 2000: 232). Gordon, Henry and Hallam (2002) recommend that we 'acknowledge Aboriginal women's different view of the use of refuges and the criminal justice system' (Gordon, Henry & Hallam 2002: 479).

Intervention strategies need to respect – rather than problematise – Aboriginal women's cultural and family obligations, even where these do not accord with the current orthodoxy on domestic violence intervention. Often the *Aboriginality* of Aboriginal women is identified as an obstacle by non-Indigenous agencies (Blagg 2000b). For many Indigenous women, choosing to leave family – with all its complexly embedded ties of mutual responsibility and obligation and connection with country and culture – is not an option. The capacity to exit family relationships (indeed, the very concept of 'choice' in such matters) – to repackage and reconstitute one's identity as an autonomous individual in some new location, is a profoundly Eurocentric construction.

Once the considerable limitations placed on Indigenous women's capacity to abrogate responsibilities to family are accepted as the starting point – rather than the problem – in victim support, it follows that community-based strategies of diversion into restorative programs are most likely to satisfy the demands of Indigenous women and their communities. Wherever possible, models of intervention should work through existing community structures. It should be acknowledged that many Indigenous people are already working to end family violence in their communities.

Crime prevention programs most suited to Aboriginal contexts are those providing a holistic framework, as Cunneen observes in relation to family violence prevention:

The common themes in evaluations of family violence programmes include the need for holistic approaches, the utilisation of community development models which emphasize self-determination and community ownership, the provision of culturally sensitive treatment which respects traditional law and customs and involves existing structures of authority such as elders, including women. (Cunneen 2001a: 9)

A recent inquiry in Queensland maintains that a 'one-size-fits-all approach to designing and delivering integrated service responses across Queensland will not work' (Queensland Government 2015: 12), and that the barriers facing women in different regions (urban, rural and remote) and from different cultural backgrounds offer contrasting challenges (Queensland Government 2015: 12).

It is increasingly becoming clear that initiatives with the greatest likelihood of success are those that genuinely engage with Aboriginal law and culture and view these as the vehicle for change. Rather than this reducing the input of government agencies, it might in fact have the opposite impact. There are vital resources (human, monetary, physical) locked up in these agencies. Aboriginal people, in my experience, want, deserve and welcome specialist skills that they cannot themselves currently offer – these include information and advice on the physical and mental effects of alcohol, drugs and unsafe sexual practices, and the input of experienced counsellors and legal practitioners: but they want these delivered in a cultural framework that enhances the community's capacities to acquire and hold on to knowledge.

One of the outcomes of the greater awareness of the safety deficit on rural and remote communities for Indigenous women, was the creation of Commonwealth funded Family Violence Prevention Legal Services (FVPLS), offering legal assistance, casework, counselling and court support to Aboriginal and Torres Strait Islander women and children who are victims-survivors of family violence: now located in 31 rural and remote locations around Australia (see <www.nationalfvpls.org/Where-We-Are.php>). The creation of these services follows on from criticism of the lack of adequate facilities in rural and remote locations, to keep women safe from violence, such as the Gordon Inquiry (Gordon et al 2002) and empirical research suggesting that services were particularly needed in remote communities (Clare, Morgan, Ferrante & Blagg 2006). In some instances, such as in Fitzroy Crossing, Western Australia, the FVPLS service is co-located with a women's refuge, offering a holistic, wrap-around service. Both are nested within the Marninwarntikura Women's Resource Centre that acts as a hub for a diversity of women's issues:

> Marninwarntikura is an agency integral to the maintenance and development of the rich cultural, social and political fabric of the Fitzroy Valley. Today it is an environment which is actively responsive to women's concerns. The organisation functions on multiple levels. It provides services and facilities for listening to fears and worries of women, while offering support through counselling and legal advice, to engage women in a process of healing, and protect them from harm. On another level, Marninwarntikura is committed to developing programs that *empower women*, economically, culturally and politically. (Marninwarntikura Fitzroy Women's Resource & Legal Centre. Marra Worra Worra Aboriginal Corporation & Nindilingarri Cultural Health Services 2009)

The emergence of place based organisations run by Indigenous women and working from within Indigenous law and culture may pose a challenge to western orthodoxies around intervention in domestic and family violence, but there are clear signs that these suit the needs of many Indigenous women (Blagg, Williams & Bluett-Boyd 2015).

The issue of Aboriginal family violence has become entangled with debates about Aboriginal customary law and a number of commentators have identified Aboriginal law as providing justification of the abuse of women and children by Aboriginal men.

Notes

1   In an interview on the ABC's 'Enough Rope' program, Lees tells of an interview with the police some weeks after the murder, she says: 'throughout that interview, I started to feel like I was a suspect ... They asked me to clarify inconsistencies in my statement, but there were no inconsistencies. It seemed as if they were trying to get a confession from me, *and then the interview ended with the question that they would like to receive closure for Pete's family and if I could tell them where Peter was*' (emphasis added). Lees lost confidence that the police were interested in finding the killer, having so clearly formed the opinion that it was her.

2   Typical was the *Sydney Morning Herald* (2004) coverage by Philip Cornford: 'Lees admits second lover' (27 May); 'Let's meet in Berlin, Lees emailed her secret lover' (28 May).

9

Aboriginal Customary Law:
From Denial to Recognition

The issue of Aboriginal Customary Law has been pushed onto the political agenda in connection with the issue of violence in Indigenous communities. But what is Aboriginal law? There have been a number of landmark inquiries into Aboriginal law, each of which has confirmed the continuing relevance of law to the daily lives of Aboriginal people. The only truly national inquiry into Aboriginal customary law was undertaken by the Australian Law Reform Commission (ALRC) in the 1980s (Australian Law Reform Commission 1986); this exhaustive inquiry has since been complemented by local inquiries in the Northern Territory and Western Australia. There have also been a number of important studies examining the relevance of Aboriginal law in sentencing offenders (Law Reform Commission of New South Wales 2000) and local justice (Fitzgerald 2001). The late 1990s, therefore, represented a new phase in the dialogue with Aboriginal people about law and justice, shifting away from debates about reform of the non-Indigenous justice system to an exploration of the ways Aboriginal law could be employed as a vehicle for change. In so doing the focus on Aboriginal law provided an alternative to reform strategies engaged in making the white system more culturally appropriate by adding elements of Aboriginal 'culture' onto an essentially unreconstructed white system.

There can be little doubt that Aboriginal law exists, in the sense of being practised and maintained in daily life: and it exists, moreover, whether 'we' give formal recognition to it or not. History shows that Aboriginal people will find ways to hang onto their law in the face of the most intense attempts to smash it. Initiatives by the federal government, in the wake of allegations of widespread violence against women and children in Central Australia, has seen the debate about Aboriginal law shifts once again – away from questions of recognition to identifying modes of abolition; general scepticism about the existence of law has been replaced by moves, in some quarters, to prevent customary law being recognised in court.

I have argued thus far that anxieties about recognising the existence of Aboriginal customary law are interwoven with colonial history and Australia's claim to sovereignty. Giving recognition to Aboriginal forms of law requires acknowledging the existence of Aboriginal society as a distinctive, functioning social system, rather than simply an ethnic subset of mainstream Australia. These anxieties have emerged again in relation to customary law and communal violence. In this chapter, I want to argue that it is not Aboriginal law that is the problem, rather it is what one commentator referred to as 'the universalist pretensions of Australian law' (McDonald cited in Northern Territory Law

Reform Commission 2005) and its refusal to reach an accommodation with traditional law that lies at the heart of the problem.

This refusal continues to seal off from exploration a potentially rich and dynamic discursive space in which new post-colonial narratives could be enunciated and shared: ensuring instead, that distorted, one-dimensional mythologies about Aboriginal law continue to circulate in the public and official imagination. This refusal has real implications for Aboriginal people. It generates situations in which Aboriginal people are subject to two laws or, worse still, exist in a state of lawlessness, where traditional law has been denied jurisdiction and the western law continues to be ineffectual. Recognising Aboriginal jurisdiction may contribute to breaking the cycle of violence in Aboriginal communities and reducing negative contact between Aboriginal people and the criminal justice system. I also want to suggest that it has been our unwillingness to establish reliable and durable mechanisms for discussing with Aboriginal people the relationship between Indigenous and non-Indigenous forms of law that has led to confusion over what Aboriginal law actually is. Discussion tends only to occur within the adversarial context of the court, where a version of Aboriginal tradition is presented to explain or justify a particular course of action by a defendant: it is raised as mitigation by defence lawyers, or where there is a threat of 'double punishment' and 'payback' violence. This, however, is only a small part of law. Rarely is Aboriginal law presented as holistic tapestry of values and beliefs in all its forms.

Customary law is difficult to define in non-Indigenous terms, as it encompasses far more than the right to inflict physical punishment: 'law' represents a grammar for living and an intricate set of religious principles that make the world intelligible (Australian Law Reform Commission 1986). Anthropologists have tended to see Aboriginal law as a mechanism for establishing and reproducing balanced relationships between social/ kinship systems, the natural environment and religious deities (Berndt & Berndt 1998). It is difficult to separate out those elements of law which are concerned with social order from those concerned with other elements of law: Aboriginal people themselves tend not to. It is hazardous to attempt a legal definition or attempt to squeeze the construct into already existing criminological categories: customary principles are not like statutes and codes (Toohey 2006). Aboriginal law does resemble other forms of law, however, in the sense that it constitutes a body of rules, even if these rules are not written down, which are widely accepted as legitimate by those who uphold them and which are enforced by sanction and penalty.

The ALRC and recognition

This approach to the issue was adopted by the 1986 Australian Law Reform Commission Inquiry, which pointed to the continuation in Aboriginal culture of a set of customary practices 'accepted as legal requirements or obligatory rules of conduct' so vital to the maintenance of Aboriginal society that they were 'treated as if they were laws'. The ALRC argued that:

> A basic precondition for the recognition of Aboriginal customary laws is the simple assertion that it exists as a real force, influencing or controlling the acts and lives of

those Aborigines for whom it is 'part of the substance of daily life'. (Australian Law Reform Commission 1986: 79)

The commission found widespread support for the recognition of Aboriginal customary law among Aboriginal people and evidence that continued non-recognition, and constant attempts to dismantle traditional practices, profoundly disadvantaged Aboriginal people by undermining social structures and systems of authority. The commission heard evidence to the effect that the western system of justice and allied agencies were ineffective in dealing with issues within Aboriginal communities. The situation in Australia since the ALRC report has also been influenced by a number of developments, which have strengthened the case for renewing debate about customary law. The 1991 Royal Commission into Aboriginal Deaths in Custody (RCIADIC) raised issues concerning both the effectiveness of the criminal justice system and the legitimacy of a system. The High Court's decision in *Mabo* raised some fundamental truths about the prior existence of systems of law and law ownership before the arrival of whites, which re-affirmed the existence of Aboriginal law. Perhaps the most exhaustive study of Aboriginal law since the ALRC's 1986 Inquiry is the Law Reform Commission of Western Australia's study, begun in 2001 and completed in 2006.

The West Australian Inquiry

In 2001 the Law Reform Commission of Western Australia began a major review of Aboriginal Customary Law in Western Australia. The overall aim of the project was to reconcile Aboriginal and non-Aboriginal systems of law. The question was not any longer *whether* Aboriginal law existed (this matter had been settled comprehensively by the Australian Law Reform Commission in the 1980s), but rather – What forms does it take? Who is bound by it? Can Aboriginal and non-Aboriginal laws co-exist? Can Aboriginal law be codified and written up in some form of statute, like its western counterpart? Underpinning the inquiry was the recognition that Aboriginal people are frequently disadvantaged in their dealings with the non-Aboriginal system of justice, this disadvantage, moreover, appears to be the product of systemic factors rather than simply a reflection of individual racist attitudes and beliefs.

A systemic analysis focuses attention on differences in structure, rather than simply on the attitudes and motives of participants. Naturally, the relationship between structure and action is a complex one. Anthony Giddens uses the concept of 'structuration' to describe the limited, but genuine, agency individuals have in reproducing the social structure (Giddens 1984). 'Agency' in the criminal justice arena involves police, judges, magistrates, social workers, Aboriginal liaison officers, elders and night patrollers, involved not just simply in replicating past practice but in shaping social change, sometimes in novel ways. They do so, however, within limits set down for them by the structures and cultures in which they operate. The links between structures and agency is also captured in Williams' notion of 'structures of feeling' (discussed earlier), or 'structures of sentiment and feeling' as Edward Said (1993) enlarges it. Centring agency and feeling is important when dealing with issues as emotive and ontologically entangled as customary law, both in terms of the deep sentiment attached to it for

Aboriginal people, and the equally powerful anxiety, fear and loathing it evokes for many non-Aboriginal people.

The West Australian Inquiry (Law Reform Commission of Western Australia 2006a) involved examination of relevant State and Commonwealth legislation on criminal law, civil law, family law, personal property law, inheritance law, laws on evidence and procedure, as well as giving recognition to the unique spiritual foundations of Aboriginal law – a daunting undertaking. Understanding these required a nuanced and variegated process, which brought together the views of Aboriginal communities and the best available expert opinion.

Community consultations were conducted across Western Australia in urban, rural and remote locations: including pre-consultation visits to establish protocols and procedures and post-consultation visits following the release of the Inquiries Discussion Paper in early 2006 (Law Reform Commission of Western Australia 2006a). Transcripts of discussions from meetings were returned to communities for commentary before becoming a formal record (2006a: 6). What these consultations revealed was that Aboriginal law still governs many aspects of daily life for many Aboriginal people, providing the maps of meaning that make communal life possible and predictable. Law provides an overarching framework of rules and obligations, forms of penalty and censure, codes of conduct, etiquette and address. It informs people about with whom they can associate and under what conditions, it informs them about their obligations and their relationship to those around them. The inquiry provided clear evidence that many Aboriginal people in Western Australia consider themselves to be bound by Aboriginal law and accept its jurisdiction over their lives. Moreover, the majority – including women – see adherence to law as a positive aspect of their lives.

The West Australian Inquiry (Law Reform Commission of Western Australia 2006a) also revealed a profound sense of alienation from the mainstream justice system. Most Aboriginal people consulted by the Law Reform Commission of Western Australia wanted to see action taken on key issues such as over-representation and the unacceptable levels of family violence in Indigenous communities, and they wanted these forms of action to be based upon close collaboration with Indigenous communities, including a commitment to fostering and nurturing local capacity for Indigenous people themselves to take the lead.

The Law Reform Commission of Western Australia Inquiry (2006a) found Aboriginal law to be a governing force in the lives of Aboriginal people living in urban, rural and remote locations. While there may be an acceptance that law does exist in the remote 'outback' (that semi-mythical space on the fringes of modernity) there is less understanding – or willingness to understand – that urban groups see law as important. Yet urban Aboriginal people continue to practice Aboriginal law in their daily lives, particularly through observation of kin obligations and duties but also through stories and language. One urban group defined law as:

> Connecting people in a web of relationships with a diverse group of people; and with our ancestral spirits, the land, the sea and the universe; and our responsibility to the maintenance of this order. (Manguri consultations)

Moreover, urban Aboriginal people see their future survival in terms of renewing relationships based on traditional law:

It [bringing Noongar customary law back] can be done ... Noongar history and teach the youth ... We have a responsibility to learn Noongar stories and pass them on ... this lady has a room full of Noongar information ... you can teach yourself the Noongar language – it should be compulsory for kids to attend cultural camps – learn language, stories, respect and hand them on to others ... some people want money for stories before they do any work ... this is wrong! ... not what Noongar culture is about ... it's an oral history ... teaching about this will bring about respect, keep children out of jail. (Rockingham consultation)

So, how do Aboriginal people today think about Aboriginal law and its relevance to their lives? In her work in the town of Roebourne, Cathy Trees (2006) notes:

For many people living in Roebourne, their customary law systems continue to regulate their lives as they had always done, even if the law is at time ignored, and for some people not well known ... [I]t is important to understand that Aboriginal people do not think of customary law in the sense that Aboriginal people think of law and the general legal system ... it is not possible to make a simple division between customary law and life generally: Aboriginal people in Roebourne do not do this. (Trees 2006: 215)

Customary law is underpinned by a rich patina of spiritual and cultural beliefs, which give meaning to daily occurrences and provide a set of explanations for problematic events:

Aboriginal people draw on spiritual or cultural beliefs to explain everyday events such as car accidents, illness and death ... they may explain a young person's anti-social behaviour (for example, breaking windows), as the result of his or her parents 'wrong way'[1] marriage and therefore inability to bring the child up properly. (Trees 2006: 217)

An inquiry into Aboriginal law in the Northern Territory (Northern Territory Law Reform Commission 2005) also found that many Aboriginal people felt bound by law in their daily lives:

Aboriginal customary law is a fact of life for most Aboriginal people in the Northern Territory, not just those in Aboriginal communities. This is because it defines people's rights and responsibilities, who a person is, and it defines a person's relationships to everybody else in the world. (Northern Territory Law Reform Commission 2005: 16)

The intricate interweaving of cultural and spiritual beliefs within Aboriginal law distinguishes it from western concepts of law. The Northern Territory Inquiry argues that, in the western system 'law' and 'custom' are radically different, even contradictory constructs, and when custom become laws through codification it ceases being customary (Northern Territory Law Reform Commission 2005: 16). In the Aboriginal context, on the other hand, no distinction is made between the two:

Aboriginal tradition is an indivisible body of rules laid down over thousands of years and governing all aspects of life, with specific sanction if disobeyed. The expression 'customary law' is therefore correct, as containing both concepts in one expression. (Northern Territory Law Reform Commission 2005: 16)

Other commentators have been less convinced that the term 'customary' should be attached to Aboriginal law. Cunneen and Schwartz (2006) maintain that the concept is 'flawed', being reliant on 'colonial assumptions about the nature of law in Indigenous communities' (2006: 430) and consequently, the construct simply reinforces the 'centrality of non-Indigenous law and legal systems': the notion of customary law is an 'imperialist concept' (2006: 430, 433).

There is general agreement that no formal code of customary laws exists. Definitions of law may shift from place to place and over time. The Aboriginal Justice Advisory Council New South Wales (AJAC) dwells on the dispute resolution aspects of Aboriginal law as most relevant to Aboriginal people living a relatively urban lifestyle:

> Aboriginal customary law is fundamentally a means of dispute resolution based on traditional spiritual beliefs and cultural traditions that provide sanction against those actions which are harmful to the community. In a criminal context fundamentally customary law is simply a means of a community establishing its set of basic values and providing a means to punish those who transgress against its established community laws. (AJAC 2000: 3)

The Law Reform Commission of New South Wales' Report into Sentencing Aboriginal Offenders (2000) also recommended that Aboriginal law be acknowledged when the criminal justice system deals with Aboriginal offenders and victims:

> Where a person, who is, or was at a relevant time, a member of an Aboriginal community, is convicted of an offence, in determining the sentence, the court shall have regard to any evidence concerning the customary laws of that Aboriginal community, and the customary laws of any other Aboriginal community of which the victim was a member at a relevant time. (Law Reform Commission of New South Wales 2000: 17)

Recognition of customary law

In its discussion, the 1986 ALRC Inquiry observed that customary law issues were taken into account within the general legal system but in an ad hoc and fragmentary fashion (Australian Law Reform Commission 1986). It concluded that Aboriginal law should be acknowledged and recognised by the legal system but rejected the idea that there should be a new and separate legal system – unless the need for such reforms was clearly demonstrated. It also came out against codification of Aboriginal law. The reasons in favour of recognition offered by the ALRC remain pertinent today. They include:

- the desirability of achieving reconciliation between Aboriginal and non-Aboriginal societies;
- the fact that Aboriginal people are often unjustly punished for following the dictates of their own law;
- the failure of the general law to reduce levels of over-representation;
- potential reductions in offending and the costs of crime;
- the fact that customary practices are taken into account already albeit in an ad hoc manner;
- the potential for non-recognition to perpetuate paternalistic and assimilationist relationships; and
- recognition would improve Australia's standing in the world.

The ALRC also raised some arguments against recognition, also pertinent today. These included:

- the possibility that we may be legitimating practices unacceptable to mainstream Australia;
- the possibility that Aboriginal people may be forced to reveal secret/sacred knowledge if Aboriginal processes are brought closer to our legal system;
- loss of Aboriginal control over customary law;
- Aboriginal women might be disadvantaged;
- recognising Aboriginal law may create 'two laws'; and
- recognition may not be relevant to many Aboriginal people who prefer the white system and may only be applicable in strictly traditional regions.

The ALRC came out against the idea that there should be two separate systems of justice, this was also the conclusion of the Northern Territory Inquiry (Northern Territory Law Reform Commission 2005: 40) The latter made the pertinent observation that there are numerous matters not covered by Aboriginal law which Aboriginal people and their communities deal with on a daily basis, including commercial contracts and faulty motor vehicles (Northern Territory Law Reform Commission 2006). The West Australian Inquiry (Law Reform Commission of Western Australia 2006a) found that many Aboriginal people wanted recognition of their law, and this was generally supported by the discussion papers commissioned by the West Australian Inquiry – with caveats regarding some aspects of so-called traditional practices, involving the abuse of women and children. Weighing up the possible options, the Law Reform Commission of Western Australia rejected administrative and statutory forms of recognition: the former because it lacked transparency and the latter because it would disempower Aboriginal people. The commission opted instead for 'functional recognition' (2006: 71) which entails 'recognition of Aboriginal customary law for practical purposes in defined areas of law' (2006: 71).

The commission argued:

> This approach allows for a variety of methods of recognition (legislative, judicial, administrative and constitutional) resulting in proposals for recognition of Aboriginal customary law that fall broadly into two categories: affirmative and reconciliatory. (Law Reform Commission of Western Australia 2006b: 71)

The affirmative aspect relates to strategies designed to empower Aboriginal communities on a host of fronts. These include:

- provisions to ensure courts and government take account of Aboriginal law;
- a whole of government approach to service delivery;
- fostering self-governance; removal of cultural bias;
- recognising Aboriginal marriage; and
- empowering elders and other respected members to be involved in the administration of justice. (Law Reform Commission of Western Australia 2006b: 72)

The reconciliatory aspects relate to the promotion of reconciliation and pride in Aboriginal culture and heritage. It includes measures to 'address the decline in cultural authority among Aboriginal people and communities' through the promotion of appropriate forms of cultural awareness training and through the creation of Independent

Office of the Commissioner for Indigenous Affairs to promote the interests of Aboriginal people. The Commission also sees an important role for constitutional change that would recognise the unique status of Indigenous people and acknowledges prior occupation and continuing connection to the land (Law Reform Commission of Western Australia 2006b: 73). One reason why the commission was reluctant to go down the path of statutory recognition was that Aboriginal people feared having their law codified, believing that it would then cease to be their law and would become the property of lawyers and the legal system.

Other inquiries have grappled with the thorny problem of how to recognise Aboriginal law without ossifying it and transforming it into its Other – western law. The Cape York Justice Study (Fitzgerald 2001) acknowledged that Aboriginal law could not be administered through the non-Aboriginal legal system without being significantly distorted:

> [A]ny attempt by the state to act as the principal machinery for the administration of Aboriginal law is highly problematic. Aboriginal customary law is not reflected through the filters of Western legal principles, procedures and institutions without significant alternation. (Fitzgerald 2001: 112)

Allowing space for what the study calls a 'vibrant decentred Aboriginal law' to flourish required commitment to a pluralistic framework, rather than one 'single imposed system' where there would be a commitment to self-determination, dialogue and community empowerment (Fitzgerald 2001: 113). The Cape York Justice Study calls for the maximum feasible devolution of authority over justice issues to what it calls 'pods of justice':

> There needs to be an institutional space or spaces created for the accommodation of Aboriginal law within the broader Australian legal system. There must be institutional design for the administration of local order by Aboriginal communities. There must be 'pods of justice' distinct in form and function, autonomous but contributing to a federal whole. Authority must be devolved to Aboriginal communities so that they may first determine the law and order issues. (Fitzgerald 2001: 113)

This argument is close to the conclusions of the Northern Territory and West Australian inquiries: both of which call for a considerable shift in power down to the community level. I will discuss the form this devolution might take later; before doing so let us first examine a crucial dimension of the debate about Aboriginal law and the relevance of human rights instrumentalities.

International human rights and Aboriginal law

Australia is party to a suite of human rights instrumentalities, a number of which have legal force in Australian domestic law. Over the past two decades in particular, scholars, activists and lawyers have turned to United Nations (UN) conventions and other instruments as a means of challenging Australian States over the treatment of Aboriginal people. Aboriginal youth has been a particular focus of this kind of intervention, issues such as the mass detention of Aboriginal youth, concentrated over-policing and denial of access to the public realm have stimulated initiatives designed to align Australian domestic law more closely with United Nations conventions (Blagg & Wilkie 1995: 6).

The creation of the offices of the Aboriginal Social Justice Commissioner in the Human Rights and Equal Opportunity Commission has provided a focal point for Indigenous concerns on human rights issues, and it has kept up pressure for the Australia to be involved in international discussions on Indigenous rights issues. The UN has been moving towards an international declaration on Indigenous rights for some time. The current draft declaration – which received strong opposition from the Australian government (under John Howard) – contains recognition of Indigenous rights to self-government, rights to participate in decision-making, rights to develop political, economic and social institutions, and the right to practice culture and custom. Of particular importance in the context of law and justice is that the declaration espouses the right of Indigenous people to nurture and develop their own institutions, structures spiritual practices and justice structures, where these do not conflict with human rights standards (Davis & McGlade 2006).

While the language of human rights has achieved international status there is a general unwillingness in Australia to countenance the existence of a body of Indigenous rights different from those applying to the mainstream. It has been a slow process, but Indigenous people have achieved a degree of recognition at the international level, as Davis and McGlade (2006) observe:

> Indigenous people enjoy a burgeoning presence in the United Nations system, with a developing corpus of Indigenous specific human rights that calls upon states to respect the right of Indigenous people to have their own customs, traditions, rules and legal systems taken into account. (Davis & McGlade 2006: 383)

It remains the case though, as Elizabeth Evatt points out, that while enormous effort has gone in to developing mechanisms to defend Indigenous rights in Australia, 'many of our most glaring failures to meet international standards concern Indigenous people' (Evatt 2001: 181).

A meta-narrative has evolved around the shared experiences of Indigenous peoples globally because, while Indigenous cultures are not homogenous and manifest extreme diversity in terms of social structure and cosmology, they share common experiences of marginalisation, dispossession and discrimination by the dominant culture: moreover they have all been subject to similar processes of failed social engineering particularly through attempts to reconstruct Indigenous family structures; having first rendered extant structures dysfunctional. The civilising mission had similarities whether it was concerned with pagan Maori, heathen First Nation Canadians or godless Aborigines. Armitage (1995) identifies 'strong and recurrent' similarities between child removal policies and practices in New Zealand, Canada and Australia while differences between policies were found to be 'a matter of emphasis and degree rather than of kind' (Armitage 1995: 217). While Stafford (in Hazelhurst 1995) points to similar experiences of systemic violence, 'powerlessness, alienation, frustration and anger', which have left a comparable legacy of social problems and self- and other-directed aggression (Stafford in Hazelhurst 1995).

Human rights instrumentalities have tended to support the recognition of customary law and practice: the right to grow up within a particular culture being acknowledged as a fundamental right under the Convention on the Rights of the Child. The major challenge in relation to Aboriginal law and human rights, according to Davis and McGlade (2006), is reconciling the recognition of customary law with notions of 'universality of human rights and core principles of non-distinction and equality before the law', as well as guaranteeing the protection of groups such as women and children and identifying cultural practices that might be 'viewed as harmful by inter-national human rights law' (2006: 383). Davis and McGlade make the useful point that, rather than attempting to impose a simple, unitary catalogue of substantive rights on Indigenous people, the most fruitful road ahead lies in developing a set of processes through which there can be ongoing consultation and dialogue as a governing principle (Davis & McGlade 2006: 384). They recognise that there will inevitably be tension between some universal human rights principles and the right to practice Aboriginal cultural, and they discuss a number of these in the context of issues such as 'promised marriages'; they conclude that the balance between these cannot be arrived at outside of processes of consultation. While this may sound simplistic they make the important point that it is precisely the lack of consistent and credible consultations mechanisms that has undermined relations between the state and Aboriginal people, 'the history of race relations … clearly illustrate that consultation has not been a fundamental value between the two' (Davis & McGlade 2006: 425). Davis and McGlade focus attention on the educative, rather than simply judicial, dynamic within the United Nations system and its instrumentalities. This is an important point because there is a genuine danger that the appeal to international human rights law – specifically in relation to men and customary law – may have the unintended consequence of reinforcing those tendencies within the Australian system to criminalise and imprison Aboriginal people, this time in the name of defending the rights of women and children.

The problems inherent in achieving a balance between international human rights principles and customary law is also discussed by Cunneen and Schwartz (2006). They maintain that the principle of self-determination represents the best position from which to address questions of Aboriginal law. They maintain that identifying whether Aboriginal law is customary or not is not the most important issue, what matters is respecting Indigenous powers to negotiate and allowing Indigenous people the right – within boundaries established by internationally recognised standards of human rights – to establish their own systems of justice (Cunneen & Schwartz 2006: 430). Cunneen and Schwartz echo Davis and McGlade's (2006) assertion that there will be areas of conflict between some aspects of Aboriginal law and those protections established in UN Standards, and they maintain that Aboriginal law must comply with these instruments. Cunneen and Schwartz conclude that the way forward lies in promoting 'Indigenous law, governance and self determination' (Cunneen & Schwartz 2006: 450) within a strong framework of negotiation. They see the current 'skeletal framework' (2006: 450) of Indigenous initiatives, such as Aboriginal Courts and Circle Courts, Night Patrols and community justice groups as significantly enhancing capacity for new forms of governance – providing these are not simply 'coopted' or 'Indigenized' (2006: 450). Here Cunneen and Schwartz are in company with a number of other commentators, who likewise see the solution in terms of expanded forms of community-owned justice mechanisms based on principles of self-determination.

Indigenous epistemologies form the bedrock of resistance to attempts by the Global North to 'standardise and homogenise' (Chomsky in Meyer and Maldonado 2010) the

Indigenous world. The world's 340 million or so Indigenous peoples vary considerably across the globe, yet they share common experiences of 'loss of land and subsistence, abrogation of treaties, and the imposition of psychologically and socially destructive assimilation policies' (Nieze 2003); historical injustices acknowledged in the UN Declaration on the Rights of Indigenous Peoples (2008) which establishes 'that indigenous peoples are equal to all other peoples, while recognizing the right of all peoples to be different, to consider themselves different, and to be respected as such' (61/295). The settler colonial state has been a poor custodian of Indigenous rights. Indigenous people globally seek *restitution* and *reparation* for a host of crimes committed by settler colonists, and their demands include: native title and land rights; the end to impunity from prosecution for human rights abuses (including genocide); a focus on state (rather than just individual) violence; a leading role for strategies of self-determination; the recognition of Indigenous sovereignty, and a willingness to acknowledge Aboriginal law as a fact of life for Indigenous peoples.

The Law Reform Commission of Western Australia also discusses the question of human rights and Aboriginal law. It argues that there are aspects of traditional law that could conflict with human rights standards – notably spearing and non-consensual child marriage – and this reinforces the argument against blanket recognition (Law Reform Commission of Western Australia 2006b: 69). Particular aspects of Aboriginal law need, therefore, to be assessed on a 'case-by-case basis' (Law Reform Commission of Western Australia 2006b: 69). The commission recommends:

> That recognition of Aboriginal customary laws and practices in Western Australia must be consistent with international human rights standards and should be determined on a case-by-case basis. In all aspects of the recognition process particular attention should be paid to the rights of women and children and the right not to be subject to inhuman, cruel or unusual treatment or punishment under international law. (Law Reform Commission of Western Australia 2006b: 69, Recommendation 5)

It is worth commenting briefly on that other obsession of white society; spearing or 'payback'. For many non-Aboriginal people 'payback' is what Aboriginal law is about. Interest in it gratifies non-Indigenous curiosity about the savage elements of Aboriginal culture and it performs the useful function of fixing Aboriginal law firmly within a framework of violence; in opposition to western law, which is, supposedly, based on principles of justice and the use of humane confinement. In Chapter 2 I made reference to Bauman's observations concerning the ways society outlaws some forms of behaviour as violent and sanitises others as not violent (legitimate force versus mindless aggression), and Cowlishaw's distinction between 'cool, cruel' correctional violence and the spontaneous violence of the street.

Many Aboriginal people see long-term confinement in prison, far from their country and the responsibilities attached to being a member of and Aboriginal community, as violent in the extreme. Moreover, they see the long-term stigma of being labelled criminal – which is confirmed rather than removed by judicial punishment in the western system – as being especially heinous. While spearing and other forms of physical punishment may offend white sensibilities they have support within some sectors of the Aboriginal community. During consultations for the Law Reform Commission of Western Australia, Aboriginal men spoke with pride when relating how they would 'stand up' or 'show a leg' for punishment. What's more, this punishment meant that the matter was over and resolved. It is difficult for non-Indigenous people to acknowledge this form of violence as a form of 'reintegration ceremony', yet for many Aboriginal people, this is precisely what these processes of ritual violence do. For Aboriginal men in particular, rituals of physical punishment mirror the physical markings of male initiation.

Long-term loss of a family member through banishment or jail is a profligate luxury that Aboriginal communities – where everyone has a role and function and multiple responsibilities – can ill afford. Traditionally, punishment ceremonies were tightly controlled and supervised by senior members of the Indigenous community. The damage done to the fabric of the Indigenous domain by colonisation has, however created deep problems. Where controls over the process have broken down due to community fragmentation these ceremonies have occasionally become alcohol charged private acts of vengeance rather than ritualised punishment. Aboriginal people today have conditions such as diabetes and heart disease making any wounding likely to increase chances of serious illness or death. Nevertheless, physical punishment is a fact of life in many parts of the Aboriginal domain and those bound by law most often consent to it being carried out. In some instances, Aboriginal offenders face 'double punishment' from within the community and from the western legal system. Many want to have matters in their own communities handled quickly; failure to do so may mean that a relative will have to face punishment. Also, those carrying out the punishment – and they may have no options within Aboriginal law not to carry out punishment – may face charges within the western legal system.

While not condoning the use of physical violence, the West Australian Inquiry acknowledged a number of inconsistencies and contradictions in mainstream opposition to spearing and recognised the need to reduce instances of double punishment. As it stands, the law maintain that a person cannot consent to a wounding. However, people do it every day when they participate in sports like boxing or karate or, more routinely, seek all kinds of body piercing and enhancement which certainly 'wound', in the sense of breaking the skin.[2] In its final report, the Law Reform Commission of Western Australia (2006b) treads cautiously and, once again, rejects blanket approval of Aboriginal punishment while seeking understanding on a case-by-case basis. The link between Aboriginal law and violence has been asserted in the context of violence against women. It is to this presumed link between Aboriginal law and violence that we next turn.

Notes

1   People marrying outside of 'skin' relationships.
2   I am grateful to Neil Morgan for raising these particular examples and for discussion about the physical punishment versus confinement debate.

10

Aboriginal Customary Law:
From Recognition to Abolition

Many Aboriginal communities, in urban, rural and remote regions of Australia exist in conditions of endemic crisis. While a string of research projects has identified violence as an issue in many Aboriginal communities, irrespective of location, it is remote, 'outback', communities that have become the focal point for concern in recent months: spurred by some particularly alarming reports of violence against women and children. Peter Sutton (2001) suggests that violence in remote communities tends to be more visible, confronting and engulfing than violence in other communities. War analogies are routinely deployed to describe daily existence in remote Aboriginal communities: one influential journalist article describes a sizable chunk of central Australia as 'a virtual war zone', a 'closed cramped realm marked out increasingly by alcoholism, boredom, domestic violence, petrol sniffing and drug abuse' (Rothwell 2006).[1] Rothwell suggests that communities be subjected to 'a system of benign social control'. There is broad agreement that something needs to be done to halt the communal violence. However, there is considerable, indeed heated, disagreement about causes and solutions. The dominant discourse on Aboriginal violence currently privileges explanations focused squarely on Aboriginal culture itself as the problem, particularly the persistence of what is frequently – and erroneously – describes as 'tribal law' which, allegedly, excuses domestic violence and the rape of children. Moreover, it is argued, the violence has been allowed to continue because the criminal justice system is soft on male Indigenous offenders who claim customary rights in mitigation. Some feminists working in the Aboriginal context also point to traditional law as the problem and a tradition of violence against women with deeps roots in Aboriginal culture (Kimm 2004). Interviewed on ABC Radio (2006a), Jane Lloyd from the Ngaanyatjarra Pitjantjatjara Yankunytjatjara (NPY) Women's Council suggests that there is 'a history and tradition of violence, especially in Western Desert cultures. It's become more extreme'. Solutions tend to be posed in terms of tougher law and order and zero tolerance policing of remote communities.

These solutions have been articulated in parallel with demands that we abandoned what is perceived to be a form of political correctness, which places criticism of Aboriginal culture off limits. Former federal Health Minister, Tony Abbott, for example, argued that political correctness has stymied criticism of the failures of Aboriginal self-management. Mr Abbott spoke of the need for a 'new paternalism' to provide effective administration for 'directionless' communities (Abbott 2006). While Abbott acknowledged past injustices, he suggested that it is communities themselves who must take responsibility for the widening gap between Aboriginal and non-Aboriginal health: about 70% of Indigenous Australians die before 65, compared with 20% of other Australians. It is not just politicians, however, who have pointed the finger at self-determination. A number of prominent academics and researchers have criticised what they see as a tendency to romanticise Aboriginal community life. The anthropologist Peter Sutton, for example, argues that we need urgently to ask a number of 'bedrock questions, with all bets off' (Sutton 2001: 125), including questioning the desirability of 'artificially perpetuating "outback ghettos" or other similar bureaucratically maintained institutions' (Sutton 2001: 125). These criticisms have paralleled increasing calls for the elimination of remote Aboriginal communities considered to be unsustainable.[2]

The attitude of the judiciary to Aboriginal violence has come in for criticism. In the wake of a number of well-publicised cases where Aboriginal men have received either short or non-custodial sentences when claiming customary rights, former Prime Minister John Howard criticised State government inaction on Aboriginal violence and for maintaining what are essentially two separate legal systems, arguing that 'the same treatment and the same law [should be] applied by the same courts to all Australians irrespective of their ethnic background' (Howard 2006). The 'two laws' issue has taken on particular resonance for many on the political Right in Australia: for whom it symbolises the unfinished business of nation-building. For these groups, the very existence of a people claiming pre-existing ownership of the continent and maintaining a set of traditional practices incommensurable with mainstream Australian values is an anathema which somehow diminishes the national totality and dilutes sovereignty. The solution is 'one law for all Australians'.

In this chapter, I critically examine the discourses currently surrounding Aboriginal communal violence in Australia and the range of solutions currently on offer to resolve the problem. I want to suggest that, in our haste to resolve the problem of violence, we should not abandon belief in Aboriginal agency as a necessary component of strategies to improve governance within Aboriginal communities. Nor should we abandon dialogue with Aboriginal law and culture. By targeting Aboriginal law and culture as the central problem, I suggest, we rob Aboriginal people of their capacity to engage with mainstream agencies from a position of cultural strength, and close off potential areas of partnerships between Indigenous communities and the justice system.

The discourse around Aboriginal law neatly inverts many of the themes about Aboriginal people found in the restorative justice movement. In place of the peace-loving Indigene and wholesome references to pre-modern rituals of dispute resolution, we find that darker Other of colonial myth, the brutal Indigenous world of ritualised abuse and violence: the image of gentle Pocahontas has been replaced by the uncivilised savage. Both sets of images conform to those Orientalist representations of the Other in its exotically idyllic or remorselessly uncivilised form.

Both pictures exist only as part of colonial discourse; they are distorted representation of Indigenous law and culture. Many Aboriginal women (said to be the principle victims of culture) maintain that it is culture and *cultural authority* that provide the basis for strategies aimed at reducing levels of violence in Aboriginal communities. In sharp contrast to many who wish to rescue them from beneath the dead weight of tradition, most Aboriginal women want to see solutions, which strengthen, not eradicate, Aboriginal law and culture. As I shall demonstrate, many of the positive initiatives taking place on Aboriginal communities have been driven by Aboriginal women, and many of these would argue that they derive their authority to act from within the very law and culture many white activists believe oppresses them, and from which they need to be rescued.

Some Indigenous commentators are suspicious of white interest in the 'plight' of Aboriginal women, and see continuities with colonial strategies of dismantling Aboriginal culture, as Pat Dodson suggests:

> [T]hroughout the 'protection', 'assimilation', 'integration' eras of the twentieth century, Aboriginal women have been consciously nominated targets of government in its pursuit to destabilise and dismantle Aboriginal society. (Dodson 1991: 377)

There is a tendency to de-culturise Aboriginal women, as though they were always the objects of cultural practice rather than active carriers and creators of culture. This returns us to the days when anthropologists theorised that law and culture were strictly the domain of men, while women remained outside law. In opposition to the picture presented in the mainstream media about Aboriginal law causing or legitimising violence disorder, I want to suggest that it is our refusal to enter into a dialogue with Aboriginal law that remains at the centre of the issue. Deliberate and protracted attempts to curtail the influence of Aboriginal law by white system of justice and governance have created not 'one law' but lawlessness and profound anomie. First let us briefly review some recent revelations concerning Aboriginal violence.

Aboriginal violence in the news

As we saw in relation to family violence, there have been a number of credible sources of information in the public and official domain detailing extreme levels of violence in Aboriginal communities. Yet, anyone observing recent media coverage of violence in remote Aboriginal communities could be forgiven for thinking that the issue had suddenly been visited upon us from the sky. The interesting question is not 'why is there violence in Indigenous communities', but 'why is the issue being aired now?' Numerous research papers have been written on the scale of the problems in central and other parts of Australia, which have not sparked this level of coverage (for a review see Memmott et al 2001). The sudden 'discovery' of Aboriginal violence in central Australia by a number of accredited white sources in May 2006, however, generated sustained coverage. This may be because the ways in which these issues were framed in the media makes them more newsworthy because they have focused on the sensational and the dramatic. They have presented Aboriginal law and culture as the essential source of the problem: helpfully exculpating – with the possible exception of white judges and defence lawyers in the Northern Territory – white society from responsibility. What is interesting about the 'debate' about violence in Aboriginal communities was that it took place between white people: the white media, white feminists, white lawyers, white journalists and white politicians framed and presented the issues largely without input from Indigenous people: they believed, as in the quote from Karl Marx, Aboriginal people were incapable of representing themselves, they had to be represented.

Revelations of entrenched sexual violence against women and children in central Australia, voiced by Northern Territory crown prosecutor Nannette Rogers in May

2006, grabbed public attention. Interviewed on ABC's *Lateline* program, when asked about the tendency to secrecy in Aboriginal communities on issues of violence she said:

> I think there are a number of reasons for that. The first is that violence is entrenched in a lot of aspects of Aboriginal society here. Secondly, Aboriginal people choose not to take responsibility for their own actions. Thirdly, Aboriginal society is very punitive so that if a report is made or a statement is made implicating an offender then that potential witness is subject to harassment, intimidation and sometimes physical assault if the offender gets into trouble because of that report or police statement. (ABC Television 2006a)

Rogers went on to document instances of extreme sexual violence against women and children. Very few of Rogers' revelations were new on their own, however, articulated together they formed a vivid and immediate portrait of an extreme crisis situation. Other examples of hyper-violence soon circulated in the media, including claims that Aboriginal men are deliberately setting fire to their wives:

> The nightmare of substance abuse among Aboriginal men has taken on another deadly dimension, with an alarming increase in the number of Indigenous women being set on fire by angry, violent partner. (Skelton & Milovanovic 2006)

No baseline date was presented against which to measure this 'increase'; the reference to the 'nightmare' of substance abuse was sufficient corroboration. Besides Nannette Rogers, the other key respondents and accredited source of information on Aboriginal culture and customary practices was Jane Lloyd of NPY Women's Council, described by Kerry O'Brien on the ABC's *7.30 Report* as 'representing' Aboriginal women on a number of remote communities. Lloyd maintains that a veil of secrecy hides the extent of violence on Indigenous communities, often attributable to customary law: violence has to be stamped out, starting at the top with the Indigenous male leadership:

> We have to make sure that the Indigenous leadership are in fact not perpetrators of abuse against women and kids. And that … from my experience … frequently Aboriginal men who hold positions of public office in remote communities and on other Indigenous bodies are in fact perpetrators of abuse, and Government continues to do business with them … So what message does that give to women and children in those communities? … That these men can hold such office and that Government then takes them seriously and does business with them. (Jane Lloyd, ABC Television 2006c)

Nanette Rogers' comments were rapidly picked up by federal Indigenous Affairs Minister Mal Brough, who maintained that 'paedophile networks and petrol barons' operated in Aboriginal communities, and there were allegations of endemic violence and networks of abusers on the Mutitjulu community in the Northern Territory, once again aired on the ABC's *Lateline* program (ABC Television 2006b).

At this stage in the debate, Aboriginal women's voices were not accorded accredited status – helpless, hopeless victims of extreme male violence these 'subalterns' could not speak, they were, at least at this stage in the coverage, spoken for. The same *Lateline* Program (ABC Television 2006b) also interviewed an anonymous source, claiming to be a 'former youth worker', who reported that on Mutitjulu those 'in control are the drug dealers and the petrol warlords and the paedophiles'. The youth worker's coyness can perhaps be explained by the fact that he wasn't a youth worker at all but a former staffer in Minster Mal Brough's office. Although Mutijulu community women unequivocally refuted the allegations that a 'paedophile ring, child sex slaves, petrol warlords, murder, kidnappings, gangs, arson and cliques of violent Aboriginal men are part of life at Mutitjulu' *(Sydney Morning Herald* 2006), their views were not covered by *Lateline*.

Aboriginal victims of Aboriginal men

The narratives surrounding responses to violence in Indigenous communities in recent years indicates that Aboriginal women and children are being acknowledged as victims of crime. The question then is: what kinds of 'victim'? The history of victimology suggests that there is no unproblematic and unified definition of a victim existing independently of the social, policing, judicial and ideological practices that structure and construct the victim in particular times and particular places. Aboriginal social relations, particularly around the control of Aboriginal women and children, have been a consistent source of anxiety for white Australia. Aboriginal women's bodies have acted as a palimpsest for the inscription of white fears of unrestrained native sexuality, as represented particularly by the tribal Aboriginal male. They come together particularly powerfully in the context of issues such as 'promised marriages', where Aboriginal girls are betrothed to older men. Anna Haebich (2000) discusses the case of the Aboriginal child Lorna, from the Northern Territory, who was fostered out by the child's family (temporarily, they believed, to a white family, until she was healthy – she was a premature birth). The family then found they could not get the child back – despite repeated attempts. There was a particularly bitter court case. Headlines in the newspaper said that the seven-year-old Lorna would be returned to a promised marriage to an older man. The white couple that had temporary care of Lorna were elevated to the status of parents, whose rights were violated by the uncivilised blacks intent on stealing 'their' child. 'Lorna', for purposes of the narrative, ceases to be an Aboriginal child from within a cluster of relationships but an isolated child in need of protection from primitives intent on imposing barbaric sexual practices on her. Haebich goes on:

> As anthropologist Les Hiatt later endeavoured to explain ... while Aboriginal girls were 'promised' to older men, marriages were not consummated before puberty and the whole system of betrothal and marriage involved complex and strictly regulated sets of social and ritual relationships conducted over many years which bound all parties in a mesh of overlapping ties and responsibilities. (Haebich 2000: 594)

The question of promised marriages continues to create tension and confusion. The practice itself is increasingly uncommon in contemporary Aboriginal society. The process of *promising* and the rituals and social ceremonies around it continue in remote areas, as part of the round of social occasions intended to cement and renew those 'overlapping ties and responsibilities' noted by Les Hiatt. It is rare, however, at least in Western Australia, for young people to go through marriage of any kind without their consent. Young people increasingly marry people they want to marry – even where this conflicts with 'skin' arrangements and creates a headache for communities. The Law Reform Commission of Western Australia notes the declining adherence to promised marriages, while maintaining that – in keeping with international law – measures need to be taken to prevent non-consensual traditional marriages and non-consensual sexual relations within any marriage (Law Reform Commission of Western Australia 2006a: 272; see also Aboriginal & Torres Strait Islander Social Justice Commissioner 2006). The commission calls for better information and education, in relation to freedom of choice, and the law in relation to sexual relations with children under the age of 16. Promised marriages – particularly where the husband claims rights of sexual access to a young girl – have been rare events in Western Australia and the Northern Territory for some years.

The interesting question is, why have *any claims by Aboriginal men* to be acting in accordance with traditional practice been accepted in some courts in the Northern Territory in cases involving sexual relations with children with such confidence and certainty? The 2002 *Pascoe* case raises some interesting issues. The case involved an Aboriginal man who violently sexually assaulted his 15-year-old promised bride and was sentenced to 13 months' imprisonment on the charge of unlawful sexual intercourse. This sentence was reduced to 24 hours on appeal, Justice Gallop accepting the defence counsel's assertions – based on 'expert' anthropological testimony – that his actions had the sanction of customary law and practice (*Hales v Jamilmara* (2003) 13 NTLR 14). The Law Reform Commission of Western Australia, in five years of consultations with remote communities in Western Australia (which included a number of meetings with senior law people, with separate men and women's gatherings) in the Kimberley region, did not hear one voice saying that non-consensual marriage or non-consensual relations (of any kind) were part of Aboriginal law.

What were utterly absent in these debates about male entitlement under customary law are the voices of Indigenous women. It is noteworthy that powerful, accredited white sources on either side of the debate in the Northern Territory – some judges, defence counsel and anthropologists on one side, other judges and lawyers, women's organisations representatives and politicians on the other – in fact shared the same beliefs about Aboriginal law and culture: that Aboriginal men under law enjoyed total possession of Aboriginal women and had unfettered access to their bodies. The only difference was that one side believed it part of Aboriginal law and therefore a mitigating factor, while the other believed it part of Aboriginal law and therefore should be over-ridden. Both sides were acting on the basis of their 'knowledge' of Aboriginal law and the Aboriginal domain, as white people standing outside of Aboriginal law and Aboriginal culture.

'Aboriginal culture: inimical to women?'

Does the moral panic surrounding presumed, culturally sanctioned, Aboriginal violence simply provide comfort to those wishing to downplay the damage wrought by colonisation and shift the focus back on Aboriginal culture itself as fundamentally misogynistic? Joan Kimm's influential book *A Fatal Conjunction: Two Laws, Two Cultures* (2004) has been picked up by a number of commentators as providing factual support for the proposition that Aboriginal men legitimate patriarchal violence against Aboriginal women through Aboriginal law. Journalists have not been slow in enlisting Kimm's work as part of a broad attack on traditional Aboriginal culture. Rosemary Neil (2006) concludes, 'it's clear that some aspects of traditional Aboriginal culture are deeply inimical to women', citing Kimm's work.

These interpretations of Kimm's work are highly selective, ignoring the emphasis she places on the impact of colonisation and the damage caused to, particularly male, roles.

Kimm sees Aboriginal women caught within two forms of patriarchal law, white and Indigenous. The extent to which traditional society routinely employed violence against women remains an issue of debate. Many Aboriginal women maintain that violence was not an accepted part of Aboriginal culture (Smallwood 1996), and there have always been misgivings in the Aboriginal community regarding the assumed impartiality, reliability and objectivity of observations made by white, male anthropologists on this topic. However, there have been instances where such observations about culture have been accorded greater status than those of Aboriginal law women (McGlade 2006).

Certainly, as we saw in relation to family violence, Aboriginal narratives on violence focus on the *breakdown* of law, the impact of colonialism and the destruction of Aboriginal community structures through alcohol abuse, the multiple and cumulative effects of government policy, the theft of land and the crushing effects of removal policies, as the landscape against which communal violence needs to be set.

Anthropologist Catherine Wohlan (2005), basing her ethnographic work with Aboriginal women and Aboriginal law in the remote Kimberley region of Western Australia, where Aboriginal law is particularly strong, makes a number of observation regarding Kimm's (2004) thesis: criticising it on three inter-related grounds. First, that the violence Kimm describes 'appears to have little *justification* under Aboriginal systems of law', there is no 'moral' basis for violence, as Kimm asserts: secondly, 'from an anthropological perspective Kimm's work suffers from Eurocentrism in *interpreting* the status of Aboriginal women' and, thirdly, Kimm's 'assertion of the centrality of the *Australian legal system* in dealing with violence' (Wohlan 2005, emphasis added). These three linked levels of criticism raise serious concerns. Based on her own work with Aboriginal women, Wohlan disputes Kimm's findings that violence against women has a place in Aboriginal law; and she critiques Kimm for imposing her own *interpretations* as a white woman on to the experiences of Aboriginal women. Finally, she questions the privileging of a non-Aboriginal structure of law as a solution to the problem of violence. Wohlan goes on to question those representations of Aboriginal women as docile and passive objects of law and culture, as only 'circumscribed by their culture', and never 'empowered by it'.

I have argued that the debate about Aboriginal violence has largely been conducted without input from Aboriginal women – and when women have been involved, as in the Mutitjulu example – they have done so largely on a terrain constructed for them by white people. It seems particularly important, therefore, that the voices of Indigenous women be given particular prominence in any future discussion of Aboriginal law and Aboriginal violence. Two recent interventions by respected Aboriginal women – Koori woman and researcher on family violence Kylie Cripps (2005) and Nyoongar woman and human rights lawyer Hannah McGlade (2006) – therefore deserve close attention. Both have been involved in critiquing representations of Aboriginal women within the white legal system and those presumptions of cultural entitlement to violence paraded in the courts in mitigation for violence against women and children.

Cripps, in her review of *A Fatal Conjunction,* argues that family violence seriously damages Aboriginal communities, and disputes the claim that violence is acceptable within Aboriginal law. She questions whether white anthropology provides a reliable source of knowledge about Aboriginal society before colonisation, particularly in rela-tion to whether traditional culture permitted violence against women, as reflective of the beliefs and power of a dominant group (Cripps 2005). She has more sympathy for Kimm's assertion that the legal system has been ineffective in dealing with violence against women – and not just Indigenous victims (see also Cripps & Taylor 2007), and, based on her own research on the topic, she states:

> Indigenous women and children receive a very clear message that the legal system is not a place where equality between the sexes or races exists; nor can the kind of justice Indigenous people are seeking be served. To the contrary, it condones the violence and relegates Indigenous women and children to the periphery of society. It is therefore not surprising that women are not choosing to use the system in their battle against family violence. (Cripps 2005: 2)

Cripps is also critical of Kimm's reliance on legal cases as the basis for hypothesis and the absence in Kimm's book of the voices of Aboriginal women and children, as well as questioning Kimm's authority to speak on their behalf.

Hannah McGlade sees the challenge in terms of a comprehensive process of human rights education and awareness within both Aboriginal communities and also within the criminal justice system to challenge distorted beliefs about cultural entitle-ments to violence, and a particular focus on the fact that traditional practices around promised marriages have changed and old practices are no longer acceptable (McGlade 2006: 10). She also makes the crucial point that – far from the issue necessitating further annexation of the Aboriginal domain by the white system of justice – there is a need to acknowledge the role that elders (particularly women elders) can play in the denunciation, censure and punishment of offenders, an idea incommensurate with the dominant trend towards actively minimising the role of Indigenous culture in the resolution of family violence matters. Here McGlade notes the important role played by 'Aboriginal justice models … such as Sentence Circles or Koori Courts', that 'allow Aboriginal Elders and communities to address their own law and order issues and play an important role within the criminal justice process' (McGlade 2006: 9). She notes that sexual assault cases are often excluded from these processes, but she suggests that they should not be 'automatically precluded' from involvement (2006: 9)

Kimm had expressed serious misgivings about how the Law Reform Commission of Western Australia's Customary Law Inquiry (2006b) would handle the issue of dialogue with 'elders and custodians of traditional law' on the issue of family violence (Kimm 2004: 144), noting that the worst violence takes place in traditional communi-ties, where law is strongest (a massive generalisation) and where 'traditional gender patterns are still intact' (Kimm 2004: 145). She asks the questions: will the inquiry reinstate customary rights to violence? Will it remove the rights of Indigenous women to protection under the law? She expresses the hope that that the inquiry offers an opportunity for women to speak independently.

Perhaps a brief report on the project will allay some of these concerns. Consul-tations with remote communities in the Kimberley region – usually said to be the most traditional – found no support for the kinds of traditional violence identified by Kimm: it also found a vibrant women's law underpinned by traditional practices of dancing, singing and observance of ceremony. Women were given space to speak independently. Separate women's meetings were held, including participation in a women's camp as part of a major cultural festival at Wuggubun in the East Kimberley. Aboriginal women with language and cultural skills were involved in the process. The commission also did a follow-up meeting in Fitzroy Crossing – the most culturally based and culturally assertive town in the Kimberly at the invitation of the community – including a string delegation of women to discuss justice issues further. This was not to berate the committee about traditional violence but to make the white justice agencies, particularly the police, accountable for their actions in relation to a death in custody, failure to intervene in drug issues and over-policing.

Many of these remote communities have been devastated by the interference of missions, land theft, child theft and attempts to dismantle them. Traditional structures have struggled to retain control over daily life in the face of the destruction of traditional rights to land, hunting and access to sacred sites, along with a host of new problems associated with employment, extreme poverty, enforced idleness, health and alcohol. The women's message was that, if anything, women enjoyed greater respect and acknowledgement in the old days than they do today, because of the increasing pressures on Aboriginal communities from the outside. The commission found no evidence of a traditional right to violence outside of those strictly regulated practices of traditional punishment. Nor did the commission hear any claims that such violence was or is justifiable and should be recognised by the white legal system. Also the commission's recommendations have not included any suggestion that Aboriginal women's protections under the law should be diluted in any way.

Perhaps the key question emerging from the debate over violence in Indigenous communities is: what is to be done? Does the empowerment of Aboriginal women and children require emancipating them from the culture, which, some claim, oppresses them and provides 'moral justification' for violence? Is the answer armouring them with the protections of the white law and extending its web of law and policing? Some observers insist that the white law is currently structurally incapable of dealing sensitively and compassionately with Aboriginal victims of violence and is itself a site of oppression and violence. As we have noted, Aboriginal women often have negative experiences of the white legal system. They are massively over-represented in the criminal justice system and do not see the police, in particular, as there to protect them.

Kimm acknowledges a need to work on a number of levels when addressing family violence and of the need to respect women's cultural integrity and autonomy (Kimm 2004: 154) and she supports many of the initiatives initiated by Aboriginal women such as Night Patrols, and the Northern Territory law and justice strategies, as well as a cluster of successful community projects on domestic violence and sexual assault. She also, rather problematically perhaps, sees a role for 'some customary laws' and cites with approval instances where communities have taken control over parts of the justice process (Kimm 2004: 156). The parts of Kimm's work, however, which have grasped attention have tended to be those aspects of her work which, however sophisticated her argument, situate violence within the moral framework afforded by customary law.

Kimm also – strangely for someone who has worked within the legal system – professes a rather touching faith in the capacity of our legal system, and its regime of punishments to deter Aboriginal offenders. Prison is, as I have already made clear, in some instances, a source of pain, but rarely of shame for Aboriginal people. The degradation ceremonies announcing arrival do not cast out or banish, they do not mortify a *public* status because few Aboriginal men have a public status to lose. Their position within the Aboriginal domain is not threatened, and occasionally it is even enhanced. Prison is but one of a range of kindred institutions introduced to capture and contain Aboriginal Australians. Aboriginal people are not deterred from offending by the currents system. Nor are they shamed by the threat of the police arriving at their door and arresting them.

Intersecting cultures

While Aboriginal law continues to provide maps of meaning for Aboriginal people in their daily lives, it does so in a dynamic relationship with the dominant culture, which constantly intrudes upon and sets limits to its influence. Many Aboriginal people, particularly, though not exclusively those living in remote regions of Australia, live still structured by traditional law and custom. I have yet to meet an Aboriginal person – as opposed to a lawyer representing an Aboriginal person – who believes the violence reported by Nannette Rogers (ABC Television 2006a), or others, is either sanctioned or excused by Aboriginal law. Women, in particular, are outraged by the proposition.

The violence we are seeing now may be less the product of Aboriginal culture, in the sense of some self-reproducing and absolutely autonomous entity, being acted out, but rather a manifestation of the damage caused to the fabric of Aboriginal law and society by the intrusion on some of the most negative and destructive aspects of non-Aboriginal culture. These have generated a number of problems which Aboriginal law and culture was never designed to handle: alcohol and drugs, unregulated sexual relationships and the impact of institutionalisation among them.

It should also be borne in mind that the meeting-ground between Aboriginal and non-Aboriginal society was, and still often is, a white institution. Aboriginal people have received socialisation within white institutions. Some of the violence we are now witnessing may be less a reflection of Aboriginal culture than the expression of rage by those who are the 'object of systematic benign or derogatory inferiorization' by white society (Cowlishaw 2003: 124). Cowlishaw's focus here on benevolent forms of 'inferiorization' – the condescension, the oppressive paternalism – sets her work apart from many other commentators:

> The subordinates' vehemence can be expressive, fearful, and shameless and is directed toward those whose control depends on a violence that is usually hidden and denied or deemed necessary and legitimate. (Cowlishaw 2003: 124)

Peter Sutton's intervention on the issue of culturally sanctioned violence is not without contradictions. He cites with approval Kunitz's (1994) statement that 'traditional modes of socialisation and social control, contribute to the problem of violence' in Aboriginal communities (Sutton 2001). However, despite the references to traditional Aboriginal culture as the problem in his 2001 essay, Sutton also subtly qualifies his approval for the Kunitz thesis when he describes patterns of violence by Aboriginal men against

Aboriginal women as 'manifestations of a particular kind of culture located *where Indigenous and non-Indigenous societies intersect*' (Sutton 2001, emphasis added). This distinctly interactive process is rather more modulated than the assertion that violence is a product of traditional Aboriginal culture *per se*. It implies that the culture of violence is generated at the 'intersection' between traditional culture and white society. Sutton does go on to reject the argument that violence is the, 'outcome of dispossession, discrimination, alienation, poverty, stress, and the historically new drugs' (Sutton 2001), and he maintains that inuring 'culture' against criticism as part of the 'official discourse' has been part of the problem.

Sutton's brief reference to points of intersection between Aboriginal and non-Aboriginal cultures could do with rather more fleshing than it receives in his work – which devotes itself largely to criticising political correctness. What does 'intersection' mean precisely in relation to the Aboriginal and non-Aboriginal worlds? Intersection assumes connecting points between two distinctive phenomena. I have already argued that intersections ('frontiers') provide a focal point for conflict, violence and hyper-marginalisation. It is precisely at these points where Aboriginal people are constantly being dispossessed, discriminated against, alienated, impoverished, traumatised, sold drugs: where they have to deal with the consequences of living in an asymmetrical relationship with a powerful alien culture, where the labels are applied, where stigma is inscribed.

Aboriginal narratives about violence in their communities constantly relate the indwelling connectedness of initial dispossession, institutionalisation, marginalisation and violence as structural processes, which join together individual biography and collective experience. The damage wrought by years of systemic racism, neglect, over-policing (in public space), under-policing (as victims), institutionalisation and deracination has created violent, oppositional sub-cultures: but these sub-cultures are, I would like to suggest, kept alive by the bleakness of much Aboriginal communal life on the one hand and interaction with non-Aboriginal systems (police, prisons) on the other. To adapt a term by Colin Tatz, it is this peculiar concentration of circumstances that makes Aboriginal violence 'different' (Tatz 2001a). It is also important to preface any discussion about violence in Aboriginal communities by recognising how frequently violence is turned inwards against the self as it is outwards towards the other: obliteration of the outside world through alcohol drugs, nihilistic violence against intimates and the intimate self. Tatz writes not of violence as 'traditional' practice, but 'a new violence, of which suicide is but one facet' (Tatz 2001a: 81). This new violence is a consequence of multiple factors and is not reducible to a single, or single group, of causes.

Sub-cultures of violence within Aboriginal communities are no more *representative* of Aboriginal culture *per se* than violent prison cultures and bikie gangs are of mainstream culture. Understanding them requires an analysis of the relationship with the dominant culture and the physical and epistemic violence brought with colonisation. As Patrick Dodson writes:

> Violence is a common factor that underlies the history of contact between Aboriginal and non-Aboriginal people. The interference over Aboriginal peoples' lives, by both church and government, has involved non-Aboriginal people using

both structured and personal acts of violence to dominate and control Aboriginal people. Communities have strong memories of the various degrees of violence they endured ... the depredations which miners, pastoralists, explorers and pearl fishers inflicted upon the people and especially the women. (Dodson 1991: 368)

These forms of violence represent the imposition of white power of Aboriginal people, across a range of sites. White society remains uneasy about exploring the role of violence in colonisation or the use of state-sanctioned violence in war and genocide within 'civilised' Europe in the 20th century. The civilising process, Norbert Elias (2000) reminds us, banned violence from the street while legitimating it within the arena of the state both in terms of day to day policing and in the military. It also sanitised violence against the weakest members of society – children – when it became redefined as pedagogy (Miller 1994) and carried out in the best interests of the recipient. There is a revealing passage in Barry Hill's magisterial biography of TGH Strehlow (Hill 2003) revealing how Strehlow's father Carl – strict Lutheran, heir to its 'long tradition of brutal parental authority' (Hill 2003: 70) and founder of the Hermansburg Mission in Central Australia – routinely thrashed his son in a manner the 'savages [sic]' found frightening and murderous: they railed against the 'sadistic pedagogy of the white man' and were excessively lenient in their approach to child rearing.[3]

In the next chapter I want to illustrate ways in which Aboriginal people – including women – are being empowered through participation in community justice mechanisms operating in the liminal space between Indigenous and non-Indigenous domains, creating hybrid initiatives of a kind that leave Aboriginal law alone while helping to resolve the issues that Aboriginal law alone cannot resolve.

Notes

1   Rothwell believes that the source of the problem lies largely with Aboriginal people themselves, the system of self-management and self-determination and the legacy of Nugget Coombs – architect of self-determination policies in the wake of the 19767 referendum – who seems to be a convenient scapegoat for problems such as Aboriginal poverty, crime, dysfunctional community syndrome, corruption and mismanagement. For a more balanced perspective on Coombs and his legacy, see Rowse (2000).

2   The *West Australian* ('Aboriginals Face Closure of Camps', 10 May 2006) reported that both State Government and Commonwealth politicians favoured shutting down many remote communities because they are economically and socially unviable.

3   'Poisonous pedagogy', for example, violence in the name of child rearing, was identified by Miller (1994) as a feature of bourgeois societies.

11

Governance from Below: Community Justice Mechanisms, Crime and Disorder

Community justice mechanisms represent locally generated alternatives mechanisms for dealing with crime and conflict and for administering justice. Their objectives are to improve security and safety in Aboriginal communities, through a diversity of practices, including:

- community justice groups;
- local justice agreements and strategies;
- diversionary projects;
- 'on-country' cultural camps;
- mediation and dispute resolution schemes;
- community capacity building initiatives;
- night patrols;
- safe houses;
- healing centres;
- family violence prevention programs; and
- Aboriginal courts.

The emergence of Aboriginal community justice mechanisms in a variety of forms across Australia may signal a significant long-term shift in the way the justice 'business' is transacted between Aboriginal communities, government and the judiciary. Community-based projects designed to involve Aboriginal communities in the criminal justice process have been in existence across Australia for a number of years; however, most of these have been relatively ad hoc and informal, they have, therefore, tended to lack sustainability, being dependent on the energies and good will of a few key players (Aboriginal and non-Aboriginal) and prey to shifts in government policies and priorities.

Community justice mechanisms draw on the strength and resilience of the Aboriginal domain as the source of their cultural mandate. Government continues to give rhetorical backing to the principle of community involvement through justice mechanisms and has become reliant on the support of communities to administer some programs. Despite this, there is a considerable gap between Aboriginal and government interpretations of the meanings attached to terms such as community involvement that have implications for the future development of community justice strategies.

Community-based or community owned?

While there is some consensus between government and Indigenous communities about the need for greater Indigenous involvement in the justice process, there is considerable uncertainty over the precise form this involvement should take. Many community justice initiatives generated by government and criminal justice agencies have tended to be, what I will refer to as, community-*based* as opposed to community *owned*. Community-based services simply relocate the service to a community setting, rather than reformulating the fundamental premises upon which the service is constructed. Expressed another way, the community setting becomes a kind of annex to the existing structures of the system. Unfortunately, many justice agencies have tended to mistake community based for community owned and have, often unwittingly, appropriated the notion of community justice to further unreconstructed administrative and legislative agendas. Aboriginal notions of justice reform should not be confused with processes simply designed to either extend the reach of the existing justice system, or make the existing justice system run more smoothly: they may in fact challenge some dominant assumptions about the role of law and justice mechanisms in Aboriginal communities.

The issue of Indigenous control and management of justice initiatives has taken on greater significance as Aboriginal people claim Native Title to their land (some 80% of the land mass of the Kimberley region of Western Australia is now subject to a Native Title determination). Many are now asking: what does Native Title mean in relation to creating spaces of Aboriginal sovereignty? Clearly, the Native Title 'recognition space' is rigorously circumscribed. I am less concerned, however, by the legal constraints than on the potential for increased Indigenous governance as the 'status' of Native Title holders is translated into action on a local level.[1] The emergence of Prescribed Bodies Corporate (PBCs) under *Native Title Act 1993*, and their potential role in creating new hybrid spaces, new meeting places, between the Indigenous domain and the mainstream, offers a glimpse of the possibilities inherent in Native Title determination. For some years now Aboriginal people have been asking the question: what impact does the possession of Native Title have on broader relationships between local Indigenous groups and the settler state? Is it possible for PBCs to leverage off Native Title to become directly involved in establishing 'on-country' programs as an alternative to mainstream community-based justice initiatives? Perhaps linking them with engagement in the hybrid economy? Does possessing Native Title and creating a PBC not give local Indigenous groups a 'moral' claim on this terrain? A seat at the table when key decisions are being made (by police, corrections, children's protection, family violence agencies) that will impact significantly on the community? Thus far, some Aboriginal groups have expressed frustration with the failure of the bureaucratic imagination to grasp the potential here, and refusal to move away from an essentially paternalistic approach to Indigenous service deliver. For example, Aboriginal people involved in the Council of Australian Governments (COAG) initiative in the Katjungka/Trurabelan region expressed disappointment that the consultation process was based on the old 'welfare mentality' where bureaucrats – not communities – defined the issues and defined the suite of policy options. It was said that the fact that people now had Native Title meant that government should approach them as equal partners and not as welfare dependents. In this instance, community mechanisms were being viewed largely in 'service delivery' terms, where community structures are viewed as mechanisms for achieving the improved delivery of services that remain fundamentally the invention of non-Indigenous organisations.

One gathering of Aboriginal women in Western Australia in the mid-1990s, who came together to discuss the problem of Aboriginal family violence, made an incisive distinction between *programmatic* solutions to issues on communities (where resources are used to expand the capacity of government agencies to resolve a particular problem) and *community* solutions (where resources are invested in communities in a way that empowers them to resolve the particular problem) (Aboriginal Women's Task Force and the Aboriginal Justice Council 1995). These women wanted to see investment in community structures, such as women's safety committees, run by Aboriginal women, Aboriginal-run safe houses and forms of policing sensitive to the needs of Aboriginal women. Perhaps PBCs will create a new liminal space where such issues can be discussed.

The Australian Law Reform Commission's (ALRC) 1986 review of Aboriginal Customary Law found a significant investment by Indigenous people in the development of what they referred to as 'local justice mechanisms', involving 'increasing Aboriginal input in various ways in application of the general law'. Indeed, the ALRC found that communities were more interested in discussing these matters than the 'application of Aboriginal customary laws or practices' (Australian Law Reform Commission 1986: 7). The Royal Commission into Aboriginal Deaths in Custody (RCIADIC) found 'the concept of community involvement in the criminal justice process is one which Aboriginal people consistently supported (Johnson 1991: Vol 4, 29.2.32). Community involvement strategies are also in-step with emerging national and international good practice where Indigenous justice is concerned: a 'synthesis and synergy' approach to reform – involving a gradual convergence of Indigenous and non-Indigenous values, beliefs and practices (Haverman 1999: 7) Community justice mechanisms provide a pathway for the construction of what the Cape York Justice Study (Fitzgerald 2001) has called a 'vibrant and decentred Aboriginal Law'.

Communities defining their own solutions

There have been a number of initiatives in Australia concerned with increasing the degree of Aboriginal involvement in justice planning, although these have tended to be localised and have had mixed success in terms of shifting government agendas toward local planning as an overall government strategy. In the Northern Territory, local justice plans have been in existence for some years through the Northern Territory's 'Law and Justice' strategy, with long-running and well-embedded processes in Lajamanu, Ali-Curung and Yuendumu – discussed in Chapter 6 in relation to Night Patrols and community conflict resolution. A recent review of Aboriginal Customary Law in the Northern Territory recommended building on these initiatives: empowering Aboriginal communities to develop their own local plans, through which, 'each Aboriginal community will define its own problems and solutions' (Northern Territory Law Reform Commission 2005). The committee saw a particular need to develop local structures which would stimulate partnerships between communities and justice agencies, and envisaged a focus on 'alternative dispute resolution, a structured system of police cautioning protocols, a panel of experts to assist magistrates on issues of customary law and so on. They are part of the community developing its own strategies' (Northern Territory Law Reform Commission 2005).

According to the consultations undertaken for the inquiry,[2] community justice mechanisms should combine a number of key ingredients, including:

- a strong focus on achieving sustainability, durability and resilience in structures, processes and programs;
- a willingness to take into account Aboriginal law and culture in the way structures, processes and programs are devised and executed;
- a commitment to nurturing the necessary governance structures; and
- a process of capacity building, both in Aboriginal communities and in the government agencies that partner with them.

In recent years there have been a number of promising developments in Australia that offer, if not exactly a road map, then certainly a number of potential pathways to change. These include:

- Developments in Queensland, following the Cape York Justice Study (Fitzgerald 2001) and the Aboriginal and Torres Strait Islander Women's Task Force on Violence (2000): particularly around the establishment of local Community Justice Groups and Negotiation Tables.
- Innovatory structures and processes introduced under Aboriginal Justice Agreements in New South Wales and Victoria, leading to initiatives such Circle Sentencing and Aboriginal Courts (already discussed), as well as some very proactive mechanisms for ensuring Aboriginal participation, such as the Regional Aboriginal Justice Advisory Councils (RAJACs) in Victoria.
- Initiatives in the Northern Territory as part of the Territory's Law and Justice Strategy, such as the Kurduju Crime Prevention Committee structure.
- A number of processes of local consultation as part of Western Australia's Aboriginal Justice Agreement and the development of a number of local justice plans. Recent initiatives by the new Youth Justice Board in Western Australia which is finding a number of 'on-country' programs run and managed by Indigenous people.

The road to justice reform in Aboriginal Australia is littered with the wreckage of promising one-off initiatives, pilot projects and local strategies that have failed to be refunded, nurtured and maintained by government. Despite the energies of both Aboriginal and non-Aboriginal people involved in running programs in Aboriginal communities, they eventually fail, leaving bitterness and disillusionment in their wake.

Community justice mechanisms are what the crime prevention literature refers to as 'bottom up', as opposed to 'top down' initiatives, in that they place stress on processes which emerge organically from within community structures and lay the groundwork for partnership with government and bureaucracy from a position of community strength. Top-down initiatives tend to be arranged and orchestrated by bureaucracies on behalf of government and *work on*, rather than *work with*, communities. They require sustained support from government to work. This point cannot be over-stated.

The weakness of the so-called self-determination approach that replaced assimilation as government policy, was the degree to which government was able to wash its hands of Aboriginal communities in the name of self-management. Sustainability, sound governance and capacity building are now widely acknowledged and may be key factors in achieving long-term success.

Preventing crime and disorder

Preventing crime and disorder in Aboriginal communities is of crucial importance. Not only is crime prevention an important goal in itself, reducing levels of crime and disorder may also be an essential pre-requisite for establishing other healthy structures on communities, which may otherwise rendered dysfunctional by alcohol and substance abuse, family violence and anti-social behaviour. A review of crime prevention and Aboriginal people by Cunneen (2001a) suggests that community-owned initiatives are needed to counter the failure of mainstream criminal justice system to reduce levels of offending and victimisation in Aboriginal communities or reduce levels of over-representation. A number of inquiries into problems of disorder and victimisation in Australian Indigenous communities have also pointed to systemic failure by the justice system (Fitzgerald 2001; Aboriginal and Torres Strait Islander Women's Task Force 2000; Memmott et al 2001). Cunneen argues that simply rolling out crime prevention programs devised for urban, non-Indigenous contexts into Aboriginal communities without considering issues related to Indigenous participation and control, the principle of self-determination and the diverse needs of Aboriginal people in urban, rural and remote locations, is a recipe for continued failure (Cunneen 2001a). Crime prevention programs most suited to Aboriginal contexts are those providing a holistic framework, as Cunneen observes in relation to family violence prevention:

> The common themes in evaluations of family violence programmes include the need for holistic approaches, the utilisation of community development models which emphasize self-determination and community ownership, the provision of culturally sensitive treatment which respects traditional law and customs and involves existing structures of authority such as elders, including women. (Cunneen 2001a: 9)

Community-based crime prevention initiatives of this kind are badly needed on Aboriginal communities. These initiatives should be tailored through consultation with Aboriginal communities to meet the specific needs of the community and focus on developing mechanisms for reducing contact with the formal criminal justice system. The Cape York Justice Study (Fitzgerald 2001) identified community crime prevention as a priority area for action on the Cape. The study astutely observes:

> In the area of crime and justice, these strategies will need to be complemented by more specific community-based crime prevention and intervention strategies and initiatives. As far as the formal criminal justice system is concerned, these community-based strategies must be supported by efforts to divert offenders to these community-based interventions as far as possible. (Fitzgerald 2001: 113)

There is recognition here that the existing criminal justice system must work with and support community initiatives and 'be more sensitive and responsive to Indigenous needs and circumstances to ensure that it does not, as is presently the case, make things worse' (Fitzgerald 2001: 113). The three key strategies identified in the study – crime prevention, diversion and improved mainstream justice – are emblematic of a new approach to Indigenous justice issues.

Crime prevention strategies may need to nurture stable community structures as a prerequisite for the successful intervention in a number of areas. However, many Indigenous communities lack the necessary infrastructure within which to embed social crime prevention initiatives. As Hazelhurst argues:

> When considering the social reconstructive potential of crime prevention, we quickly realise that that it may well be futile to attempt to separate objectives to reduce crime from social development issues. In the absence of a 'community base', 'community based crime prevention' is a theory in search of reality. (Hazelhurst 1995a: xxi)

Thinking differently about crime prevention may involve having to nurture the community base at the same time as developing crime prevention strategies. This is a complex process (which is why we so often get it wrong) requiring considerable inter-agency coordination and constant attention to the issues of participation and control highlighted in Cunneen's study. Reviewing practice on a global level related to Indigenous crime prevention, Capobianco and Shaw (2003) argue:

> Given the severity of the problems facing Indigenous populations, the arguments for building programmes which are cross-cutting and 'whole of government' are even greater. The urgency of a proactive approach to community safety which recognises the strong links between social and economic factors, and the health of their communities, is greater among Indigenous populations than in any other population group. (Capobianco & Shaw 2003: 6)

Expanding the notion of crime prevention to include broader issues of community safety is very much a feature of contemporary crime prevention thinking in Australia and stems from work on international best practice (Tilley 2005).

Multiple risk factors

It is now widely accepted, for example, that risk factors linked to unemployment, family breakdown, disengagement from education, poverty and social exclusion are impor-tant in shaping criminal careers and contribute to repeated forms of victimisation. Studies involving Indigenous communities identify additional, multiple risk factors. These encapsulate the above but also involve a catalogue of issues linked to the specific historical experiences of Indigenous people and their ongoing marginalisation; includ-ing forced removal policies, dispossession and institutional racism. These experiences are rarely taken into account in criminal justice programs as situating factors. '[M]any contemporary criminal justice systems use classification systems ... based on research on general offending populations rather than minority groups' (Capobianco & Shaw 2003: 7).

On the other hand, the criminal justice system has also been slow to evolve strategies which work to the particular strengths of Indigenous cultures, particularly possible sources of cultural resilience (Homel, Lincoln & Heard 1999). Working *with* Aboriginal culture, as opposed to working against the cultural grain, will also require an understanding that Aboriginal people may view invitations to become involved in local crime prevention initiatives with some misgivings. As Hommel et al suggest, the very term 'crime' turns many Aboriginal people off due to its association with over-policing and deaths in custody, also many crime prevention strategies have involved excluding Aboriginal people as the stereotype 'crime problem', in urban shopping malls and the streets of country towns (Blagg & Wilkie 1995, 1997).

An emphasis on community safety will see stress placed on the neglected issue of Aboriginal victimisation and on the 'multiple' – rather than simply criminogenic – risks factors identified by Capobianco and Shaw. I have called these elsewhere those 'multiple and compound' forms of crisis that tend to exist in the Aboriginal context (Blagg 2000a). Indeed, some important preventive programs may not even describe themselves as crime prevention initiatives at all: structured youth activities programs, for example, (always in high demand on remote communities) may not be directly targeted at crime reduction but may reduce crime nonetheless as a spin-off of positive engagement with young people.

Value adding

Critical writing on Aboriginal community initiatives has focused attention on the need for government to relinquish control and allow Aboriginal communities to define the issues for themselves and then work in partnership with government agencies to implement strategies. The principle of self-determination underpins this approach.

Self-determination does not necessarily imply complete independence, indeed such a process could be devastating for communities: it speaks, instead, to Aboriginal aspirations for a renewed social contract between Aboriginal and non-Aboriginal Australia. One prominent commentator suggests that:

> self-determination does not necessarily entail secession or the creation of separate states but can be articulated through the *restructuring and renewal* of existing relations between Indigenous organizations and Government to create arrangements to reflect and support a diversity of Indigenous circumstances. (Aboriginal and Torres Strait Islander Social Justice Commissioner 2004: 2, emphasis added)

'Restructuring and renewal' has a similar resonance to Haverman's (1999) notion of 'synthesis and synergy', noted above. Both imply dialogue and a willingness to think imaginatively (in current parlance, to 'think outside the square') when dealing with Aboriginal communities and let go of pre-existing forms of 'common sense'. Self-determination also involves being aware of the different life circumstances of Aboriginal people – there cannot be a 'one fits all' solution. Fitzgerald's vision of devolution here, shifts discussion firmly in the direction of negotiated settlements with Aboriginal communities: creating what he calls new 'sub-contracts' with Indigenous communities, with '[c]entral government deferring to local institutions to organize local life to the greatest extent possible' (Fitzgerald 2001: 113).

Similarly, the Aboriginal and Torres Strait Islander Social Justice Commissioner argues for an approach based on the development of 'governance structures and regional autonomy' and goes on to identify community justice mechanisms as 'an integral component of Indigenous governance' (Aboriginal and Torres Strait Islander

Social Justice Commissioner 2004: 2). They are essential, the commissioner insists, to deal with the damage that both violent communal behaviour and the practices of the justice system continue to inflict on Indigenous communities. However, to be success-ful, community justice mechanisms must, he asserts, 'be accompanied by a return of control and decision making processes to Indigenous communities' (Aboriginal and Torres Strait Islander Social Justice Commissioner 2004: 3). Current forms of govern-ment control are, he suggests, based upon the 'perpetuation of the marginalised position of Indigenous people, combined with a denial of any collective or historical dimension to Indigenous people's experience' (Aboriginal and Torres Strait Islander Social Justice Commissioner 2004: 3).

Law and justice planning

The significance of the law and justice planning process lies in its capacity to finely tune strategies to meet the requirements of individual communities and work to the grain of local culture and tradition. Each plan is unique to that particular community, however, there are a number of common processes and strategies. A typical remote community Law and Justice Committee would have a dual role, one formal and the other informal. On the one hand, it would act as the point of interface with the formal criminal justice system, be involved in pre-court conference, make recommendations to the courts, develop diversionary strategies and act as a focal point for community justice issues. On the other hand, the committee would be involved in community-level dispute resolution, coordinate community responses to law and order issues, and maintain relations with outside agencies (police, corrections, family and children services, and others) (Ryan, undated).

The Northern Territory Law Reform Commission

The 2005 *Report of the Committee of Inquiry Into Aboriginal Customary Law*, on behalf of the Northern Territory Law Reform Commission, supports the practice of law and justice planning on communities. Furthermore, the committee sees Aboriginal custom-ary law playing a role in this process. Recommendation 4 states that:

> Aboriginal communities should be assisted by government to develop law and justice plans which appropriately incorporate or recognise Aboriginal customary law as a method of dealing with issues of concern to the community or assist or enhance the application of Australian law within the community. (Northern Territory Law Reform Commission 2005: 18)

The committee noted that issues on communities differ enormously and that there cannot be a 'one fits all' solution, rather solutions needed to be tailored to meet community-defined need, '*in anyway that the community thinks appropriate*' (italics in the original):

> *The Inquiry's general view is that each community will define its own problems and solution.* Models may deal with alternative dispute resolution, family law issues, civil law, criminal law, or with relationships between Aboriginal communities and government officers/private contractors while in Aboriginal communities, and so on (Northern Territory Law Reform Commission 2005: 6, italics in the original).

The committee recognised – based upon a wealth of oral and written testimony – that traditional law and its forms of dispute resolution can work very effectively on some community issues. For example, the committee envisaged scenarios where, suitably resourced, communities would develop protocols with police on the cautioning of juvenile offenders – a practice also advocated in the Cape York Justice Study (Fitzgerald 2001). The only limitation placed by the committee on community plans was that they should not infringe human rights (Northern Territory Law Reform Commission 2005: 21).

Women, violence and community justice

The Northern Territory Inquiry saw limitations of the community justice approach in the area of family violence, there were fears that – given concerns that customary practices in this area – community control may simply reinforce the power of male elders, who may themselves be perpetrators. At the same time the committee acknowledged that Aboriginal dispute resolution mechanisms (that have a basis in traditional law) have been effective in family violence on some communities (Northern Territory Law Reform Commission 2005: 15). As we have seen the Ngaanyatjarra Pitjantjatjara, Yankunytratjara (NPY) Women's Council has been a consistent advocate for white law and white police to deal with issues it sees as being beyond the competence of Aboriginal law in the NPY region. Other Aboriginal women's voices, however, argue that Aboriginal law can be effective in combating family violence. Wohlan (2005) found two community initiatives in the Kimberley region of Western Australia; the Peninsula Women's Group and the Fitzroy Valley Action Group. The former was established by women on the Dampier Peninsula in 2002 in light of allegations of sexual abuse on the peninsula. Wohlan reports that the women were 'very angry' and that 'the cultural logic to address the issues was very Aboriginal' (2005: 43). There was little faith in the criminal justice system to resolve the problem and the focus was on Aboriginal law. Wohlan records the action at a women's bush meeting:

> A senior woman regarded as being knowledgeable about law issues addressed the meeting and stated that child sexual abuse is not part of Aboriginal culture … Ideas emerged such as involving the families; getting people together for meetings; having the 'story' collected and 'right'; ways of keeping children safe; and ostracising perpetrators from the community for a time as punishment for child abuse. The role of non-Aboriginal support agencies was canvassed as well. (Wohlan 2005: 43)

The women ran into difficulties as soon as they had to deal with non-Aboriginal bureaucracies and funding bodies, and the initiative has found it difficult to sustain itself. However, it is interesting that, when given space to speak, Aboriginal women are able to articulate solutions from within Aboriginal law and culture. The Fitzroy Valley Action Group also emerged on the basis of women's concerns about alcohol and violence. Fitzroy women have been active participants in the local Community Patrol and the safe house, however they also wanted to see more done to address the causes of alcohol-fuelled violence and have been pushing the police and other agencies to work with them to develop an alcohol reduction strategy (Wohlan 2005: 44). One initiative that received no coverage whatsoever during the moral panic about violence in central Australia was the Kurduju Committee.

The Kurduju Committee

The Kurduju Committee enjoyed its heyday approximately between 2000 and 2010, bringing together the Warlpiri communities of Ali-Curung, Lajamanu and Yuendumu. 'Kurduju' means 'Shield' in Warlpiri language. Each community, as noted in Chapter 6 on Night Patrols, has been involved in developing law and justice strategies for some years under the Territory's Aboriginal Law and Justice Strategy. Each community has its own law and justice committee which implements the community's law and justice plan. The Kurduju Committee was formed because of frustration with government strategies on family violence in remote communities, particularly the lack of recognition given to already existing work on communities that has proven successful.[3] The aim was to give greater power to Elders, whose influence was being eroded by outside intervention. The community committees felt that the image being portrayed of Aboriginal women in remote communities was one of helpless, docile victims of traditional violence, incapable of developing strategies to combat violence. The implication being that only law and policing strategies driven from outside the community and based upon the general law could be effective. In its submission to the Northern Territory's Committee of Inquiry into Aboriginal Customary Law (2005), the Kurduju Committee rejects this view. It also raises questions about the relevance of strategies devised in urban areas to the realities of life in remote communities. This was particularly the case in regards to policies and programs on family violence based upon western feminist principles and targeted towards increased criminalisation of family violence. The submission is particularly critical of 'legal services' that are simply dropped on to communities with no understanding of the cultural context or the fact that these communities operate under two, not one, law. The committee sees its role as fostering better coordination and cooperation between agencies and the communities and providing sound advice on appropriate strategies. It sees a need for community capacity building, improved access to legal services (providing these are willing to work within a community building paradigm) and mechanisms for ensuring that matters relating to Aboriginal law are taken fully into account by the courts and other justice agencies (Kurduju Committee 2001).

Community structures

As I have intimated earlier, we have to be on-guard against tendencies to impose non-Aboriginal definitions of 'community' onto Indigenous communities: the term is problematic when used in connection with Aboriginal notions of collectivity, obligation and loyalty. The notion of community is heavily value laden and resonates with images of collective solidarity and *gemeinschaft* that are quite inappropriate to Indigenous communal practices, which tend to be labile and fluid and only consistent in relation to the demands made by family, clan and skin.[4] Moreover, Aboriginal townships are artificial constructs, fractured along numerous demographic, racial, religious, affiliate and elective fault-lines, as Mosey writes in relation to the *Kutjungka* region in the East Kimberley:

> The word 'community' is very deceptive when applied to the conglomerate of language groups, ages, families, and vastly differing agendas, both Aboriginal and non-Aboriginal, existing in the Kutjungka region. In fact, most 'communities' seem to only operate as a community of people with a common purpose when they are supporting their football team, or for the purposes of external administration and funding service provision. (Mosey 2002: 8)

Another dimension of this issue that needs to be addressed is the way government administration also created 'regional' structures that do not correspond to Aboriginal patterns of life. Aboriginal communities in desert regions of Western Australia and the Northern Territory voice concerns that they are governed from salt-water regions along the coast, where Indigenous politics is determined by groups with different forms of law and different priorities. In contrast, the arbitrary lines in the sand that demarcate States and Territories artificially separate groups with strong clan, skin and family connections. It is only recently that this problem has been addressed at the level of law enforcement through developments such as the multi-jurisdictional, 'cross border' policing protocols between Western Australia, the Northern Territory and South Australia, which allow joint policing of the NPY lands, although this multi-jurisdictional approach has yet to be employed to strengthen Indigenous community governance across borders.

A number of professionals with significant experience working in the desert/ spinifex areas of the State voiced enthusiasm for some governance structures linking communities from the Balgo area, through to Wiluna and Warburton, rather than constantly feeding initiatives through existing regional governance structures (which run from west to east).[5] The abolition of ATSIC regional councils in June 2005 raises particular concerns in this regard. ATSIC regional councils represented one of the only alternatives to the rigid geographical administration of government. There is a real danger that future regional structures that replace ATSIC regions will bear little relation to the traditional groupings of Aboriginal people. The government's defined regions are artefacts of the bureaucratic imagination and bear little resemblance to the lines of connection operating in Indigenous communities. Community consultations suggested that 'town' agencies (Broome and Hedland for example) – even Aboriginal ones – did not understand desert issues where Aboriginal law still governed most aspects of daily life. A number of remote communities consulted by the Law Reform Commission of Western Australia wanted to see some big meetings organised specifically to deal with the law issues that faced people living in these 'remote' regions.

Desert meetings and desert facilities

For example, elders at the Kunawaradji community consultation wanted to convene a 'bush meeting' where all elders in the area met with members of the judiciary, to talk about Aboriginal law, the meeting would be open to all communities in the East Pilbara. Similarly, in the Goodabinya community (Marble Bar), the men's meeting wanted to hold a big meeting involving all the East Pilbara communities and representatives from the key agencies, police and judiciary, to discuss a range of issues, they were especially concerned with issues of alcohol, drugs (ganja, amphetamines) and anti-social behaviour. Jigalong community had been discussing the possibility of establishing an Outstation Program for some years, and there had been regular discussions with government agencies regarding the process. A camp at Puntawari, some 40 km east of the community had been established but with only rudimentary infrastructure. One potential use of the Puntawari camp was as a place to send young 'troublemakers' to be taught the traditional ways by elders, away from town influences. There had also been plans to use Puntawari as a 'family healing centre': a place to take families who had been experiencing family violence, as well as men after release from prison – the view being that many were not ready to be just dropped back into family/community life. The problem was that government agencies saw this as too costly: places such as Puntawari being too 'remote' from existing centres. Aboriginal people in these areas want to see the necessary capacity generated for such structures to be viable.

This was also said in relation to prison building during the Law Reform Commission of Western Australia's meetings with prisoners: there were demands for investment in rural and remote facilities as well as outstations:

> Instead of prisons, build a community facility that can be used regionally or by several communities. Its main purpose is rehabilitation and restoration through education/training, employment training, courses for employment opportunities, drug, alcohol, violent and sex offending. Staffed by trained Aboriginal people and non-Aboriginal people who are not prejudiced. A place that family can come to and stay especially when death occurs in or out of prison, or when children are born so people in facility can do the cultural business and family is not made to suffer because person is in prison.

and

> Why build a new prison in Roebourne, when could build a facility run by elders, out in the desert? Allow people to shame their own people, relations might be best (for this). (Prisoner consultations)[6]

The need for sound coordination and capacity building processes is now widely acknowledged (in theory, if not always in practice) by government. A 2002 inquiry into child abuse and family violence in the Aboriginal community (Gordon, Henry & Hallam 2002) assigns considerable importance to capacity building and the improved coordination of services as a necessary step to reducing family violence in the long term (Gordon et al 2002). The capacity-building approach informs new initiatives around work with children, young people and families by the Department of Community Development (DCD). The approach is intended to 'work with', rather than 'work for', these groups and find common solutions (Department for Community Development 2004). There is little one can take issue with in these ideals: the problems begin when the ideals are operationalised.

Community justice from the ground up

Community-owned justice mechanisms, I have suggested, should not be seen as points of delivery for government services or simply sounding boards for ideas generated at the centre (which always, for Indigenous people, remains a colonial centre). They should be considered as nodal points in a fabric created by Aboriginal law and culture, situated at those liminal points of connection between Aboriginal and non-Aboriginal domains. While the language of 'bottom up' 'top down' is useful in imagining the flow of power and influence between localities and the state it is not always a useful way of conceptualising relationships between domains. Aboriginal power and influence, I have suggested, tends to remain horizontal and flows in a circular rather than linear directions, taking in decentred clusters of authority and influence depending upon context. Power asserted within one cluster cannot be assumed to have salience in another. In discussing the ways community justice structures operate I find myself falling into topographic representations, I am a white male researcher after all. It is easy and convenient to envisage a situation where local community justice groups feed 'upwards' to regional then State-level representative bodies. This is not how they should be read, however. The aim of justice mechanisms is to feed the local systems, by providing a range of resources, advice and support and by resolving problems between local people and powerful agencies that cannot be resolved locally. Local solutions may require the mobilisation of resources, government coordination (and the coordination of government) and changes in law, etc.

Community justice mechanisms should constitute the bedrock for strategies intended to shift power towards the Aboriginal domain. Through its consultations with Aboriginal people, the Law Reform Commission of Western Australia arrived at this conclusion, so too have inquiries in the Northern Territory, Queensland and New South Wales.

Community Justice Groups operate widely in Queensland and New South Wales: they represent a mechanism for grass-roots involvement in the local justice system and a means whereby Aboriginal people can run their own justice processes:

> Under the proposal any Aboriginal community will be able to set up a community justice group if they wish to. It is anticipated that community justice group members will be selected by their community and will be representative of all relevant family, social or skin group in the community. In addition ... community justice groups must comprise an equal number of men and women from each relevant grouping. (Law Reform Commission of Western Australia 2006a: 134)

The Law Reform Commission envisages Community Justice Groups becoming 'directly involved in the operation of the criminal justice system':

> A community justice group could provide crime prevention, rehabilitative and diversionary programs. A community justice group could also, where appropriate, play a role in supervising offenders while on bail or subject to court orders. (Law Reform Commission of Western Australia 2006a: 136)

The groups would create local rules and sanctions which would replace the current system of by-laws. The advantages of Community Justice Groups, according to the Law Reform Commission, lies in the extent to which they allow Aboriginal people to develop their own processes for dealing with justice issues in their locality, recognise the practical role of Aboriginal Customary Law, increase the potential for diversion from the system, and enhance governance capacity in Aboriginal communities.

These initiatives 'fill out' the liminal space between Aboriginal and non-Aboriginal domains while not further colonising Aboriginal law and its spiritual base. The trick

Figure 11.1: Community Justice Mechanisms

will be to nurture these hybrid initiatives which sit closest to the core of Aboriginal domain and that are generated, nurtured and reproduced through Aboriginal culture and Aboriginal social relationships. As I have taken pains to point out, hybrid structures may require *more* not *less* input from government but this input should be mainly in the form of support for Indigenous process rather than outside control. The importance of locally situated structure cannot be over-estimated. Depending on a host of factors, localities will vary in their capacities to take on responsibilities for certain functions. Particular groups will take their own stance on the boundaries between domains and what the responsibilities of each should be. We have tended to equate Aboriginal self-determination in narrowly Eurocentric terms: Aboriginal people will copy the kinds of system we use but deliver these systems themselves; this has been the experience notably in Canada and the United States. As I have suggested, however, Aboriginal people in some regions see self-determination differently. In the Fitzroy Valley, as we have seen, they envisage situations where white organisations deliver mainstream service, while they provide the cultural base, work on cultural health, provide models of policing based on prevention rather than intervention, and strengthen Aboriginal law.

Notes

1   Under the *Native Title Act 1993* (NTA) PBCs are established for each native title determination in order to hold in trust or manage the native title rights and interests on behalf of the native title holders.

2   Aboriginal Customary Law, Thematic Summaries of Community Consultations, at <www.lrc. justice.wa.gov.au>.

3   During a visit to Lajamanu and Ali-Curung by the author in 2000, the law and justice committees expressed some unease at the views being expressed in urban areas about the inability of communities and community structures to work on family violence issues. In one instance a Family Violence Prevention lawyer in Katherine publicly suggested that Lajamanu was incapable of dealing with family violence and that the male elders ran the policy on family violence, to their own ends. This outraged the women on the committee who ran their own Night Patrol and safe house and worked with the police to combat the problem. The lawyer was forced to publicly retract her statement.

4   The notion of community within the 'western' tradition is heavily imprinted simultaneously with images of the rural idyll and what Benedict Anderson (1991) called the 'imagined community' of the nation state: neither construct necessarily complies with Aboriginal notions of community, indeed there is a significant tension between these different notions.

5   Thanks to Trevor Jewel for discussing this issue.

6   Law Reform Commission of Western Australia, Thematic Summaries of Consultations, at <www.lrc.justice.wa.gov.au>.

Concluding Comments:
Moving Forward

In this book I have argued that meaningful reductions in the numbers of Aboriginal people being arrested and imprisoned and in rates of violence within Aboriginal communities requires systemic change and a genuine decolonisation of relationships between Aboriginal and non-Aboriginal people. I have counter-posed the mainstream notion of restorative justice with what I have termed a restorative vision, where reforms focus attention on systemic and structural, as opposed to individual and institutional, change. Such changes can only take place incrementally, however. Many Aboriginal communities exist in conditions of multiple and compounded crisis, where damaging life events pile up on one another and internal structures of care and control – particularly in families – frequently collapse under the strain. We do Indigenous people no favours if we assume that a 'decolonised' justice system would be one where the white mainstream simply walks away from the catastrophes it has helped create. It bears repetition that is *the way* we interact with the Aboriginal domain that is the problem, not interaction *per se*. It has to be acknowledged that many families have been rendered dysfunctional due to inter-generational trauma that can be linked backwards to the founding violence of colonisation and subsequent eliminatory practices. Problems such as Foetal Alcohol Spectrum Disorders (FASD) are not restricted to the Aboriginal community but their impact is exacerbated due to a constellation of social and cultural factors that ensure that the impact of FASD is that much more destructive.

I have maintained that engagement with Aboriginal people on criminal justice related matters requires investment in Aboriginal *owned* community justice mechanisms. I have also suggested that, far from requiring that Aboriginal people be left alone to resolve problems, engagement of this nature necessitates greater, not diminished, involvement and commitment from a diversity of mainstream organisations. Aboriginal autonomy in decision-making, Aboriginal self-management and Aboriginal self-determination remain fundamental principles, allowing communities to determine what problems exist and in setting out the parameters for action. Non-Aboriginal organisations, government agencies and the judiciary have a crucial role to play in providing resources (financial, human, administrative, and legal) for initiatives to succeed. Aboriginal communities want to be able to access the knowledge and resources locked up in government organisations on issues of great importance to them, such as the impact of alcohol and drugs on their young people and on how the western legal system actually operates.

There is a tendency for government to think of capacity building and governance in extremely narrow terms and equate them simply with enhanced service delivery

(Aboriginal and Torres Strait Islander Social Justice Commissioner 2004). In opposition to this, we need to define a notion of community capacity building, which sets out to strengthen and nurture the capacities of Aboriginal people to define their problems and develop, in partnership with government, likely solutions. Law and justice structures and process constitute primary links in the chain of governance, and are, as such, prerequisites for the development of healthy communities.

I have argued that establishing community justice mechanism involves a focus on achieving sustainability, durability and resilience in structures, processes and programs; acknowledging that many Aboriginal communities operate on two laws, rather than one; being committed to nurturing the necessary governance structures; and, being willing to participate in capacity building processes both in Aboriginal communities and in government agencies. I have suggested that both the language and the practice of community *based* services often work to ensure that power and control are retained by government agencies; perpetuating that meticulously embroidered fiction that it is possible both to 'empower' communities and not to give up any of one's own. Many forms of 'consultation' by government agencies are about manufacturing consent to ideas and practices defined in advance by those organisations.

The new approach to partnership requires that we accept the *radical alterity* of Aboriginal people and do not try to squeeze them in to structures and processes evolved in the non-Aboriginal domain. The concept of 'Aboriginal domain', I have suggested, represents a useful means of imagining the distinction between Aboriginal and non-Aboriginal worlds and worldviews. Many of the perspectives and theories evolved within western scholarship to conceptually realise the life-world of the outsider, need to be radically recast if they are to have relevance in the Indigenous context. Simply imposing western theories on to the Aboriginal context risks reproducing the very colonial discourse we might have set out to unseat. This does not make western theory redundant – far from it. Western social sciences have relevance to understanding aspects of Indigenous experience, particularly experiences on the frontiers, hybrid zones and liminal spaces between Indigenous and non-Indigenous domains and the syncretised cultures that emerge at the porous boundaries between domains. On the other hand, western theories and western forms of knowledge, with their basis in enlightenment rationalism, need to be decentred from their privileged place at the centre of all inquiry – a kind of Copernican revolution is required – and space created for the subjugated and denied knowledge of those who lived in the shadows of modernity to be granted respect.

Any theoretical enterprise wishing to make sense of Indigenous experience in and around western law and western justice systems simply must figure the role these processes had – and in some respects continue to have – in the management of dispossession and in legitimising the theft of continents. One of the abiding attractions of western theories and mainstream approaches is that they magically subtract a number of unpleasant and unfortunate truths. The domain assumptions of mainstream criminology, for example, were fashioned in relation to the experience of diaspora and in the construction of complexly stratified societies within and around the urban conurbations of western cities. The imagination of criminology hesitates at the borders of a landscape inscribed not with diaspora but with dispossession and genocide: where the dispossessed demand not simple formal equality, but the right to a radical differ-ence based upon a pre-existing relationship with the land. This is made more complex because the colonised also demand not simply equality in western law but the additional recognition that they are subject to a separate law which continue to govern daily life. Aboriginal people continue to assert an identity that differentiates them from others: they are not simply a disadvantaged ethnic minority within society, but a distinctive, subordinated society with its own values, beliefs and law.

Little wonder then that many criminologists wish to pretend that these issues do not exist and prefer to focus on discrete and decontextualised elements of the 'problem': so that it becomes a problem of educational achievement, alcohol and drug abuse, domestic violence, marginalisation; thus permitting us to work on familiar terrain (sometimes quite literally since we need only 'review the data', not engage in the messy business of dealing with people) which gives us a sense of control.

I have also suggested that criminologists should engage (but not uncritically) with the anthropological tradition – while acknowledging the traditional biases of this tradi-tion as a science concerned with mapping and appropriating Indigenous knowledge on behalf of the coloniser – to make sense of the complex web of connections that tie Aboriginal people to law, land and kin and the equally complex points of intersection between Aboriginal collectivity and the non-Aboriginal world. I focused principally on the insights of Tim Rowse (1998) and those of Davenport, Johnson and Yuwali (2005) in relation to the meanings Aboriginal people attach to the giving and taking of goods, services and rations. Rowse, you will recall, deliberated that the processes connected with rationing established a set of dynamic relationships between Arranda and white people, which, while on one level confirming Arranda subordination, left, nonetheless, significant room for differences of meaning regarding the deeper implica-tions of this transaction to exist. Davenport et al illustrated the process at work at the Jigalong Mission: here, the missionaries believed that the provision of goods and services entitled them to the souls of the Martu, whereas the Martu had other ideas; they were willing, within limits, to forgo some autonomy but were utterly unwilling to surrender their law – the core of their identity as Aboriginal people. In both instances white authorities provided services on the implicit, if not always explicit, premise that Aboriginal people recognised, and would be willing to accept, the implications of the contract they had entered into by virtue of being in receipt of the goods and services: Aboriginal people would assimilate, give up their current existence and become like us. Implicit in this exchange also was the belief – on the part of white colonists – that Aboriginal people recognised the superiority of western culture.

The rich examples provided by Rowse and Davenport et al raise some intriguing questions. Because Aboriginal people participate in, utilise or consume a service (will-ingly or unwillingly) does this mean they that they attach the same meanings to this involvement or accept the goals (usually involving some kind of change in identity) underpinning the service from a white perspective? Aboriginal people were involved in a struggle for survival in a world usurped by a powerful alien culture with genocidal propensities (it simply had to be taken seriously): it was also a culture that had access to seemingly limitless supplies of food and newly desired objects such as tobacco, sugar, flour. Many Aboriginal people took advantage where they could of the bounty on offer, but they did so to retain and safeguard, *not surrender*, their Aboriginality. I want to suggest that we look critically at a host of institutions and services we provide with this in mind. Many, implicitly if not always deliberately, give a strong message that 'Aboriginality' itself is the price of entry: think like we do, live like we do, structure family life as we do. Increasingly, the focus of attention is on Aboriginal cultures as the problem: *if only Aboriginal people would stop being Aboriginal then we could help them.* Aboriginal people are often penalised for their incapacity/unwillingness to live like us; *our solution to Aboriginal people's 'problems' is still that Aboriginal people cease to be Aboriginal.*

We volunteer services, we put Aboriginal people in prison and other kindred institutions, we establish an array of consultative structures: implicitly assuming that, in consuming services, in being sentenced to prison of detention, or participating in our consultation processes, that they therefore share the meanings we inscribe in them – a refuge is for purpose x, a prison for purpose y, a consultative process is to arrive at solution z, etc: when, clearly, they don't. What if there were a number of incommensurate meanings submerged beneath surface 'participation' in our social institutions, processes of denigration, rituals of stigmatisation, forms of consultation? What if Aboriginal people are able to draw upon a range of alternative beliefs, systems of knowledge and cultural practices, which allow them to neutralise the dominant message and communicate an alternative set of meanings?

The issue of policing has featured prominently in recent debates about violence in Indigenous communities, particularly remote communities. There are increasing calls for the introduction of mainstream models of policing in remote areas. Most Aboriginal people want to see a police presence in their communities, but they also want a say in how policing is conducted and the how the inevitable wagon train of institutions freighted in with policing is dispersed. Will it simply impose a new set of demands that their social and economic situation, and their culture and law prevent them from meeting? If so, then we may see the wagons forming the familiar circle with the whites on the inside and the Indigenous people still on the outside.

Federal government policy (under John Howard) towards remote communities suggested a new attempt to further assimilate and discipline Aboriginal communities. New 'shared responsibility agreements' where Federal government dealt directly with individual communities and represented an attempt to impose neo-liberal responsibilisation strategies. Communities had to address issues, such as rubbish and getting kids to school, before being eligible for government support. Many critics of the move saw it as patronising and assimilationist in philosophy and content, playing on and amplifying dominant cultural perceptions about Aboriginal communities as stifled by passive welfare and unwilling, unless coerced to do so, to resolve deep-seated problems of which they themselves are largely responsible.

Shared responsibility as a form of neo-liberal governance has paralleled attempts by government to bypass Aboriginal representative structures (indeed, their introduction swiftly followed on from the abolition of the Aboriginal and Torres Strait Islander Commission (ATSIC) in 2005). Rowse (2006) placed a more optimistic gloss on the changes, suggesting that the government's agenda (under John Howard) of 'practical reconciliation' was not to be mistaken for simple mainstreaming or assimilationism:

one reason being that the Howard Government had to accept the existence and relevance of the 'Indigenous sector' and the premise that, 'Indigenous Australians make up a clientele whose needs of government are significantly different from those of non-Indigenous Australians' (Rowse 2006: 173). While ATSIC may have disappeared, this has not yet stripped away the network of Aboriginal organisations providing a diverse mix of services to Aboriginal communities, this, he suggests is a very different picture to one of mainstreaming. Rowse's comments provide a necessary corrective to excessive intellectual pessimism and offer a focal point for an optimism of the will: reminding us that Indigenous people have shown extraordinary resilience in developing a rich plethora of organisations, culturally embedded in the Indigenous domain and able to acts as nodal points for Indigenous innovation on issues as diverse as policing and security, women's safety, family violence, cultural health and wellbeing and employment.

In June 2007, the federal government under John Howard introduced the National Emergency Response Bill: a raft of measures designed to combat the sexual abuse of children in the Northern Territory. The revelations concerning sexual violence in central Australia (discussed in Chapter 10) had prompted a major inquiry in the Northern Territory (Wild & Anderson 2007), which called for a host of reforms to the investigation of child abuse, but also supported the creation of community-owned justice mechanisms of the kind outlined in Chapter 11. The Howard Government, however, employed a different strategy and introduced sweeping changes to the governance structures of Indigenous communities. In 2006 it had made increased funding (for police stations, drug and alcohol services etc) conditional on States removing references to customary law from Crimes Acts in each State and Territory (something they refused to do). The Intervention introduced widespread alcohol restrictions in the Northern Territory, made health checks for children compulsory and tightened access to welfare.

It confirmed the Howard Government's commitment to abolishing the Community Development Employment Projects (CDEP) scheme (an Australian government-funded initiative for unemployed Indigenous people in selected locations). But it also increased the powers of the federal government to decide how communities are governed. Space precludes an examination of these measures and the response of Aboriginal communities in the Northern Territory. It is clear, though, that while many Aboriginal communities welcome the additional resources and the focus on children and child health, there is also widespread cynicism about the deeper motives – revealed in those aspects of the strategy which diminish self-government, take over Aboriginal land and reduce the capacities of communities to restrict access to their land through the abolition of the permit system. The Rudd Labor Government was committed to re-establishing the permit system and keeping CDEP for the foreseeable future – although it committed itself also to retaining the general shape of the intervention measures. Although rebadged as 'Stronger Futures' and 'Closing the Gap', many of the coercive elements of the Intervention remain intact, without much discernable improvement in regards to key milestones such as health, education and employment, but a massive increase in the Indigenous prison population.

My major preoccupation has been to sketch out a rationale for building initiatives in the liminal space between Aboriginal and non-Aboriginal domains. Aboriginal people simply do not want to their law 'recognised' where this involves processes of codification and writing. They want their law left alone. What they want is support when dealing with the white man's law and in managing the tensions between white law and the dictates of Aboriginal law. I have suggested that we engage in partnerships with Aboriginal people in building hybrid initiatives within the labile and fluid meeting grounds between Aboriginal and non-Aboriginal domains, which are not Aboriginal law in the traditional sense, but which allow Aboriginal values, beliefs and forms of cultural authority to intervene constructively in the shared space between domains.

In Figure 11.1 (see Chapter 11), I sketched out the place of community justice mechanism within an expanded Aboriginal justice domain, offering options for the criminal justice system (itself, of course, reformed in crucial ways to accommodate Indigenous practices) to divert offenders and victims in partnership with Indigenous communities. The diagram also shows that Aboriginal people, through their own initiatives, should be diverting their own people into their own alternative systems of care and control, through Community Patrols and similar initiatives, without having contact with the general system – something that already takes place on a local basis. In diverting Aboriginal people from contact with the criminal justice system they divert them also from those excessive, punitive and disabling tendencies towards Aboriginal capture, inherent in mainstream modes of policing. Diversion, in this respect, has a powerfully decolonising dimension, both literally and symbolically. Figure 2.1 (see Chapter 2) represents a means of visualising the liminal space between domains and situating initiatives along a continuum of hybridity. Those most likely to achieve ownership in Indigenous communities are those situated closely to the Aboriginal domain.

It deserves repetition that Aboriginal people tend to see long-term survival in terms of strengthening and safeguarding Aboriginal law and culture. A dangerous, if often unintended, consequence of the current focus on law, culture and violence, lies in the potential for further eroding Indigenous forms of cultural authority and stripping Aboriginal people of capacity to deal with problems in their communities. I have attempted instead to highlight those initiatives – based on partnership between domains – that actively seek to strengthen Aboriginal law and culture. Aboriginal women, assumed always to be the passive, docile and helpless victims of culture (the only accredited means by which Aboriginal women can be currently accorded victim status) are active participants in processes intended to reduce levels of violence in urban, rural and remote Indigenous communities. Most do so on the basis of law and culture and on the forms of authority flowing from them.

Reducing levels of contact between Indigenous young people and the criminal justice system has a particularly urgent claim on the time, energies and resources of government. As I have pointed out, the youth detention system in States such as Western Australia is an Aboriginal youth detention regime. We are faced with the bankruptcy of those 'diversionary' strategies which evolved in the early part of the 1990s, based upon the expansion of police discretionary powers, the multi-agency approach and restorative justice, which were intended to meaningfully increase Indigenous diversion from the justice system. Instead these initiatives cemented Indigenous people's subordinate position within the system, and offered new ways for the police to mark off Indigenous youth as offenders and expand the net of controls. Diversion and restorative justice have been successful in removing many young offenders from the system but these tend not to be Aboriginal young people.

Youth diversion needs to be situated with the expanded Aboriginal justice domain, outlined above, with a greater role for Indigenous self-policing initiatives and a greatly enlarged network of Aboriginal-owned initiatives on out-stations and similar culturally secure environments. I have argued that Aboriginal people themselves are often way ahead of us in developing local practices. They are also insistent that local initiatives need to be nurtured and supported using the resources of local agencies – appropriately resourced and supported community justice groups provide the best available mechanism for achieving this aim. Aboriginal people have also been active in developing regional and State forums and councils where big picture issues are discussed. I have mentioned the success of the system of Regional Aboriginal Justice Councils in Victoria in supporting initiatives such as the Koori Courts. It is ironic that it has been from within the court system – that much targeted site of inflexibility and bureaucratic inertia – that some of the most far-reaching reforms have emerged. The NSW Aboriginal Justice Advisory Council has enjoyed a similar role in relation to community justice groups and Circle Sentencing Courts. This kind of reform is, by nature, incremental and slow, but there is an overwhelming need for such reform.

The prison remains a highly damaging and disruptive influence on Aboriginal domain. While, paradoxically, offering sites of safety in some instances (particularly for women), offering opportunities for a form of Aboriginal domain to exist (particularly between men), providing access to goods and services; it does not fulfil the function it purports to fulfil, it neither deters, reforms or shames Aboriginal offenders. What it does do is to drain off the human capital of Aboriginal communities and provide an enclave in which some of the most damaging mythologies about Aboriginal male entitlement to violence can circulate. It provides a material environment for the development and dispersal of violent attitudes and practices that mix eventually with the youth culture in the world outside to form aggressive counter-cultures. These cultures are not easily challenged or changed by the intervention of the non-Aboriginal control system. Evidence suggests the opposite. Aboriginal youth continue to live out a form of opposition fuelled by resistance to what is perceived to be an unjust justice system imposed by non-Aboriginal systems of power, to defend white privilege. These beliefs, that sustain and legitimate violent practices and are extraordinarily damaging to the fabric of the Aboriginal community, are difficult to challenge from within the non-Aboriginal domain employing the techniques and technologies, beliefs and values, forms of language and structures of sentiment and feeling that characterise the white domain. We urgently require a new, decolonised vision of justice, founded upon respect for, and recognition of, the Aboriginal domain and its laws and cultures, and we need to do it now.

References

Abbott, T (2006) 'Misplaced Tact Stands in the Way of Help', *Sydney Morning Herald*, 21 June.

ABC News Online (2006) 'Aboriginal Leaders to Join Court Process', 2 November, <www.abc.net.au/news/stories/2006/11/02/1779437.htm>.

ABC Radio (2006a) *PM*, 'Culture of Violence Revealed in Central Australia', 16 May, <www.abc.net.au/pm/content/2006/s1640070.htm>.

ABC Radio (2006b) *The World Today*, 'WA Aboriginal Girl Charged Under Racial Vilification Laws', 2 August, <www.abc.net.au/worldtoday/content/2006/s1704187.htm>.

ABC Television (2006a) *Lateline* interview with Nannette Rogers by Tony Jones, 15 May, <www.abc.net.au/lateline/content/2006/s1639127.htm>.

ABC Television (2006b) *Lateline* 'Sexual Abuse Reported in Indigenous Community' by Suzanne Smith, 21 June, <www.abc.net.au/lateline/content/2006/s1668773.htm>.

ABC Television (2006c) *7.30 Report* interview with Jane Lloyd by Kerry O'Brien, 21 June, <www.abc.net.au/7.30/content/2007/s1958592.htm>.

Aboriginal and Torres Strait Islander Commission (1996) *Indigenous Deaths in Custody, 1989 to 1996,* Aboriginal and Torres Strait Islander Commission: Canberra.

Aboriginal and Torres Strait Islander Social Justice Commissioner (2001) *Social Justice Report 2001,* Human Rights and Equal Opportunity Commission: Sydney, <www.hreoc.gov.au/>.

Aboriginal and Torres Strait Islander Social Justice Commissioner (2004) *Social Justice Report 2004*, Human Rights and Equal Opportunity Commission: Sydney, <www.hreoc.gov.au/>.

Aboriginal and Torres Strait Islander Social Justice Commissioner (2006) *Ending Family Violence in Aboriginal and Torres Strait Islander Communities*, Human Rights and Equal Opportunity Commission: Sydney, <www.hreoc.gov.au/>.

Aboriginal and Torres Strait Islander Women's Task Force on Violence Report (2000), *Full Report*, Department of Aboriginal and Torres Strait Islander Policy: Brisbane, <www.datsip.qld.gov.au/pdf/taskforce.pdf>.

Aboriginal Justice Advisory Council New South Wales (2000) *Strengthening Community Justice – Some Issues in the Recognition of Aboriginal Customary Law in New South Wales*, Discussion Paper, Aboriginal Justice Council of New South Wales: Sydney <www.lawlink.nsw.gov.au/ajac.nsf/pages/publications>.

Aboriginal Justice Advisory Council New South Wales (2002) *News No 41*, December, <www.lawlink.nsw.gov.au/ajac>.

Aboriginal Justice Council (1997) *Getting Stronger on Justice, The 1997 Monitoring Report of the Aboriginal Justice Council on the Recommendations of the Royal Commission into Aboriginal Deaths in Custody*, Aboriginal Justice Council Secretariat: Perth.

Aboriginal Justice Council (1999) *Our Mob Our Justice: Keeping the Vision Alive. The 1998 Monitoring Report of the Aboriginal Justice Council on the Recommendations of the Royal Commission into Aboriginal Deaths in Custody*, Aboriginal Justice Council Secretariat: Perth.

Aboriginal Legal Service of Western Australia (ALS) (2006) *The 'Move On' Law and its Impact on Aboriginal People in Western Australia,* Submission to the Human Rights and Equal Opportunities Commission, Aboriginal Legal Service of Western Australia: Perth.

Aboriginal Women's Task Force and the Aboriginal Justice Council (1995) *A Whole Healing Approach to Family Violence,* Aboriginal Justice Council: Perth.

Agamben, G (1998) *Homo Sacer: Sovereign Power and Bare Life,* Translated by Daniel Heller-Roazen, Stanford University Press: Stanford.

Allen Consulting Group (2010) *Independent Review of Policing in Remote Indigenous Communities in the Northern Territory: Policing Further into Remote Communities, Report to the Australian Government and the Northern Territory Government*, Allan Consulting Group Pty Ltd: Sydney, Melbourne and Canberra.

Althusser, L (1971) *Lenin and Philosophy*, New Left Books: London.

Althusser, L (1974) *For Marx,* New Left Books: London.

Anderson, B (1991) *Imagined Communities: Reflections on the Origins and Spread of Nationalism,* Verso: London.

Anthony, T (2013) *Indigenous People, Crime and Punishment,* Routledge: Abingdon, Oxford.

Anthony, T and Blagg, H (2012) *Addressing the Crime Problem of the Northern Territory Intervention: Alternate Paths to Regulating Minor Driving Offences in Remote Indigenous Communities,* Report to the Criminology Research Council, Grant: CRC 38/09-10, Canberra.

Anthony, T and Blagg, H (2013) 'STOP in the Name of Who's Law? Driving and the Regulation of Contested Space in Central Australia' 22(1) *Social and Legal Studies* 43.

Arendt, H (1973) *The Origins of Totalitarianism,* Harvest Books: New York.

Armitage, A (1995) *Comparing the Policy of Aboriginal Assimilation: Australia, Canada and New Zealand*, UBC Press: Vancouver.

Ashcroft, B, Griffiths, G and Tiffin, H (eds) (1995) *The Post-colonial Studies Reader,* Routledge: London.

Ashcroft, B, Griffiths, G and Tiffin, H (1998) *Key Concepts in Post-colonial Studies,* Routledge: London.

Ashworth, A (2003) 'Responsibilities, Rights and Restorative Justice' in Johnson, G (ed), *A Restorative Justice Reader: Texts, Sources, Context,* Willan Publishing: Cullompton.

Atkinson, J (1990) 'Violence Against Aboriginal Women: Reconstitution of Aboriginal Law', *Aboriginal Law Bulletin* (2): 6-9.

Atkinson, J (1991) 'Stinkin' Thinkin' – Alcohol, Violence and Government Responses', *Aboriginal Law Bulletin* (3): 8-11.

Atkinson, J (1993) *The Political And the Personal: Racial Violence Against Aboriginal and Torres Strait Islander Women and Women of Non-English-Speaking-Backgrounds*, National Committee on Violence and the Office of the Status of Women: Canberra.

REFERENCES

Atkinson, J (2000) *Trauma Trails, Recreating Song Lines: The Transgenerational Effects of Trauma in Indigenous Australia,* Spinifex Press: Melbourne.

Australian Bureau of Statistics (ABS) (2006, 2009, 2011, 2012, 2013) *Prisoners in Australia, 2011.* Cat No 4517.0, Canberra.

Australian Government Productivity Commission (2014) *Report on Government Services.* Australian Government Productivity Commission: Canberra.

Australian Law Reform Commission (ALRC) (1986) *Recognition of Aboriginal Customary Law,* ALRC 31, Australian Law Reform Commission: Sydney.

Baldry, E and Cunneen, C (2014) 'Imprisoned Indigenous Women and the Shadow of Colonial Patriarchy', *Australian and New Zealand Journal of Criminology* 47: 2, 276-298.

Bauman, Z (1995) *Life in Fragments: Essays in Postmodern Morality,* Blackwell: Oxford.

Bauman, Z (1997) *Postmodernity and its Discontents,* Polity Press: Cambridge.

Bauman, Z (2001) *Modernity and the Holocaust,* Cornell University Press: Cornell.

Bauman, Z (2004) *Wasted Lives: Modernity and its Outcasts,* Polity: Oxford.

Bayley, DH and Shearing, CH (2001) 'The Future of Policing', *Law and Society Review,* (30)3.

Bazemore, G and Walgrave, L (eds) (1999) *Restorative Juvenile Justice: Repairing the Harm of Youth Crime,* New York Criminal Justice Press.

Beck, U (2000) *What is Globalization?,* Polity: Cambridge.

Becker, H (1963) *Outsiders: Studies in the Sociology of Deviance,* Macmillan: London.

Beresford, Q and Omaji, P (1996) *Rites of Passage, Aboriginal Youth, Crime and Justice,* Fremantle Art Centre Press: Fremantle.

Berndt, RM and Berndt, CH (1988) *The Speaking Land: Myth and Story in Aboriginal Australia,* Methuen: Sydney.

Beyer, L (2003) *Inadequacies of Published Statistics: Policy and Debate on Heroin in the Community,* Paper presented at the Evaluation in Crime and Justice: Trends and Methods Conference, AIC & ABS: Canberra, 24-25 March.

Bhabha, HK (1994) *The Location of Culture,* Routledge: London.

Blagg, H (1997) 'A Just Measure of Shame? Aboriginal Youth and Conferencing in Australia', *British Journal of Criminology,* (37)4: 381-501.

Blagg, H (1998a) 'Restorative Visions and Restorative Justice Practices: Conferencing, Ceremony and Reconciliation in Australia', *Current Issues in Criminal Justice,* (10)1: 5-14.

Blagg, H (1998b) *Working With Adolescents to Prevent Domestic Violence, Vol 2, The Aboriginal Town Model,* Attorney-General's Department: Canberra.

Blagg, H (2000a) *Crisis Intervention in Aboriginal Family Violence, Summary Report and Strategies and Models for Western Australia,* <www.padv.dpmc.gov.au/projects/crisis_interv_summ.pdf> and <www.padv.dpmc.gov.au/projects/crisis_interv_ab_fv_wa.pdf>.

Blagg, H (2000b) 'Aboriginal Youth and Restorative Justice: Critical Notes from the Australian Frontier', in Morris, A and Maxwell, G (eds) *Restorative Justice for Juveniles: Conferencing, Mediation and Circles,* Hart: Oxford.

Blagg, H (2000c) *Pilot Counselling Programs for Mandated and non-Mandated Indigenous Men – Research and Program Development,* Report Prepared for the Domestic Violence Prevention Unit: Perth.

Blagg, H (2002) 'Restorative Justice and Aboriginal Family Violence: Opening a Space for Healing' in Strang, H and Braithwaite, J (eds) *Restorative Justice and Family Violence*, Cambridge University Press: Cambridge.

Blagg, H (2005) 'A New Way of Doing Justice Business? Community Justice Mechanisms and Sustainable Governance in Western Australia', *Background Paper No 8*, Law Reform Commission of Western Australia: Perth.

Blagg, H (2012) 'Re-imagining Youth Justice: Cultural Contestation in the Kimberley Region of Australia Since the 1991 Royal Commission into Aboriginal Deaths in Custody' 16(4) *Theoretical Criminology* 481.

Blagg, H (2015) 'From Terra Nullius to Terra Liquidus? Liquid Modernity and the Indigenous Other' in Erikson, A (ed) *Punishing the Other: The Social Production of Immorality Revisited*, Routledge Frontiers of Criminal Justice, Routledge: London.

Blagg, H and Ferrante, A (1995) *Aboriginal Youth and the Juvenile Justice System of Western Australia*, Aboriginal Affairs Department: Perth.

Blagg, H and Smith, D (1989) *Crime, Penal Policy and Social Work*, Longman: Essex.

Blagg, H and Wilkie, M (1995) *Young People and Police Powers*, Australian Youth Foundation: Sydney.

Blagg, H and Wilkie, M (1997) 'Young People and Policing in Australia: the Relevance of the UN Convention on the Rights of the Child', *Australian Journal of Human Rights*, (3)2: 134-157.

Blagg, H and Valuri, G (2002) *Evaluating Community Patrols in Western Australia*, Department of Indigenous Affairs: Perth.

Blagg, H and Valuri, G (2003) *An Overview of Night Patrols in Australia*, National Crime Prevention Branch and ATSIC, Attorney General's Department: Canberra, <www.ncp.gov.au>.

Blagg, H and Valuri, G (2004a) 'Self-Policing & Community Safety: the Work of Aboriginal Patrols in Australia', *Current Issues in Criminal Justice*, 15(3).

Blagg, H and Valuri, G (2004b) 'Aboriginal Community Patrols in Australia: Self-policing, Self-determination and Security', *Policing and Society*, (14)4: 313-329.

Blagg, H, Morgan N, Cunneen, C and Ferrante, A (2004) *Systemic Racism as a Factor in the Over-Representation of Aboriginal People in the Victorian Criminal Justice System*, Draft Paper prepared for the Equal Opportunity Commission and the Aboriginal Justice Forum: Melbourne.

Blagg, H and Anthony, T (2016) *Decolonising Criminology: Re-imagining Justice in a Postcolonial World*. Palgrave Macmillan: Basingstoke.

Bolger, A (1991) *Aboriginal Women and Violence*, Australian National University, North Australian Research Unit: Darwin.

Bond, C and Jeffries, S (2011a) 'Indigeneity and the Judicial Decision to Imprison: A Study of Western Australia's Higher Courts', *British Journal of Criminology* 51: 256-277.

Bond, C and Jeffries, S (2011b) 'Indigeneity and the Likelihood of Imprisonment in Queensland's Adult and Children's Courts', *Psychiatry, Psychology and Law*, 19: 169-183.

Bourgois, P (1999) *In Search of Respect: Selling Crack in El Barrio*, Cambridge University Press: Cambridge.

Bradley, HB, Chief Magistrate (2007) *Community Court Darwin: Guidelines,* <www.nt.gov.au/justice/ntmc/docs/community_court_guidelines_27.05.pdf>.

Brady, M (1989) *Heavy Metal: The Social Meaning of Petrol Sniffing in Australia,* AIATSIS: Canberra.

Brady, M, Nichols, R, Henderson, G and Byrne, J (2006) 'The Role of a Rural Sobering-Up Centre in Managing Alcohol-Related Harm to Aboriginal People in South Australia', *Drug and Alcohol Review* (25): 201-206.

Braithwaite, J (1999) 'Restorative Justice: Assessing Optimistic and Pessimistic Accounts', in Tonry, M (ed), *Crime and Justice: A Review of Research,* University of Chicago Press: Chicago, (25): 1-127.

Braithwaite, J and Mugford, S (1994) 'Conditions for a Successful Reintegration Ceremony', *British Journal of Criminology,* 32: 453-472.

Briggs, D and Auty, K (2005) *Koori Court Victoria – Magistrates Court (Koori Court) Act 2002,* International Society for the Reform of Criminal Law, <www.restorative-justice.org/articlesdb/articles/5560>.

Broadhurst, RG (1994) 'Aborigines, Cowboys, "Firewater" and Jail: The View from the Frontier', *Australian and New Zealand Journal of Criminology* 27(3): 50-56.

Broadhurst, RG (1999) 'Crime, Justice and Indigenous Peoples: The "New Justice" and Settler States', *Australian and New Zealand Journal of Criminology* 32(3): 105-108.

Broadhurst, RG (2002) *Crime and Indigenous People* in Graycar, A and Grabosky, P (eds), *Handbook of Australian Criminology,* Cambridge University Press: Melbourne, Ch 12: 256-280.

Bull, S (2004) 'The Land of Murder, Cannibalism, and All Kinds of Atrocious Crimes: Maori and Crime in New Zealand, 1853-1919', *British Journal of Criminology* (44)4: 496-519.

Burbank, V (2006) 'From Bedtime to On Time: Why Many Aboriginal People Don't Especially Like Participating in Western Institutions' *Anthropological Forum* (16)1: 3-20.

Burbank, V (1988) *Aboriginal Adolescence: Maidenhood in an Australian Community,* Rutgers University Press: New Brunswick.

Burbank, V (1994) *Fighting Women: Anger and Aggression in an Australian Community,* University of California Press: Burbank.

Busch, J (2002) *Northbridge: Shaping the Future,* Department of the Premier and Cabinet: Perth.

Butler, B (1994) *Aboriginal Children: Still in Terra Nullius,* Paper presented to the Aboriginal Justice Issues II Conference: Townsville, 14-17 June.

Canclini, NG (2005) *Hybrid Cultures: Strategies for Entering and Leaving Modernity,* University of Minnesota Press: Minnesota.

Capobianco, L and Shaw, M (2003) *Crime Prevention and Indigenous Communities: Current International Strategies and Programmes Final Report,* International Centre for the Prevention of Crime, <www.crime-prevention-intl.org/>.

Castells, M (1999) 'Grassrooting the Space of Flows', *Urban Geography,* 4:294-302.

Castells, M (2010) *The Rise of The Network Society* (2nd ed), Cambridge University Press: Cambridge.

Caulthord, G (2014) *Red Skin, White Masks: Rejecting the Colonial Politics of Recognition,* University of Minnesota Press: Minnesota.

Cavadino, M and Dignan, J (2006) 'Penal Policy and Political Economy', *Criminology and Criminal Justice* (6)4: 435-457.

Chakrabarty, D (1992) 'Provincializing Europe: Postcoloniality and the Critique of History' *Cultural Studies* 6(3), October 1992: 337-357.

Chakrabarty, D (2006) 'Foreword' to Lea, T, Kowal, E and Cowlishaw, G (eds) *Moving Anthropology: Critical Indigenous Studies,* Charles Darwin University Press: Darwin.

Chantrill, P (1997) *The Kowanyama Justice Group: A Study of the Achievements and Constraints on Local Justice Administration in a Remote Aboriginal Community,* Paper presented to the Australian Institute of Criminology's Occasional Seminar series.

Christie, N (1986) 'The Ideal Victim' in Fattah, E (ed), *Crime Policy to Victim Policy: Reorienting the Justice System,* St Martin's: New York.

Clarke J, Bainton D, Lendvai N and Stubbs P (2015) *Making Policy Move: Towards a Politics of Translation and Assemblage,* Policy Press: Bristol.

Clarke, S and Varos, G (1995) *Kimberley Regional Domestic Violence Plan,* Domestic Violence Prevention Unit: Perth.

Cohen, P (1972) *Sub-cultural Conflict and Working Class Community, Working Papers in Cultural Studies No 2,* University of Birmingham: Birmingham.

Cohen, P and Robbins, D (1978) *Knuckle Sandwich: Growing Up in the Working Class City,* Penguin: Harmondsworth.

Cohen, S (2001) *States of Denial: Knowing About Atrocities and Suffering,* Polity Press: Cambridge.

Coleman, A (2002) '*Sister it Happens to Me Everyday': An Exploration of the Needs of, and Response to, Indigenous Women in Brisbane's Inner City Public Space,* Department of Aboriginal and Torres Strait Islander Policy: Brisbane, <www.indigenous.qld.gov.au>.

Comaroff, J and Comaroff, J (2011) *Theory from the South: Or, How Euro-America is Evolving Toward Africa,* Paradigm Press: Boulder.

Community Development and Justice Standing Committee (2010) '*Making Our Prisons Work': An Inquiry into the Efficiency and Effectiveness of Prisoner Education, Training and Employment Strategies,* Report No 6 in the 38th Parliament, Government of Western Australia: Perth.

Cowlishaw G, Kowal, E and Lea, T (2006) 'Double Binds' in Lea T, Kowal, E and Cowlishaw, G (eds) *Moving Anthropology: Critical Indigenous Studies,* Charles Darwin University Press: Darwin.

Cowlishaw, G (2003) 'Disappointing Indigenous People: Violence and the Refusal of Help', *Public Culture,* (15)1: 103-125.

Crime Research Centre and Donovan Research (1999) *Young People's Attitudes to Domestic Violence,* Attorney Generals Office: Canberra.

Cripps, K (2005) 'Review of J Kimm, "A Fatal Conjunction: Two Laws, Two Cultures"', *QUT Law and Justice Journal* (5)1, <www.law.qut.edu.au/about/ljj/editions/v5n1>.

Cripps, K and Taylor, SC (2007) 'White Man's Law, Traditional Law, Bullshit Law: Customary Marriage Revisited', *Balayi: Culture, Law and Colonialism Journal of Law* 12.

Cunneen, C (1989) 'Constructing a Law and Order Agenda', *Aboriginal Law Bulletin* (38).

Cunneen, C (1994) 'Enforcing Genocide? Aboriginal Young People and the Police' in White, R and Alder, C (eds), *The Police and Young People in Australia,* Cambridge University Press: Melbourne.

Cunneen, C (1997) 'Community Conferencing and the Fiction of Indigenous Control', *Australian and New Zealand Journal of Criminology* 30: 292-311.

Cunneen, C (1999) *Diversion and Best Practice for Indigenous People: A Non-Indigenous View,* Paper presented to the 'Best Practice in Corrections for Indigenous People' Conference, Adelaide, Australian Institute of Criminology and Department for Corrections: SA.

Cunneen, C (2001a) 'The Impact of Crime Prevention on Indigenous Communities', Institute of Criminology: Sydney, <www.lawlink.nsw.gov.au/ajac.nsf/pages/reports>.

Cunneen, C (2001b) *Conflict, Politics and Crime: Aboriginal Communities and the Police,* Allen & Unwin: Sydney.

Cunneen, C (2001c) *Review of Best Practice Models for Indigenous Diversion Programs,* Report for Corrective Services Commission Victoria: Melbourne.

Cunneen, C (2006) 'Racism, Discrimination and the Over-representation of Indigenous People in the Criminal Justice System: Some Conceptual and Explanatory Issues', *Current Issues in Criminal Justice* (17)3: 329-347.

Cunneen, C (2011) 'Postcolonial Perspectives for Criminology' in Bosworth, M and Hoyle, C (eds) *What Is Criminology?,* Oxford: OUP.

Cunneen, C and Kerley, K (1994) 'Indigenous Women and Criminal Justice: Some Comments on the Australian Situation' in Hazelhurst, K (ed), *Perceptions of Justice,* Avebury: Aldershot.

Cunneen, C and Macdonald, D (1996) *Keeping Aboriginal and Torres Strait Islander People out of Custody: An Evaluation of the Implementation of the Royal Commission into Aboriginal Deaths in Custody,* ATSIC: Canberra.

Cunneen, C and Robb, T (1987) *Criminal Justice in North-West New South Wales,* NSW Bureau of Crime Statistics and Research, Attorney General's Department: Sydney.

Cunneen, C and Schwartz, M (2006) 'Customary Law, Human Rights and International Law; Some Conceptual Issues', Law Reform Commission of Western Australia Background Paper No 11, *Aboriginal Customary Law Background Papers,* Law Reform Commission of Western Australia: Perth, p 94.

Cunneen, C and White, R (1995) *Juvenile Justice, An Australian Perspective,* Oxford University Press: Sydney.

Cunneen, C et al (2013) *Penal Culture and Hyperincarceration: The Revival of the Prison,* Ashgate: London.

Curtis, D (1993) 'Julalikari Council's Community Night Patrol' in McKillop, S (ed), *Aboriginal Justice Issues: Proceedings of a Conference, 23-25 June,* AIC Conference Proceedings No 21, Australian Institute of Criminology: Canberra.

Daly, K (2002) 'Restorative Justice – The Real Story', *Punishment and Society,* 4: 55-79.

Davenport, S, Johnson, P and Yuwali (2005) *Cleared Out: First Contact in the Western Desert,* Aboriginal Studies Press: Canberra.

Davis, M and McGlade, H (2006) 'International Human Rights Law and the Recognition of Aboriginal Customary Law' Law Reform Commission of Western Australia Background Paper No 10, *Aboriginal Customary Law Background Paper*, Law Reform Commission of Western Australia: Perth, p 94.

Davis, M (2004) 'Planet of Slums', *New Left Review* (26)1: 357-372.

Department for Community Development (DCD) (2004) *Draft Capacity Building Strategic Framework*, Department for Community Development: Perth.

Department of Indigenous Affairs (2010) *Closing the Gap in Western Australia*. Perth: Department of Indigenous Affairs, <http://www.dia.wa.gov.au/PageFiles/923/DIACOAG%20Report.pdf>.

Dickson-Gilmore, J and La Prairie, C (2005) *Will the Circle be Unbroken? Aboriginal Communities, Restorative Justice, and the Challenges of Conflict and Change*, University of Toronto Press: Toronto.

Dodson, M (2003) *Violence, Dysfunction, Aboriginality*, Paper presented to the National Press Club: Canberra, 11 June, <http://law.anu.edu.au/anuiia/dodson.pdf>.

Dodson, M (2006) 'Keynote Address', *Positive Ways: An Indigenous Say Conference, Darwin 11-13 September 2006*, Victims of Crime NT: Darwin.

Dodson, P (1991) *Regional Report of Inquiry into Underlying Issues in Western Australia 2 Volumes*, Royal Commission into Aboriginal Deaths in Custody, AGPS: Canberra.

Drugs and Crime Prevention Committee (2001) *Inquiry into Public Drunkenness, Final Report*, Government Printer: Melbourne.

Eades, D (1995) (ed) *Language in Evidence: Issues Confronting Aboriginal and Multicultural Australia*, University of New South Wales Press: Sydney.

Elias, N (2000) *The Civilising Process*, Blackwell Publishing: London.

Escobar, A (2001) 'Culture Sits In Places: Reflections On Globalism And Subaltern Strategies Of Localization', *Political Geography*, 20: 139-74.

Evans, J (2005) 'Colonialism and the Rule of Law: The Case of South Australia', in Godfrey, BS and Dunstall, G (eds) *Crime and Empire 1840-1940: Criminal Justice in Local and Global Context*, Willan Publishing: London.

Evatt, E (2001) 'The Current Debate Surrounding Australia's Participation in the UN Committee System, *Public Law Review* 12: 177-190.

Fanon, F (1990) *The Wretched of the Earth*, Penguin: Harmondsworth.

Feeley, M and Simon, J (1992) 'The New Penology: Notes on the Emerging Strategy of Communication and its Implications', *Criminology* (30): 449-474.

Ferrante, A, Loh, N, Maller, M, Valuri, G and Fernandez, J (2004) *Crime and Justice Statistics for Western Australia: 2003*, Crime Research Centre: Perth.

Ferrante, A, Loh, N, Maller, M, Valuri, G and Fernandez, J (2005) *Crime and Justice Statistics for Western Australia: 2004*, Crime Research Centre: Perth.

Ferrante, A, Morgan, F, Indermaur, D and Harding, R (1996) *Measuring the Extent of Domestic Violence*, Hawkins Press: Sydney.

Finnane, M (ed) (1987) *Policing in Australia: Historical Perspectives*, New South Wales University Press: Sydney.

Finnane, M and McGuire, J (2001) 'The Uses of Punishment and Exile' *Punishment & Society* (3)2: 279-298.

Fitzgerald, T (2001) *The Cape York Justice Study,* Department of the Premier, Brisbane, <www.datsip.qld.gov.au>.

Ford, L (2010) *Settler Sovereignty: Jurisdiction and Indigenous People in America and Australia, 1788-1836, Vol 166,* Harvard University Press: Cambridge.

Foucault, M (1991) *Discipline and Punish: The Birth of the Prison,* Penguin: Harmondsworth.

Frank, AG (1971) *Sociology of Development and Underdevelopment of Sociology,* Pluto: London.

Frazer, N (1992) 'Rethinking the Public Sphere: A Continuation of the Critique of Actually Existing Democracy' in Calhoun, C (ed), *Habermas and the Public Sphere,* MIT Press: London.

Freud, S (1989) *Civilisation and its Discontents,* WW Norton & Company: London.

Garland, D (2001) *The Culture of Control: Crime and Social Order in Contemporary Society,* Oxford University Press: Oxford.

Gayle, F, Bailey-Harris, R and Wundersitz, J (1990) *Aboriginal Youth and the Criminal Justice System,* Cambridge University Press: Cambridge.

Giddens, A (1984) *The Constitution of Society. Outline of the Theory of Structuration,* Polity Press: Cambridge.

Giddens, A (1998) *The Third Way: The Renewal of Social Democracy,* Polity Press: Cambridge.

Giddens, A (1999) *Sociology,* 3rd ed, Polity Press: Cambridge.

Giddens, A (2001) *The Global Third Way Debate,* Polity Press: Cambridge.

Goffman, E (1990) *Stigma: Notes on the Management of Spoiled Identity,* Penguin: Harmondsworth.

Goldstein, H (1990) *Problem Oriented Policing,* McGraw-Hill: London.

Gordon, S, Henry, D and Hallam, K (2002) *Putting the Picture Together: Inquiry into Response by Government Agencies to Complaints of Family Violence and Child Abuse in Aboriginal Communities,* Department of the Premier and Cabinet: Perth.

Gray, J (1995) *Enlightenment's Wake: Politics and Culture at the Close of the Modern Age,* Routledge: London.

Green, N (1995) *The Forrest River Massacres,* Fremantle Arts Centre Press: Fremantle.

Gullestad, M (2006) *Plausible Prejudice: Everyday Practices and Social Images of Nation, Culture and Race,* Universitetsforl: Oslo.

Haebich, A (2000) *Broken Circles: Fragmenting Indigenous Families 1800-2000,* Fremantle: Arts Centre Press: Fremantle.

Hall, S and Jefferson, T (1978) (eds) *Resistance Through Rituals; Youth Sub-Cultures in Post-War Britain,* Hutchinson: London.

Hall, S (1995) 'The Whites of Their Eyes – Racist Ideologies and the Media' in Dines, G and Humez, JM, *Gender, Race and Class in Media – A Text Reader,* Sage Publications, Thousand Oaks, London and New Delhi.

Hall, S, Critcher, C, Jefferson, T, Clarke, J and Robert, B (1978) *Policing the Crisis: Mugging, the State and Law and Order,* Palgrave Macmillan: London.

Harding, R (ed) (1992) *Repeat Juvenile Offenders: The Failure of Selective Incapacitation in Western Australia,* University of Western Australia: Crime Research Centre: Perth.

Harding, R and Maller, R (1997) 'An Improved Methodology for an Analyzing Age – Arrest Profiles: Application to a Western Australian Offender Population', *Journal of Quantitative Criminology* (13)4: 349-372.

Harding, R, Broadhurst, R, Ferrante, A and Loh, N (1995) *Aboriginal Contact with the Criminal Justice System and the Impact of the Royal Commission into Aboriginal Deaths in Custody*, Hawkins Press: Sydney.

Harris, M (2004) 'From Australian Courts to Aboriginal Courts in Australia – Bridging the Gap?', *Current Issues in Criminal Justice* (16)1: 26-42.

Harris, M (2006) *A Sentencing Conversation': Evaluation of the Koori Courts Pilot Program, October 2002-October 2004,* Department of Justice: Victoria.

Haunani-Kay, T (2003) 'Review of "Talking up to the White Woman"', *Contemporary Pacific,* Fall: 474-476.

Haverman, P (1992) 'The Indigenization of Social Control in Canada' in Silverman, RA and O'Neilson, M (eds), *Aboriginal Peoples and Canadian Criminal Justice,* Harcourt, Brace & Co: Toronto.

Haverman, P (ed) (1999) *Indigenous Peoples' Rights in Australia, Canada and New Zealand,* Oxford University Press: Auckland.

Hazel, S and Rodriguez, L (1997) *Understanding and Responding to Aboriginal Family Violence,* Hedland College Social Research Centre: South Hedland.

Hazelhurst, K (ed) (1995) *Legal Pluralism and the Colonial Legacy,* Avebury: Sydney.

Higgens, D & Associates (1997) *Best Practice for Aboriginal Community Night Patrols and Wardens Schemes,* A Report to the Office of Aboriginal Development, Office of Aboriginal Development: Darwin.

Hill, B (2003) *Broken Songs: TGH Strehlow and Aboriginal Possession*, Random House: Sydney.

Hogg, R (2005) 'Policing the Rural Crisis', *Australian and New Zealand Journal of Criminology* (38)3: 340-361.

Homel, R, Lincoln, R and Herd, B (1999) 'Risk and Resilience: Crime and Violence Prevention in Aboriginal Communities', *Australian and New Zealand Journal of Criminology* (32)2: 111-122.

Hope, A (2004) *Record of Investigation into the Deaths of Owen James Gimme and Mervyn Miller,* Coroners Court of Western Australia: Perth.

Hope, A (2008) *Inquest into the Deaths of 22 Aboriginal People,* Coroners Court of Western Australia: Perth.

House of Representatives Standing Committee on Aboriginal and Torres Strait Islander Affairs (2011) *Doing Time, Time for Doing: Indigenous Youth in the Criminal Justice System,* Parliament of the Commonwealth of Australia: Canberra.

Howard, J (2006) 'Act on Sex Abuse, or Get Out, PM Tells States', *West Australian,* 29 May.

Hudson, B (2003) *Justice in the Risk Society,* Sage: London.

Hulls, R (2002) 'Koori Courts. A Responsive System', *Alternative Law Journal* (27)4: 188.

Human Rights and Equal Opportunity Commission (HREOC) (1991) *Racist Violence: Report of the National Inquiry into Racist Violence,* AGPS: Canberra.

Human Rights and Equal Opportunity Commission (HREOC) (1997) *Bringing Them Home: Report of the National Inquiry into the Separation of Aboriginal and Torres*

Strait Islander Children from their Families, Human Rights and Equal Opportunity Commission: Sydney.

Human Rights and Equal Opportunity Commission (HREOC) (2005) submissions to *The Northern Territory Inquiry into Customary Law*, Human Rights and Equal Opportunity Commission: Sydney.

Human Rights and Equal Opportunity Commission (HREOC) and the Australian Law Reform Commission (1997) *Seen and Heard: Priority for Children in the Legal Process*, Report No 84, Human Rights and Equal Opportunity Commission: Sydney.

Hunter, EM (1993) *Aboriginal Health and History: Power and Prejudice in Remote Australia*. Melbourne: Cambridge University Press.

Indermaur, D and Roberts, L (2003) 'Drug Courts in Australia: the First Generation', *Current Issues in Criminal Justice*, 15(2): 136-154, 138.

Jackson, M (1992) 'The Colonization of Maori Philosophy' in Odie, G and Perret, R (eds), *Justice, Ethics and New Zealand Society*, Oxford University Press: Auckland.

Jackson, M (1995) 'Justice and Political Power: Reasserting Maori Legal Processes', in Hazelhurst, K (ed), *Legal Pluralism and the Colonial Legacy*, Avebury: Aldershot.

Jackson, M (1999) 'Canadian Aboriginal Women and their "Criminality": The Cycle of Violence in the Context of Difference', *Australian and New Zealand Journal of Criminology* (32)2: 197-209.

Jarman, N (2007) 'Policing, Policy and Practice: Responding to Disorder in North Belfast', *Anthropology in Action* 13(1-2).

Jensen, L (2005) *Unsettling Australia: Readings in Australian Cultural History*, Atlantic Publishers: New Delhi.

Johnson, E (1991) *Royal Commission into Aboriginal Deaths in Custody National Report*, AGPS: Canberra.

Johnston, L and Shearing, C (2003) *Governing Security: Explorations in Policing and Justice*, Routledge: London.

Jonas, W (2002) *Community Justice, Law and Governance: A Rights Perspective*, Paper presented to the 'Indigenous Governance Conference', 3-5 April 2002: Canberra.

Jones, T and Newburn, T (2002) 'Policy Convergence and Criminal Control in the USA and UK: Streams of Influence and Levels of Impact', *Criminal Justice* (2)2: 173-205.

Keel, M (2004) *Family Violence and Sexual Assault in Indigenous Communities: 'Walking the Talk'*, Australian Centre for the Study of Sexual Assault, Briefing, No 4, Australian Institute for Family Studies: Melbourne.

Kickett-Tucker, S (1998) 'Research and Urban Aboriginal School Children: Considerations and Implication', *Australian Association for Research in Education National Conference*: Adelaide, 29 November-3 December 1998.

Kimm, J (2004) *Fatal Conjunction: Two Laws, Two Cultures*, Federation Press: Sydney.

King M, Freiberg A, Batagol B, Hyams R (2009) *Non-adversarial Justice*, Federation Press, Sydney.

Kunitz, S (1994) *Disease and Social Diversity. The European Impact on the Health of Non-Europeans*, Oxford University Press: Oxford.

Kurduju Committee (2001) *Reports*, The Combined Communities of Ali-Curung, Lajamanu and Yuendumu Law and Justice Committees, Kurduju Committee:

Northern Territory, <www.dcdsca.nt.gov.au/dcdsca/intranet.nsf/Files/RDPublications/$file/Kurduju.pdf>.

La Prairie, C (1989) 'Some Issues in Aboriginal Justice Research: The Case of Aboriginal Women in Canada', *Women in Criminal Justice,* (1)1: 54-67.

Langton, M (1992) 'The Wentworth Lecture: Aborigines and Policing: Aboriginal Solutions From Northern Territory Communities', *Australian Aboriginal Studies,* (2)14.

Law Commission of Canada (2002) *In Search of Security: The Roles of Public Police and Private Security,* Law Commission of Canada: Ontario.

Law Reform Commission of New South Wales (2000) *Sentencing: Aboriginal Offenders,* Report 96, Law Reform Commission of New South Wales: Sydney, October: 96.

Law Reform Commission of Western Australia (2006a) *Aboriginal Customary Laws: Discussion Paper: No 94,* Law Reform Commission of Western Australia: Perth.

Law Reform Commission of Western Australia (2006b) *Aboriginal Customary Laws: Final Report: The Interaction of Western Australian Law and Culture,* Law Reform Commission of Western Australia: Perth.

Lawrie, R (2002) *Speak Out, Speak Strong: Researching the Needs of Aboriginal Women in Custody,* New South Wales Aboriginal Justice Advisory Council: Sydney.

Leach, P (2003) 'Citizen Policing as Civic Activism: An International Inquiry', presented at *In Search of Security: An International Conference on Policing and Security,* Canada Law Commission: Montreal.

Lendvai, N and Stubbs, P (2007) 'Policies as Translation: Situating Trans-national Social Policies' in Hodgson, S and Irving, Z (eds), *Policy Reconsidered: Meanings, Politics and Practices,* Bristol: Policy, 173-189.

Lilles, H (2001) 'Circle Sentencing: Part of the Restorative Justice Continuum' in Morris, A and Maxwell, G (eds), *Restorative Justice for Juveniles: Conferencing, Mediation and Circles,* Hart: Oxford.

Lingiari Foundation (2004) *The Munjurla Study: A Scoping, Profiling and Planning Process in respect of the WA COAG Site Trial for the Purposes of Informing the Negotiation of a Comprehensive Regional Agreement,* Lingiari Foundation: Broome.

Loh, N and Ferrante, A (2003) *Aboriginal Involvement in the Western Australian Criminal Justice System: A Statistical Review, 2001,* Crime Research Centre: Perth.

Macdonald, G (2002) 'Economies and Personhood: Demand Sharing Among the Wiradjuri of New South Wales' in Wenzel, G, Hovelsrud-Broda, G and Nobuhiro, K (eds), *The Social Economy of Sharing: Resource Allocation and Modern Hunter-Gatherers,* Ethnological Studies, (53): 78-111.

Macpherson, Sir William Of Cluny (2003) *The Stephen Lawrence Inquiry,* Home Office: London, <www.archive.officialdocuments.co.uk/document/cm42/4262/4262.htm>.

Marchetti, E and Daley, K (2004) 'Indigenous Courts and Justice Practices in Australia', *Trends and Issues in Criminal Justice,* (277), Australian Institute of Criminology: Canberra, <www.aic.gov.au>.

Marshall, T and Merry, S (1990) *Crime and Accountability: Victim/Offender Mediation in Practice,* HMSO: London.

Marshall, T (1996) 'Criminal Mediation in Great Britain', *European Journal on Criminal Policy and Research,* 4(4): 37-53.

Marshall-Beier, J (2004) 'Beyond Hegemonic Statements of Nature: Indigenous Knowledge and the Non-state Possibilities in International Relations', in Chowdhry, G and Nair, S (eds) *Postcolonialism and International Relations: Reading Race, Gender and Class,* Routledge: London.

Martin, D (2004) 'Designing Institutions in the "Recognition Space" of Native Title', in Toussaint, S (ed), *Crossing Boundaries: Cultural, Legal and Practice Issues in Native Title,* Melbourne University Press: Melbourne.

McCold, P (1996) 'Restorative Justice and the Role of Community' in Galaway, B and Hudson, J (eds) *Restorative Justice: International Perspectives,* Criminal Justice Press: New York.

McCoy, BF (Undated). *'If We Come Together Our Health Will Be Happy': Aboriginal Men Seeking Ways to Better Health,* School of Population Health, University of Melbourne: Melbourne.

McElrea, F (1996) 'The New Zealand Youth Court: A Model for Use with Adults' in Galaway, B and Hudson, J (eds), *Restorative Justice: International Perspectives,* Criminal Justice Press: New York.

McGlade, H (2006) 'Aboriginal Women, Girls and Sexual Assault: the Long Road to Equality within the Criminal Justice System', *Aware,* ACSSA Newsletter (12), Institute of Family Studies: Melbourne.

McGregor, R (2005) 'Avoiding Aborigines: Paul Hasluck and the Northern Territory Welfare Ordinance, 1953', *Australian Journal of Politics and History* 51(4): 513-529.

McGregor, R (1997) *Imagined Destinies: Aboriginal Australians and the Doomed Race Theory, 1880-1939,* Melbourne University Press: Melbourne.

McIntyre, G (2005) 'Aboriginal Customary Law: Can it be Recognised?', Background paper No 9, *Aboriginal Customary Law Background Papers,* Law Reform Commission of Western Australia, p 94.

McMullen, S and Jayerwardene, C (1995) 'Systemic Discrimination, Aboriginal People, and the Miscarriage of Justice in Canada' in Hazlehurst, K (ed), *Perceptions of Justice: Issues in Indigenous and Community Empowerment,* Avebury: Aldershot.

McNamara, L (1995) 'Aboriginal Justice Reform in Canada: Alternatives to State Control', in Hazelhurst, K (ed), *Perceptions of Justice: Issues in Indigenous and Community Empowerment,* Avebury: Sydney.

Memmott, P and Fantin, S (2001) *'The Long Grassers': A Strategic Report on Indigenous 'Itinerants' in the Darwin and Palmerstone Area,* Memmott and Associates: St Lucia.

Memmott, P, Stacy R, Chambers, C and Keys, C (2001) *Violence in Aboriginal Communities,* Attorney-General's Department, Canberra.

Merlán, F (1998) *Caging the Rainbow: Places, Politics, and. Aborigines in a North Australian Town.* University of Hawai'i Press, Honolulu.

Merton, R (1957) *Social Theory and Social Structure,* Free Press: New York.

Meyer L and Maldonado Alvarado B (2010) (eds), *New World of Indigenous Resistance: Noam Chomsky and Voices from North, South, and Central America,* San Francisco, CA: City Lights Books and Open Media Series.

Miller, A (1994) *Thou Shalt Not Be Aware: Society's Betrayal of the Child,* Verso: London.

Miller, J (2001) 'Bringing the Individual Back In: A Commentary on Wacquant and Anderson', *Punishment and Society,* 3(1): 153-160.

Mignolo, W (2007) 'The Decolonial Option and the Meaning of Identity in Politics, *Anales Nueva Epoca* (Instituto Iberoamericano Universidad de Goteborg) 9/10: 43-72.

Mignolo, W (2011) *The Darker Side of Western Modernity: Global Futures, Decolonial Options,* Latin America Otherwise Duke University Press.

Moore-Gilbert, B (1997) *Postcolonial Theory: Contexts, Practices, Politics,* London: Verso.

Moreton-Robinson, A (2000) *Talkin' Up to the White Woman; Indigenous Women and Feminism,* University of Queensland Press, St Lucia.

Moreton-Robinson, A (2003) 'I Still Call Australia Home: Indigenous Belonging and Place in a White Postcolonising Society' in Ahmed, S, Cataneda, C, Fortier, AM and Shelley, M (eds) *Uproot-ings/Regroupings: Questions of Postcoloniality, Home and Place,* Berg: London and New York.

Morphy, F (2007) 'Performing Law: The Yolngu of Blue Mud Bay Meet the Native Title Process' in Smith, BR and Morphy, F (eds) *The Social Effects of Native Title: Recognition, Translation, Coexistence,* CAEPR Research Monograph No 27, ANU E-Press: Canberra.

Morphy, F and Morphy, H (2013) 'Anthropological Theory and Government Policy in Australia's Northern Territory: The Hegemony of the "Mainstream"', *American Anthropologist* 115:2 174-187.

Morgan, N and Mottram, J (2006) 'Aboriginal People and Justice Services: Plans, Programs and Service Delivery' in Law Reform Commission of Western Australia, *Aboriginal Customary Law Background Papers,* Law Reform Commission of Western Australia: Perth.

Morgan, N (2000) 'Mandatory Sentences in Australia: Where Have We Been and Where Are We Going?', *Criminal Law Journal,* (24)3.

Morgan, N (2002) 'Going Overboard? Debates and Developments in Mandatory Sentencing', *Criminal Law Journal,* (26)5: 293-311.

Morgan, N, Blagg, H and Williams, V (2001) *Mandatory Sentencing in Western Australia,* Aboriginal Justice Council: Perth.

Morrison, W (2004) '"Reflections with Memories": Everyday Photography Capturing Genocide', *Theoretical Criminology,* 8(3): 341-358.

Morrow, E (1984) *The Law Provides,* Hesperian Press: Perth.

Mosey, A (1994) *Remote Area Night Patrols,* DASA: Alice Springs.

Mosey, A (2002) Dry Spirit: *Petrol Sniffing Interventions in the Kutjungka region, WA, 1999-2000,* Mercy Community Health Service, Kutjungka Region, Western Australia & Office of Aboriginal Health, Health Department of Western Australia, Perth.

Mosko, M (2001), 'Syncretic Persons: Sociality, Agency and Personhood in Recent Charismatic Ritual Practices Among North Mekeo – PNG', *Australian Journal of Anthropology,* (12): 30-45.

Mouzos, T (2001) *Homicide in Australia: 2000-2001 National Homicide Monitoring Program (NHMP),* Annual Report No 46, <www.aic.gov.au>.

Mow, KE (1992) *Tjunparni: Family Violence in Indigenous Australia: A Report and Literature Review for the Aboriginal and Torres Strait Islander Commission,* Aboriginal and Torres Strait Islander Commission: Canberra.

Muncie, J (1999) *Youth and Crime: A Critical Introduction*, Sage: London.

Muncie, J and Goldson, B (2006) (eds) *Comparative Youth Justice*, Sage: London.

Musgrove, F (1974) *Ecstasy and Holiness: Counter Culture and the Open Society*, Methuen and Co, Newton: London.

Myers, K (1996) *An Overview of Corrections Research and Development Projects on Family Violence*, Solicitor General of Canada: Canada, <www.scg.gc.ca>.

Nancarrow, H (2006) 'In Search of Justice for Domestic and Family Violence: Indigenous and non-Indigenous Australian Women's Perspectives', *Theoretical Criminology*, (10): 87-106.

National Drug Research Institute (2000) *The Review of Services provided by Jungarni-Jutiya Alcohol Action Council Aboriginal Corporation*, Curtin University of Technology: Perth.

Neil, R (2006) 'Aboriginal Violence has a Lengthy History', *The Australian*, 19 May.

Niezen, R (2003) 'The Origins of Indigenism: Human Rights and the Politics of Identity', Berkeley: University of California Press.

Northern Territory Law Reform Commission (2005) *Report of the Committee of Inquiry into Aboriginal Customary Law: Report on Aboriginal Customary Law*, Northern Territory Law Reform Commission: Darwin.

O'Dea, J (1991) *Individual Death Reports, Western Australia*, AGPS: Canberra.

O'Malley, P (1992) 'Risk, Power and Crime Prevention', *Economy and Society*, (21)3: 252-275.

O'Malley, P (1996) 'Indigenous Governance', *Economy and Society*, (25)1: 310-326.

O'Malley, P (1998) (ed) *Crime and the Risk Society*, The International Library of Criminological, Criminal Justice and Penology, Ashgate: Dartmouth.

O'Malley, P (2002) 'Globalizing Risk?: Distinguishing Styles of "Neo-Liberal" Criminal Justice in Australia and the USA', *Criminal Justice*, (2)2: 205-223.

Office of the Inspector of Custodial Services (2005), *Directed Review of the Management of Offenders in Custody*, Report No 30, Office of the Inspector of Custodial Services; Perth: 5.

Palmer, D (2010) *'Opening Up to Be Kings and Queens of Country': An Evaluation of the Yiriman Project*, Report One, November. Fitzroy Crossing: KALACC.

Park, RE (1915) 'The City: Suggestions for the Investigation of Human Behaviour in the Urban Environment', *American Journal of Sociology*, 20: 577-612.

Parliament of Victoria Drugs and Crime Prevention Committee (2001) *Inquiry into Public Drunkenness: Final Report*, Government Printer for the State of Victoria: Melbourne.

Pearson, N (2006) 'Travesty on Palm Island', *The Australian*, 23 December.

Petersen, N (2000) 'An Expanding Aboriginal Domain: Mobility and the Initiation Journey', *Oceania*, March.

Peterson, N (1991) 'Cash, Commoditisation and Authenticity: When do Aboriginal People Stop Being Hunter-Gatherers?' in Peterson, N and Matsuyama, T (eds), *Cash, Commoditisation and Changing Foragers*, National Museum of Ethnology: Osaka: 67-90.

Pilay, S (2015) *Decolonising the University*, University of Cape Town, <http://africasa-country.com/2015/06/decolonizing-the-university/>.

Pilkington, J (2009) *Aboriginal Communities and the Police's Taskforce Themis: Case studies in remote Aboriginal community policing in the Northern Territory*. Darwin: North Australian Aboriginal Justice Agency and Central Australian Legal Aid Service.

Pilmer, RH (1998) *Northern Patrol: An Australian Saga*, edited and annotated by Clement, C and Bridge, P, Hesperian Press: Perth.

Polina, A and Perdrisat, I (2004) *A Report of the Derby/West Kimberley Project: Working With Adolescents to Prevent Domestic Violence*, Attorney-General's Department: Canberra, <www.ncp.gov.au>.

Polk, K, Adler, C, Muller, D and Rechtman, K (2001) *Early Intervention: Diversion and Youth Conferencing – A National Profile and Review of Current Approaches to Diverting Juveniles from the Criminal Justice System*, National Crime Prevention: Canberra.

Potas, I, Smart, J, Brignell, G, Thomas, B and Lawries, R (2003) *Circle Sentencing in New South Wales: a Review and Evaluation*, Judicial Commission: Sydney, <www.lawlink.nsw.gov.au>.

Povinelli, E (2001) 'Radical Worlds: The Anthropology of Incommensurability and Inconceivability', *The Annual Review of Anthropology*, (30): 319-334.

Povinelli, E (2006) 'Finding Bwudjut: Common Land, Private Profit, Divergent Objects' in Lea T, Kowal, E and Cowlishaw, G (eds), *Moving Anthropology: Critical Indigenous Studies*, Charles Darwin University Press: Darwin.

Pratt, J (1998) 'Assimilation, Equality, Sovereignty, The Maori and the Criminal Justice and Welfare Systems' in Haverman, P (ed), *New Frontiers: Constitutionalising Aboriginal Rights in Australia, Canada and New Zealand 1975-1995*, Oxford University Press: Auckland.

Pratt, J (2006) 'The Dark Side of Paradise: Explaining New Zealand's History of High Imprisonment', *British Journal of Criminology*, 46: 541-560.

Raferty, J (2006) *Not Part of the Public: Non-Indigenous Policies and Practices and the Health of Indigenous South Australians, 1836-1973*, Wakefield Press: Adelaide.

Regional Domestic Violence Coordinating Committee (1997) *Domestic Violence Resource Directory*, Regional Domestic Violence Coordinating Committee: Broome.

Report of the Aboriginal Issues Unit of the Northern Territory (1991) 'Too Much Sorry Business' in Johnson, E (ed), *Royal Commission into Aboriginal Deaths in Custody*, AGPS: Canberra.

Reynolds, H (2013) *Forgotten War*, Sydney: New South Publishing.

Richards, K (2005) 'Unlikely Friends? Oprah Winfrey and Restorative Justice', *Australian and New Zealand Journal of Criminology*, 38(3): 381-399.

Rigakos, G (2003) *The New Para-Police: Risk Markets and Commodified Social Control*, University of Toronto Press: Toronto.

Roche, D (2004) *Accountability in Restorative Justice*, Clarendon Studies in Criminology, Oxford University Press: Oxford.

Rothwell, N (2006) 'Generation Lost in the Desert', *Weekend Australian*, 15-16 April 2006.

Rowse, T (1998) *White Flower, White Power: from Rations to Citizenship in Central Australia*, Cambridge University Press: Cambridge.

Rowse, T (2000) *Obliged to be Difficult: Nugget Coomb's Legacy in Indigenous Affairs,* Cambridge University Press: Cambridge.

Rowse, T (2002) *Indigenous Futures: Choice and Development for Aboriginal and Islander Australia,* University of New South Wales Press: Sydney.

Rowse, T (2006) 'The Politics of Being "Practical": Howard's Fourth Term Challenge' in Lea, T, Kowal, E and Cowlishaw, G (eds), *Moving Anthropology: Critical Indigenous Studies,* Charles Darwin University Press: Darwin.

Ryan, N, Head, B, Keast, R and Brown, K (2006) 'Engaging Indigenous Communities: Towards a Policy Framework for Indigenous Community Justice Programmes', *Social Policy & Administration,* (40)3, June: 304-321.

Ryan, P (2001) *Lajamanu Night Patrol Service,* Office Of Aboriginal Development: Darwin.

Ryan, P (2005) *The Evolving Role and Functions of Remote Area Community Patrols in Dispute Resolution: a Discussion Paper,* Department of Justice: Darwin.

Ryan, P (Undated) *Indigenous Community Engagement in Safety and Justice Issues: A Discussion Paper,* Aboriginal Law and Justice Strategy: Darwin.

Ryan, P and Antoun, J (2001) *Law and Justice Plans: an Overview,* Office of Aboriginal Development: Darwin.

Sagger, S and Gray, D (1998) *Dealing with Alcohol: Indigenous Usage in Australia, New Zealand and Canada,* Cambridge University Press: Cambridge.

Said, E (1984) *The World, the Text, and the Critic.* Harvard University Press: Harvard.

Said, E (1993) *Culture and Imperialism,* Vintage: London.

Said, E (2003) *Orientalism,* Penguin: Harmondsworth.

Sam, M (1992) *Through Black Eyes: A Handbook of Family Violence in Aboriginal and Torres Strait Islander Communities,* Secretariat of the National Aboriginal and Islander Child Care: Melbourne.

San Roque, C (2004) *Petrol Sniffing: An Exercise in Surviving Psychic Pain,* Carpa Manual, Background Paper, Intjartnama Aboriginal Corporation: Alice Springs.

Sercombe, H (1995). 'The Face of the Criminal is Aboriginal' in Bessant, J, Carrington, C and Cook, S (eds), *Cultures of Crime and Violence: The Australian Experience,* A Special Edition of the Journal of Australian Studies, 76-92.

Shaw, C and McKay, H (1942) *Juvenile Delinquency and Urban Areas,* Chicago University Press: Chicago.

Shearing, CH (1994) 'Reinventing Policing: Policing as Governance', *Conference on Privatisation,* Beilfield: Germany, 24-26 March.

Shearing, CH (2001) 'Transforming Security: A South African Experiment' in Braithwaite, J and Strang, H (eds), *Restorative Justice and Civil Society,* Cambridge University Press: Cambridge.

Shearing, CH and Stenning, PC (1981) 'Modern Private Security: Its Growth and Implications' in Tonray, M and Morris, N (eds), *Crime and Justice: An Annual Review of Research,* University of Chicago Press: Chicago.

Sherman, K, Gottfredson, D, MacKenzie, D, Eck, J, Reuter, P and Bushway, S (1997) *Preventing Crime: What Works, What Doesn't, What's Promising,* National Institute of Justice: Washington.

Simon, J (2007) *Governing Through Crime: How the War on Crime Transformed American Democracy and Created a Culture of Fear*, New York: Oxford University Press.

Skelton, R and Milovanovic, S (2006), 'Aboriginal Women "Set on Fire"', *The Age*, 17 May.

Smallwood, M (1996) "Violence is Not Our Way" in Thorpe, R and Irwin, J (eds), *Women and Violence: Working for Change*, Hale and Ironmonger: Sydney.

Smith, LT (1999) *Decolonizing Methodologies: Research and Indigenous Peoples*, New York & London: Zed Books.

Sparks, R and Newburn, T (2002) 'How Does Crime Policy Travel?', *Criminal Justice*, (2)2: 107-111.

Spivak, GC (1996) *The Spivak Reader: Selected Works of Gayatri Chakravorty Spivak*, Landry, D and Maclaen, G (eds), Routledge: London.

Sputore, B, Gray, D, Bourbon, D and Baird, K (1998), *Evaluation of Kununurra-Waringarri Aboriginal Corporation and Ngnowar-Aerwah Aboriginal Corporation's Alcohol Project*, funded by National Drug Strategy: Canberra.

Stafford, C (1995) 'Colonialism, Indigenous Peoples, and the Criminal Justice Systems of Australia and Canada' in Hazelhurst, K (ed) *Legal Pluralism and the Colonial Legacy*, Avebury: Sydney.

Stanner, WEH (1969) *The Boyer Lectures 1968 – After the Dreaming*, Australian Broadcasting Commission: Sydney.

Staples, R (1994) 'Black Male Genocide: The Final Solution to the Race Problem in America?' in Baker, D (ed), *Reading Racism and the Criminal Justice System*, Canadian Scholars Press: Toronto.

Stratton, J and Ang, I (1996) 'On the Impossibility of a Global Cultural Studies: British Cultural Studies in an International Frame' in Morley, D and Chen, KH (eds), *Stuart Hall: Critical Dialogues in Cultural Studies*, Routledge: London.

Sumner, C (1982) (ed) *Crime, Justice and Underdevelopment*, Heinemann: London.

Sutton, P (2001) 'The Politics of Suffering: Indigenous Policy in Australia since the 1970s', *Anthropological Forum*, (11)2: 125-173.

Sydney Morning Herald (2006) 'Mutitjulu Women Hit Back at Pedophilia Claims', 16 September.

Tatz, C (2001a) *Aboriginal Suicide is Different: A Portrait of Life and Self-Destruction*, Aboriginal Studies Press: Canberra.

Tatz, C (2001b) 'Aboriginal Youth Suicide', *Life Matters*, ABC Radio National, 6 August.

Tatz, C (2003) *With Intent to Destroy: Reflecting on Genocide*, Verso: London.

Tauri, J (1999) 'Explaining Recent Innovations in New Zealand', *Australian and New Zealand Journal of Criminology*, 32: 25-46.

Taylor, I, Walton, P and Young, J (1971) *The New Criminology*, Routledge and Kegan Paul: London.

Taylor, M and Walsh, T (2007) (eds) *Nowhere to Go: The Impact of Police Move on Powers on Homeless People in Queensland*, Queensland Public Interest Law Clearing House Homeless Person's Clinic and the University of Queensland: Brisbane.

Taylor, SC (2004) *Court Licensed Abuse*, Peter Lang: New York.

Thompson, R (ed) (1999) *Working in Indigenous Perpetrator Programs: Proceedings of a Forum, Adelaide: 4 & 5 August*, Ministerial Council for Aboriginal and Torres Strait Islander Affairs: Darwin.

Tilley, N (2005) (ed) *Handbook of Crime Prevention and Community Safety*, Willan Publishing: Cullompton.

Tonkinson, R (2006) *'Difference' and 'Autonomy' Then and Now: Four Decades of Change in a Western Desert Society*, Wentworth Lecture, <www1.aiatsis.gov.au/exhibitions/wentworth/2006WentworthLectureProfBobTonkinson.pdf>.

Toohey, J (2006) 'Aboriginal Customary Law Reference: An Overview', *Aboriginal Customary Law Background Papers*, Law Reform Commission of Western Australia, 94.

Trees, C (2006) 'Contemporary Issues Facing Customary Law and the General Legal System: Roebourne – A Case Study', Law Reform Commission of Western Australia Background Paper No 6, *Aboriginal Customary Law Background Papers*, Law Reform Commission of Western Australia: Perth, p 94.

Trigger, D (1986) 'Blackfellas and Whitefellas: the Concepts of Domain and Social Closure in the Analysis of Race Relations', *Mankind* 16(2): 99-117.

Trigger, D (1992) *Whitefella Comin': Aboriginal Responses to Colonialism in Northern Australia*, Cambridge University Press: Cambridge.

Turner, V (1967) *The Forest of Symbols: Aspects of Ndembu Ritual*, Cornell University Press: New York.

Turner, V (1969), *The Ritual Process: Structure and Anti-Structure*, Aldine: Chicago.

Tyler, W (1995) 'Community Based Strategies in Aboriginal Criminal Justice: The Northern Territory Experience', *Australian and New Zealand Journal of Criminology*. (28): 127-142.

Victorian Aboriginal Justice Agreement (VAJA) (1999) *Victorian Aboriginal Justice Agreement: An Agreement Between the Victorian Government and the Koori Community*, Victorian Department of Justice, Indigenous Issues Unity: Melbourne, <www.justice.vic.gov.au>.

Van Gennep, A (1960) *The Rites of Passage*, Republished English language edition, University of Chicago Press: Chicago.

Van Ness, D, Morris, A and Maxwell, G (2001) 'Introducing Restorative Justice', in Morris, A and Maxwell, G (eds), Restoring Justice for Juveniles: Conferencing, Mediation and Circles, Oxford, Hart Publishing.

Van Swaaningen, R (1997) *Critical Criminology: Visions from Europe*, Sage: London.

Victorian Department of Justice (2002) Koori Court Discussion Paper, Victorian Department of Justice: Melbourne.

Victorian Implementation Review Team (2004) *Discussion Paper*, Review of the Recommendations from the Royal Commission into Aboriginal Deaths in Custody: Melbourne.

Victorian Law Reform Commission (2006) *Review of Family Violence Laws; Final Report*, Victorian Law Reform Commission: Melbourne.

Von Sturmer, J (1984) 'The Different Domains', *Aborigines and Uranium, Consolidated Report on the Social Impact of Uranium Mining on the Aborigines of the Northern Territory*, AIAS: Canberra.

Wacquant, L (2001) 'Deadly Symbiosis: When Ghetto and Prison Meet and Mesh', *Punishment and Society*, 2: 95-133.

Walgrave, L (1999) 'Community Service as a Cornerstone of a Systemic Restorative Response', in Bazemore, G and Walgrave, L (eds), *Restoring Juvenile Justice; Repairing the Harm of Youth Crime*, New York Criminal Justice Press: New York.

Walker, J and Forrester, S (2002) *Tangentyere Remote Area Night Patrol*, Paper presented to the Crime Prevention Conference, Convened by the Australian Institute of Criminology and the Commonwealth Attorney General's Department, Sydney, 12-13 September, AIC: Canberra.

Walsh C (2010) 'Development as Buen Vivir: Institutional Arrangements and (De) Colonial Entanglements', *Development*, 53(1), (15-21)

Waters, A (2001) 'Ontology of Identity and Interstitial Being', *Newsletter on American Indians in Philosophy*, Spring, No 2, <www.apa.udel.edu/apa/publications/newsletters/v00n2/amindians/index.asp>.

Weatherburn D, Fitzgerald J and Hua, J (2003) 'Reducing Aboriginal Over-Representation in Prison', *Australian Journal of Public Administration*, 62(3): 65-73.

Weatherburn D (2014) *Arresting Incarceration: Pathways out of Indigenous Imprisonment*. Aboriginal Studies Press: Canberra.

Webb, RD (2003) *Maori Crime: Possibilities and Limits of an Indigenous Criminology*, PhD Thesis, University of Auckland: Auckland.

West Australian (2006) *Aboriginals Face Closure of Camps*, 10 May.

White, R (2003) 'Communities, Conferences and Restorative Social Justice', *Criminal Justice*, 3(2): 139-160.

Wild, R and Anderson, P (2007) *Ampe Akelyernemane Meke Mekarle 'Little Children are Sacred'*, Report of the Northern Territory Government Inquiry into the Protection of Aboriginal Children from Abuse, Northern Territory Government: Darwin.

Willhelm, SM (1994) 'The Economic Decline of Blacks in America: A Prelude to Genocide?' in Baker, D (ed) *Reading Racism and the Criminal Justice System*, Canadian Scholars Press: Toronto.

Williams, R (1976) *Culture and Society*, Penguin: Harmondsworth.

Williams, MN (1986) *The Yolngu and Their Land: A System of Land Tenure and the Fight for its Recognition*, Stanford University Press: Stanford.

Willis, P (1981) *Learning to Labour: How Working Class Kids Get Working Class Jobs*, Columbia University Press: Columbia.

Wohlan, C (2005) 'Aboriginal Women's Interest in Customary Law Recognition', *Background Paper No 13*, Law Reform Commission of Western Australia: Perth.

Wood, J and Font, E (2003) 'Building Peace and Reforming Police in Argentina: Opportunities and Challenges for Shantytown', presented at *In Search of Security: An International Conference on Policing and Security*, February, Canada Law Commission: Montreal.

Wolfe, P (2008) 'Settler Colonialism And The Elimination Of The Native', *Journal of Genocide Research* (2006) 8: 387-409.

Worrall, A (2000) 'What Works at One Arm Point: A Study in the Transportation of a Penal Concept', *Probation Journal*, (47)4: 243-249.

Young, J (1999) *The Exclusive Society: Social Exclusion, Crime and Difference in Late Modernity,* Sage: London.

Young, R (1990) *White Mythologies: Writing History and the West,* Routledge: London.

Young, R (1995) *Colonial Desire: Hybridity in Theory, Culture and Race,* Routledge: London.

Young, R (2001) 'Just Cops Doing "Shameful" Business? Police-led Restorative Justice and the Lessons of Research' in Morris, A and Maxwell, G (eds), *Restorative Justice for Juveniles: Conferencing, Mediation and Circles,* Hart: Oxford.

Zdenkowski, G (1994) 'Customary Punishment and Pragmatism – Some Unresolved Dilemmas: The Queen v Wilson JagamaraWalker', *Aboriginal Law Bulletin.* 3(68):26.

Zedner, L (2006) 'Liquid Security: Managing the Market for Crime Control', *Criminology and Criminal Justice,* (6)3: 267-288.

Zeher, H and Mika, M (1998) 'Fundamental Concepts of Restorative Justice', *Contemporary Justice Review,* 1: 47-55.

Index